The Epidemic of Rape and Child Sexual Abuse in the United States

Diana E. H. Russell
Rebecca M. Bolen

Sage Publications, Inc.
International Educational and Professional Publisher
Thousand Oaks ▪ London ▪ New Delhi

For information:

Sage Publications, Inc.
2455 Teller Road
Thousand Oaks, California 91320
E-mail: order@sagepub.com

Sage Publications Ltd.
6 Bonhill Street
London EC2A 4PU
United Kingdom

Sage Publications India Pvt. Ltd.
M-32 Market
Greater Kailash I
New Delhi 110 048 India

Printed in the United States of America

Library of Congress Cataloging-in-Publication Data

Russell, Diana E. H.

The epidemic of rape and child sexual abuse in the United States / by Diana E. H. Russell and
　Rebecca M. Bolen.
　　p. cm.
　Includes bibliographical references and index.
　ISBN 0-7619-0301-1 (cloth: alk. paper)
　ISBN 0-7619-0302-x (pbk.: alk. paper)
　　1. Rape—Research—United States—Evaluation. 2. Child sexual
abuse—Research—United States—Evaluation. 3. Victims of crimes
surveys—United States—Evaluation. I. Bolen, Rebecca M.
II. Title.
　HV6561 .R86 2000
　364.15'32'072073—dc21　　　　　　　　　　　　　　　　　　00-008111

This book is printed on acid-free paper.

00　01　02　03　04　05　06　7　6　5　4　3　2　1

Acquisition Editor:	Nancy Hale
Production Editor:	Nevair Kabakian
Editorial Assistant:	Cindy Bear
Typesetter:	Tina Hill
Indexer:	Do Mi Stauber
Cover Designer:	Michelle Lee

DEDICATIONS

To Mary Koss, for her exemplary research on rape and other forms of sexual coercion; for her dedication to furthering society's understanding of these crimes and how widespread they are; for her persistence despite ongoing attacks by those who want to turn back the clock to the good old days when rape was seen as a rare problem; and for her leadership in exposing the scandalous underestimation of rape by the federal government-funded annual National Crime Victimization Surveys.

—Diana E. H. Russell, Ph.D.

To the survivors.

—Rebecca M. Bolen, Ph.D.

CONTENTS

PART II: The Scope of Child Sexual Abuse

PART III: Conclusion

LIST OF TABLES AND FIGURES

TABLES

TABLES IN APPENDIXES

Appendix 1. Tables About Rape

Appendix 2. Tables About Child Sexual Abuse

FIGURES

PREFACE

In 1977, I received funding from the National Institute of Mental Health (grant R01MH 28960) to conduct research into the prevalence of rape and other forms of sexual assault in San Francisco. A probability sample of 930 adult women residents of San Francisco were interviewed about their experiences with incestuous abuse, extrafamilial child sexual abuse, unwanted sex with authority figures, pornography-related abuse, and rape by strangers, acquaintances, friends, dates, lovers, ex-lovers, husbands, and ex-husbands. In 1980, I was funded by the National Center on Child Abuse and Neglect (grant 90-CA-813/01) to analyze the data on incestuous abuse gathered in this survey.

Because a campaign to make rape in marriage illegal was launched in the early 1980s, and because of the dearth of accurate information on wife rape, I decided to give first priority to analyzing my survey data on wife rape. After completing the manuscript for *Rape in Marriage* in 1981, I was selected as an expert consultant on sexual violence for the California Commission on Crime Control and Violence Prevention. The Commission had undertaken an investigation into "the root causes of crime" to guide their formulation of recommendations aimed at preventing these crimes in California. My book *Sexual Exploitation: Rape, Child Sexual Abuse, and Workplace Harassment* (1984) was a revised version of the report I wrote for the Commission.

In 1995, Peter Labella, my then-editor at Sage, requested that I update *Sexual Exploitation*. Rebecca Bolen, an advanced and gifted doctoral student in social work at the University of Texas at Arlington at that time (now an Assistant Professor of Social Work at Boston University), had previously requested permission to analyze my survey data on child sexual abuse for a research practicum she wanted to do that was funded by a doctoral fellowship from the National Center on Child Abuse and Neglect. Familiarizing her with my survey methodology provided me with the opportunity to observe that she was well qualified to assist me with a second edition of *Sexual Exploitation.* Happily, Rebecca agreed to take on this responsibility.

The first edition of *Sexual Exploitation* focused on the prevalence and causes of rape, child sexual abuse, and sexual harassment in the workplace. Rebecca completed a first draft of an update of the research for this book, minus a few selected chapters. However, when it was my turn to revise the manuscript, I discovered that there were so many new rape prevalence studies to be described and compared with my 1978 survey, that this section of the manuscript soon expanded into several chapters. The same applied to prevalence studies of child sexual abuse.

This development forced us to realize that the task of updating *Sexual Exploitation* had become impossible. After discussing this problem with Peter Labella, we decided to focus on the incidence and prevalence of rape and child sexual abuse and to omit the causal theories of these sex crimes. To reflect this considerable change in the subject matter of our book, the title was changed to *The Epidemic of Rape and Child Sexual Abuse in the United States.* Aside from a lengthy description of the methodology of my study, and a comparison of its incidence rate with the statistics gathered by the FBI's *Uniform Crime Reports* and the Bureau of Justice's annual National Crime Survey Data, *The Epidemic of Rape and Child Sexual Abuse in the United States* ended up having little resemblance to *Sexual Exploitation.*

This radical change in our project was very distressing because Rebecca had already invested considerable time and effort in revising *Sexual Exploitation.* This was one of many factors that extended the time it took us to complete *The Epidemic.*

Because Rebecca used my database on child sexual abuse for her research practicum, she did a thorough analysis of it to check that the final version was free of mysteries and inconsistencies. She noted (and I was reminded) that small corrections had been made from time to time in publications that followed the publication of *Sexual Exploitation* in 1984 (e.g., Russell, 1986). This explains the small discrepancies between some of the analyses in this volume and *Sexual Exploitation.*

We are happy to say that our evaluations of different surveys of the prevalence of rape and child sexual abuse have resulted in our being able to make definitive statements about several very important research and policy issues—for example, the severe problems that persist with the revised methodology of the National Crime Victimization Surveys, the neglected issue of child rape, the now commonly accepted view among contemporary rape researchers that rape is primarily a problem for children and adolescent females, and the best methodology to use for studies of the incidence and prevalence of sexual crimes.

—Diana E. H. Russell

1

◆

INTRODUCTION: FROM REVOLUTION TO BACKLASH

Research has revealed the alarming frequency of sexual coercion in women's lives and the various guises in which rape occurs.

Mary Koss, Lori Heise, & Nancy Russo, 1994, p. 510

Whether or not one in four college women has been raped . . . is a matter of opinion, not a matter of mathematical fact.

Katie Roiphe, 1993, p. 54

The estimates of sexual assault calculated by feminist researchers are advocacy numbers, figures that embody less an effort at scientific understanding than an attempt to persuade the public that a problem is vastly larger than commonly recognized. . . . Under the veil of social science, rigorous research methods are employed to measure a problem defined so broadly that it forms a vessel into which almost any human difficulty can be poured.

Neil Gilbert, 1991c, p. 63

In 1974, after Russell completed her first study of rape (Russell, 1975), she was struck by the sharp divergence in views between some feminists who believed that rape was a widespread problem, and most other people who considered it to be rare. The latter view was supported by most of the research literature available at that time (e.g., Amir, 1971; MacDonald, 1971). Eugene

Kanin (1957, 1970, 1971; Kirkpatrick & Kanin, 1957; Kanin & Parcell, 1977), however, was an outstanding exception. This motivated Russell to conduct the first study (in 1978) of the prevalence of rape ever to be based on a probability sample (Russell, 1983b). Besides rape, she also attempted to ascertain the prevalence of child sexual abuse, and, to a lesser extent, sexual abuse by authority figures and wife abuse (Russell, 1982, 1983a, 1984, 1986). Russell found astonishingly high rates of rape and child sexual abuse in her San Francisco sample.

Many other surveys on the prevalence of rape, sexual assault, lesser forms of sexually coercive behavior, and child sexual abuse have been conducted since Russell completed her pioneering study. The percentage of women who disclosed having been victimized by completed or attempted rape at some time in their lives has ranged from a low of 2.6% (Breslau, Davis, Andreski, Federman, & Anthony, 1991) to a high of 44% (Russell, 1984), while the percentage of women who disclosed a history of child sexual abuse has ranged from 2% (George & Winfield-Laird, 1986) to 62% (Wyatt, 1985). Given the fact that rape has long been known to be the most underreported of the violent crimes identified by the FBI, and that many girls and women also fail to disclose their experiences of child sexual abuse to anyone, studies that have obtained high incidence and/or prevalence rates of these crimes have tended to receive more attention than the studies finding very low rates.

Feminists in the early 1970s, together with large numbers of rape survivors who started speaking out about their victimization experiences, transformed our understanding of this widespread form of misogynist behavior. In the late 1970s and early 1980s, these same forces transformed our understanding of child sexual abuse. In addition, empirical research began to validate the high prevalence of these forms of sexual victimization (e.g., Finkelhor, 1979; Koss, Gidycz, & Wisniewski, 1987; Russell, 1983a, 1983b).

The combination of feminist theory and empirical research challenged the myth that rapists and child molesters are a relatively small group of deviant, pathological males whose behavior is altogether different from males in general. Research has also challenged the view that many rape and child sexual abuse survivors collude in their victimization. And it has discredited the common belief that incarcerating and/or treating rapists is a feasible and effective way to handle these widespread problems, given the extraordinarily high numbers of rapists and child molesters in the population.

We believe that the development of sound rape and child sexual abuse theories, as well as effective social policies and activist strategies to combat these crimes, all require accurate knowledge of their prevalence. With regard to rape, Mary Koss, Lori Heise, and Nancy Russo (1994) emphasize that obtaining accurate data on rape prevalence is important in raising awareness about the problem and providing a rational basis for policy decisions about the allocation of resources for services and prevention of rape. In contrast, Mary Koss et al. (1994) contend that inaccurately low prevalence rates

> are a cruel hoax for women. The low numbers invalidate women's experience, indicate a lack of commitment and concern for women's well-being, and fuel illusions that rape is a minor issue on which feminists are overly focused. As a result, rape activists are less able to speak authoritatively about the need for social changes or to command financial resources for intervention and prevention services. (pp. 527-528)

Trying to measure the prevalence of child sexual abuse is equally important for the same reasons. Kevin Gorey and Donald Leslie (1997) consider establishing a sound estimate of its prevalence as the number one research priority in the field, maintaining that it "would go a long way toward facilitating effective practice as well as other research in this field" (p. 396). According to Jeffrey Haugaard and N. Dickon Reppucci (1988),

> Much of today's increased interest in the identification and treatment of sexually abused children, as well as in the prevention of sexual abuse, can be attributed to the research on prevalence, as it has shown that child sexual abuse occurs in all segments of our society and that children in any family can experience sexual abuse. (p. 32)

These authors also maintain that

> the results of the research and the subsequent public acceptance of child sexual abuse as a significant problem have made it increasingly easy for sexually abused children, or adults, to be taken seriously, and to seek help if it is needed. Interviews with many sexual abuse victims reveal that they often believe themselves to be the only ones who have suffered abuse. Making the true prevalence known may have helped many victims take steps to ameliorate the effects of their earlier abuse as they came to see their experience and their reaction to it as less unique. (p. 32)

In short, well-constructed rigorous, scientific studies on the prevalence of rape and child sexual abuse are extremely important in the understanding, treatment, and prevention of these forms of sexual violence.

The two denunciations of feminist prevalence research on rape that open this chapter—targeting feminist research that has obtained high prevalence rates—reflect the powerful backlash against the researchers and their find-ings that the United States is plagued by an epidemic of rape. Those who most vociferously denounce studies that have documented the widespread preva-lence of rape (e.g., Bonilla, 1993; Gilbert, 1991c; Paglia, 1992; Roiphe, 1993; Schoenberg & Roe, 1993; Sommers, 1994) appear to be unfamiliar with the sizeable social scientific literature on this crime, much of which has contributed to revolutionizing our knowledge about rape from the early 1970s until today. Nor have they themselves ever conducted any research on rape. Consequently, they sometimes make scientifically naive statements, such as Roiphe's (1993) claim that the prevalence of rape experienced by col-lege women is just "a matter of opinion, not a matter of mathematical fact" (p. 54).

Philosophy professor Christina Hoff Sommers (1994) argues that re-searchers should base their estimates of the prevalence of rape on women respondents' self-identification as rape victims. "Believing what women actually say is precisely *not* the methodology by which some feminist advo-cates get their incendiary statistics," Sommers declares (p. 223). She appears unaware that a large body of research shows that many women do not concep-tualize as rape many sexual attacks that meet the legal definition of rape (Kilpatrick, Resnick, Saunders, & Best, 1998; Koss et al., 1987; Resnick, Kilpatrick, Dansky, Saunders, & Best, 1993; Russell, 1982). Hence, requir-ing that rape victims self-identify as such would result in a considerable underestimation of the prevalence of rape, particularly that perpetrated in intimate relationships.

Furthermore, Sommers (1994) endorses the outdated pathological model of rapists. More specifically, she asserts that, "Rape is perpetrated by crimi-nals, which is to say, it is perpetrated by people who want to gratify them-selves in criminal ways and who care very little about the suffering they inflict on others" (p. 225). Sommers's revival of this myth is contradicted by a large body of research that shows that large percentages of male college stu-dents report some likelihood of raping a woman if they could be sure of get-ting away with it (Briere & Malamuth, 1983; Malamuth, 1986), as well as re-search showing that large percentages of male high school students believe they are entitled to rape girls in many different circumstances (Goodchilds & Zellman, 1984). Clearly, if large percentages of male students are willing to admit that there is some likelihood that they would rape a woman if they could get away with it (a *majority* [60%] of male students in one experiment admit-ted that there was some likelihood that they would rape or force sex acts on fe-males if they could be sure of getting away with it [Briere & Malamuth,

1983]), this invalidates Sommers's (1994) implicit assumption that rape is desired only by "criminals . . . who care very little about the suffering they inflict on others" (p. 225). There are no data that support the notion that all males who rape females are psychopaths.

Neil Gilbert is a vociferous critic of all research that shows a high incidence or prevalence of rape and child sexual abuse. For example, Gilbert (1991a) writes that, "With a much larger sample [than Koss's] and a much smaller ax to grind than the *Ms.* survey [in which some of Koss's findings were reported], the BJS's [Bureau of Justice Statistics] findings reveal that approximately one in 1,000 women are victims of rape and attempted rape annually" (p. A14). While Gilbert (1991c) concedes that "the problem of sexual assault may well be greater than is suggested by the [BJS's] National Crime Survey figures," he declared that "it has certainly not reached the epidemic proportions indicated by the advocacy numbers" (p. 65). Gilbert offers no justification for his opinionated conclusion. Nor does he criticize the highly defective methodology of the BJS (which will be described in Chapter 5). Only studies with relatively high prevalence rates have been subject to his criticism.

Camille Paglia's (1992) contribution to this debate is to criticize feminists for failing to appreciate what she considers the male perspective on rape: "Feminism does not see what is for men the eroticism or fun element in rape, especially the wild, infectious delirium of gang rape," Paglia maintains (p. 63). She goes on to enthuse about the risks she used to take in the sixties when she wandered "those dark streets understanding that not only could I be raped, I could be *killed*" (p. 65). Paglia then proceeds to castigate feminists for having "no idea that some women like to flirt with danger because there is a sizzle in it" (p. 65). Elsewhere she maintains that "if you get raped, if you get beat up in a dark alley in a street, it's okay" (p. 63).

The following statement reveals Paglia's (1992) prefeminist view that rape is limited to "either stranger rape or the intrusion of overt sex into a nonsexual situation." Paglia also contends "that women should take full responsibility for the dating experience" (pp. 69-70). Hence, Paglia discounts the occurrence of rape in intimate relationships, including rape in marriage, and considers women to be responsible for any experiences they may have of forced intercourse, intercourse because of threat of force, and intercourse when the woman is unable to consent because she is incapacitated.

Unfortunately, because the media has promoted such attacks by critics unfamiliar with rape research, these critics' ill-informed skepticism about the fact that rape in the United States is a very widespread and serious problem has been embraced by many others in the 1990s. As Katha Pollitt (1993) notes with regard to the enthusiastic public response to Roiphe's polemical book, *The Morning After* (1993):

> These explosive charges have already made Roiphe a celebrity. *The New York Times Magazine* ran an excerpt from her book as a cover story: "Rape Hype Betrays Feminism." Four women's glossies ran respectful prepublication interviews. . . . Clearly, Katie Roiphe's message is one that many people want to hear: sexual violence is anomalous, not endemic to American society, and appearances to the contrary can be explained away as a kind of mass hysteria, fomented by man-hating fanatics.[1] (p. 220)

The so-called "man-hating fanatics" are, of course, feminists. Despite the fact that very few of the major surveys on the magnitude of the rape problem in the United States have been conducted by feminists, many of the attacks on the claim that there is an epidemic of rape in this country hold feminists—including feminist researchers—responsible for manufacturing this alleged myth. Consider the following four examples of titles of articles in newspapers, magazines, and scholarly journals in the 1990s:

"Cultural Assault: What Feminists Are Doing to Rape Ought to Be a Crime" (Bonilla, 1993)

"The Phantom Date Rape Epidemic: How Radical Feminists Manipulated Data to Exaggerate the Problem" (Gilbert, 1991b)

"The Truth About Date Rape: Radical Feminist Ideology Encourages Sexual Assaults" (Fox, 1991)

"Rape Hype Betrays Feminism: Date Rape's Other Victim" (Roiphe, 1993)

Blaming feminists for being among the first to document the widespread prevalence of rape in the United States appears to be more palatable to many individuals in the 1990s than a careful assessment of the validity of their findings as well as those of other social scientists.

THE PURPOSE OF THIS BOOK

We stand at a critical historical juncture. While rape and child sexual abuse have a long history of being minimized and overlooked as societal problems, the emergence of the contemporary phase of the feminist movement succeeded in challenging this obliteration of female victimization. As increasing numbers of survivors of these sexual crimes broke their silence, a new era of research started to be conducted by feminists and nonfeminists on many different aspects of rape and child sexual abuse. This research included Russell's (1975) first volunteer-based study of rape survivors, followed by her NIMH-funded study of the prevalence of rape and child sexual abuse in San Francisco.

For the first time in history, a substantial volume of research has found high rates of rape and child sexual abuse in the United States, spearheading an angry backlash against these so-called advocacy statistics allegedly propagated by radical feminist researchers and activists. Moving beyond this argument requires a close and critical analysis of representative incidence and prevalence surveys of rape and child sexual abuse in the United States, with a special focus on the strengths and weaknesses of their methodology. Our evaluations in this book provide a rational basis for attempting to arrive at the soundest estimate of the prevalence of rape and child sexual abuse in this country.

Because women and girls constitute the vast majority of rape and child sexual abuse survivors, the data on the incidence and prevalence of rape to be analyzed in this book will focus on female survivors.

In order to qualify for inclusion in our study sample, surveys had to meet the following criteria:

1. They had to be based on representative samples of the general population in a city, county, state, or in the entire nation.
2. They had to provide prevalence data on rape and/or child sexual abuse.
3. They had to provide data on the rape and/or child sexual abuse of females separate from males.
4. They had to provide data on these crimes in the United States.
5. The range of ages between a study's youngest and oldest respondents had to be at least 18 years. (Wyatt's [1985] study of women aged 18 to 36 only just qualified by this criterion.)
6. The studies had to be published.

We excluded unpublished surveys from those to be analyzed, mostly for the practical reason that they are difficult to obtain. In addition, unpublished papers, such as those written for presentation at conferences, are sometimes so flawed that the authors may have deliberately chosen not to publish them and/or they may have been unable to get them published. Gorey and Leslie

(1997) also excluded unpublished articles on surveys from their comparison of 16 surveys because they believed that published peer-reviewed articles provided a "measure of quality assurance" (p. 393).[2]

Only 10 surveys on the prevalence of rape, two of which were limited to the prevalence of child rape, and nine surveys on the prevalence of child sexual abuse qualified by our six criteria. There were only 10 studies on the prevalence of rape because several other studies estimated the prevalence of sexual assault, not rape. Although legal usage of the term *sexual assault* is synonymous with rape, in the prevalence literature "the term sexual assault often is treated as a generic term that subsumes rape as well as lesser degrees of unwanted and pressured sexual contacts not involving penetration" (Koss & Harvey, 1991, p. 23).

Because there is a wide range in the magnitude of the incidence and prevalence rates found in these studies, our task includes evaluating methodological soundness, analytical accuracy, and the validity of researchers' interpretations of their findings on the incidence and prevalence of these two crimes. The findings of surveys that fail to meet satisfactory standards on these counts will be excluded from consideration when we evaluate whether or not the incidence/prevalence of rape and child sexual abuse have achieved epidemic proportions in the United States.

We are using the term *epidemic* simply to mean "widely prevalent" (*The American Heritage Dictionary*, 1992). Clearly, readers with more specific definitions of this term can decide for themselves if they agree or disagree with our conclusion regarding whether or not the term epidemic is appropriate.

DEFINING INCIDENCE AND PREVALENCE

In the forthcoming chapters of this book, we will compare studies, most of which assessed the lifetime prevalence of rape and/or child sexual abuse. We will also be comparing the few studies that reported incidence rates for these two forms of sexual victimization.

Incidence is usually defined as the number of new cases that occur within a specified period of time—usually a year (Sedlak & Broadhurst, 1996b, p. 3-2, fn. 2). It is typically translated into an incidence *rate* per 1,000 individuals, whereas *prevalence* is expressed as a percentage. (Incidence rates are computed "by dividing the number of victimizations occurring in a specific population by the number of persons in that population" [BJS, 1996, p. 6].) Translating numbers into rates and percentages enables researchers to make comparisons between studies and to assess changes over time.

For example, the *Uniform Crime Reports* provides the number of rape incidents that are reported each year as well as the rate of rape per 100,000 inhabitants in the United States. To ascertain whether rapes have increased since the previous year, the rape rates must be compared. Comparing the numbers of incidents can be deceptive. For example, there may be an *increase* in the number of rapes reported for a particular year, but a decline in the rape *rate* because the rape rate takes account of fluctuations in the size of the U.S. population.

With regard to child sexual abuse, numerous ethical and methodological problems (e.g., designing an interview schedule or questionnaire that is appropriate for children of various ages) as well as the fact that babies and very young children have no—or minimal—mastery of language, and little or no reliable memory before the age of four years old or so—make it impossible for researchers to obtain incidence rates in the prior 12 months for such youngsters. In addition, using the reports of parents to obtain data on incidence is extremely unreliable, and using official reporting agencies to establish estimates of child sexual abuse incidence leads to a vast underestimate of the problem. Hence, measuring the scope of child sexual abuse in a community or society requires calculating the prevalence, not the incidence, of this form of sexual victimization.

The term *incident* in the context of rape and child sexual abuse refers to an experience of one of these forms of sexual victimization. Whereas *incidence* is an incident-based measure, prevalence is a person-based measure. If all victims of rape and child sexual abuse were victimized once only, the number of victims on which prevalence estimates are based, and the number of incidents on which the incidence rate is based, would be the same. However, the greater the number of multiple victimizations, the more the number of victims and incidents on which these two measures are based, diverge.

Unfortunately, there is no agreement among sexual victimization researchers about how best to *count* incidents. Dissimilar methods of counting victimizations constitute a very serious hidden problem that can thwart simple comparisons of the incidence rates obtained by different studies. Following is a concocted case in which a woman—whom we will call Robin—

was raped on five different occasions by her lover and once on another occasion by two strangers. Robin was also raped by her lover three times on the last occasion that he raped her. The first time Robin's lover raped her, she was with her sister, whom he also raped. The second time, both he and a buddy of his raped her. The last time, he raped her once vaginally, once anally, and once orally.

Following are five ways in which the number of rape incidents perpetrated on Robin can be counted.

1. According to the rules of counting incidents followed by some researchers, Robin was raped only twice. The implicit definition of an incident used by these researchers is the number of incidents in which rapes are perpetrated by different rapists. A second rule is that multiple rapists of the same incident are counted as if they are only one. This incident count remains the same whether or not it is limited to the most recent 12 months. This method of counting incidents, used by Russell in her survey, is more conservative than all the others, omitting many rape experiences from the count. Hence, some would consider that it underestimates the true extent of the rape problem. For example, consider how odd it would seem if five robberies by the same person and two robberies by a neighbor counted as only two cases.

2. By the rules of counting used by some researchers, Robin was raped six times—five times by her lover and once by a stranger (e.g., Tjaden & Thoennes, 1998a). Other researchers, including Russell, probably consider that this method overestimates the true extent of the rape problem. For example, if a woman estimates that she was raped by her husband about once a week during the period of a year, adding 52 rapes to the incidence count seems questionable. Imprecise estimates, such as, "it happened between 5 and 10 times" or "more than 10 times," also pose a problem. Yet how researchers handle these decisions can have a great impact on the number of incidents they report. While coding rules can be devised to quantify imprecise data, it does not seem appropriate for a few such cases to have an inordinate impact on the number of incidents counted and/or the incidence rate calculated.

3. The simultaneous raping of Robin and her sister by Robin's lover can be counted as either one or two incidents. One can argue that it constitutes only one incident with two victims and one perpetrator, or that since two rapes were perpetrated, it should be counted as two incidents. The Bureau of Justice Statistics, which administers the National Crime Victimization Surveys, counts this kind

of assault as two incidents despite considering this to be "strictly speaking incorrect" (Michael Rand, personal communication, December 14, 1998).

4. Robin's rape by her lover three times on one occasion can be counted as one incident—because there was only one perpetrator and because the rapes occurred on one occasion, or each of the three rapes can be counted as separate incidents.

5. When Robin was raped on one occasion by her lover and his buddy, this experience can be counted as one incident because it was perpetrated at one time. On the other hand, it can also be counted as two incidents because Robin was raped twice.

The BJS's National Crime Victimization Surveys use a combination of the different ways of counting incidents listed above. They use the term *series victimizations* when at least six rapes that are similar in nature occur within a 6-month period and when "the respondent cannot recall details of each crime" (Tjaden & Thoennes, 1998a, p. 4). Such cases are counted as only one rape. However, if there are fewer than six rapes, each one counts as a separate incident. The same applies to six or more rapes that share no similarities (Michael Rand, personal communication, December 14, 1998).

These different ways of counting the incidents of rape obviously have a great impact on the number of rapes identified and the magnitude of the incidence rates obtained. Researchers typically assume that there is consensus on the way the term incident is used, and they therefore fail to clarify the rules they follow for counting these incidents. This problematizes making comparisons between the incidence rates reported by different studies.

Hence, it is vitally important that researchers become more aware of the choices available to them with regard to defining incidents, and that they describe their choices when writing up their research. Doing this could be the first step toward researchers eventually arriving at a consensus on how best to standardize the way in which incidents are counted, thereby facilitating more valid comparisons between the incidence rates obtained by different studies.

Despite the lack of agreement among researchers on how best to count incidents, prevalence researchers only have to add a question such as: "Did the rape (any of the rapes) that you mentioned occur in the last 12 months?" to obtain data on the incidence of rape. More prevalence researchers who have obtained sufficiently large sample sizes should add such a question to enable them to compare their findings with those of the FBI (reported in the annual *Uniform Crime Reports*) and the BJS's National Crime Victimization Surveys.

THE PREVALENCE OF RAPE AND CHILD SEXUAL ABUSE

Most prevalence researchers define *prevalence* as *the percentage of individuals known to have been victims of rape or child sexual abuse in the total population or other specified populations (e.g., women, mental patients, children between the ages of 1 to 15 years) during a specified period of time (e.g., a year) or at some time during their lives.* Prevalence rates that apply to individuals at some time during their lives are referred to as *lifetime* prevalence rates. For example, David Finkelhor (1994) defined prevalence rates of child sexual abuse obtained by retrospective representative samples as the "proportion of the adult population that have been victims of sexual abuse at some time in their lives" (p. 36, Table 1).

For practical and theoretical reasons, most rape researchers favor studies that assess prevalence rather than incidence rates. Studies of incidence require much larger sample sizes to generate a sufficient number of cases from which to calculate reliable estimates of incidence rates than do prevalence studies covering many years. Incidence studies are therefore much more costly than prevalence studies. In addition, Koss et al. (1994) favor obtaining prevalence rates for rape because they consider the longer time frame of prevalence studies to be more appropriate since "the aftereffects of rape may extend for many years beyond the [rape] incident or series of incidents" (p. 509). In addition, there is far more consensus in the field regarding how to measure prevalence than incidence.

With regard to child sexual abuse, the fact that young children cannot be interviewed about their victimization experiences, and that interviewing their parents is totally unsatisfactory as a method of obtaining prevalence rates, constitutes another important reason why retrospective prevalence studies are preferred over incidence studies.

As skeptical as many people are about the value of gathering statistics (consider the common cliche, "You can prove anything with statistics"), it is vitally important that we have sound estimates of the prevalence of rape and child sexual abuse. When they are seriously inaccurate, however, they can be harmful to women and children. The findings of several studies that obtained data on the prevalence and/or incidence of rape and/or the prevalence of child sexual abuse will be reported and their methodology evaluated in several chapters of this book. Arriving at the soundest estimates of the incidence and prevalence of rape and child sexual abuse in the United States is a major objective of these evaluations and comparisons.

RECALL PROBLEMS

Survivors' abilities to recall rape and child sexual abuse experiences, particularly those that occurred long ago, is one of the most serious methodological problems for prevalence studies, particularly those estimating lifetime prevalence. Clearly, studies of the incidence of rape over the 6 months or 12 months prior to the respondents' interviews are at a great advantage when it comes to recall. In their discussion of criminal victimization studies, Jan van Dijk and Patricia Mayhew (1993) note that

> findings about the last year will be most accurate, because less serious incidents which took place some time ago tend to be forgotten. This memory loss explains the fact that victimisation rates over [more than] five years are much less than five times higher than calendar year rates: five-year rates are on average [only] about three times higher [than one-year rates]. (pp. 9-10)

Experiences that are kept secret and even denied—as so many adult rapes and experiences of child sexual abuse are—are probably also forgotten much more readily than equally traumatic experiences that people feel able to talk about (e.g., injuries sustained as a result of a natural disaster or in a serious auto accident for which another driver is responsible) because of the rehearsal effect that enhances people's recollections of an event each time they describe it.

Hence, because of secrecy and/or denial as well as recall problems, researchers' findings on the prevalence of lifetime rape and child sexual abuse are likely to be considerable underestimates of these crimes. Furthermore, the longer the periods of secrecy, the greater the underestimation is likely to be.

THE IMPORTANT ROLE OF CRITICISM

A few excellent review articles have been done comparing studies of the prevalence of child sexual abuse (e.g., Finkelhor, 1994; Peters, Wyatt, & Finkelhor, 1986; Wyatt & Peters, 1986a, 1986b) in the United States. However, with the exception of Koss (e.g., Koss, 1992, 1996), equivalent reviews have not been done comparing studies of the prevalence of rape.

Most of the representative studies of the incidence and/or prevalence of rape evaluated in this volume were published in articles or reports, not books. Articles and reports typically make it possible to get the studies into the public domain more rapidly than books. However, the inevitable page limitation imposed on authors by journals means that researchers reporting on their data have little choice but to do cursory reviews of other studies germane to their work. Hence, their evaluations of each study they refer to in their literature reviews tend to be superficial and limited to providing a rationale for their own research. In short, there is little payoff for journal authors who are reporting the results of their research to embark on thorough evaluations of related studies.

On the other hand, the above rationale does not explain why researchers on child sexual abuse have undertaken critical review articles, but researchers on rape have not. Whatever the explanation for this, it is rare to find any indication that rape researchers have checked the accuracy of their colleagues' calculations (where this is possible), scrutinized the comprehensibility and correctness of their descriptions of their sampling methods and participation rates, checked to see that the conclusions they drew from their findings are justified, and so on.

Detailed and comprehensive critiques of certain research studies on the incidence and/or prevalence of sexual assault have been made, however, by those who are strongly ideologically opposed to the findings. Some examples of these critics were cited at the beginning of this chapter. Most of them appear to have borrowed criticisms from Neil Gilbert, who is the initiator of these often hostile attacks.

Something is very wrong if most of the substantive criticism of the methodologically challenging research on the prevalence of sexual assault is almost exclusively being made by those outside the field. Russell will argue in Chapter 16 that most (but not all) of their criticisms are without merit.

In the field of child sexual abuse, particularly incestuous abuse, Russell (1999) has elsewhere emphasized some of the destructive consequences that have resulted from the failure of researchers and clinicians, in what is sometimes referred to as the child sexual abuse recovery movement, to be critical of some of their colleagues' assumptions, theories, methodologies, and clinical work (pp. xvii-xlvi). For example, the theory that all recovered memories of child sexual abuse are true has come under increasing scrutiny. In the 1980s and early 1990s, those in the recovered memory movement typically assumed that children's and adults' memories of child sexual abuse could all be believed. Research on the memory processes of young children and adults, however, has made it increasingly clear that memories are not stored intact and that memory is indeed fallible.

In recent years, the use of hypnosis to assist adults in therapy to recall previously unremembered childhood experiences of sexual abuse has been greatly criticized. The increasing use of hypnosis and other suggestive techniques often used by therapists has coincided with allegations of increases in false memories of childhood sexual abuse by mostly female clients. This, in turn, resulted in a countermovement of critics spearheaded by the False Memory Syndrome Foundation whose members claimed that many, most, or all recovered memories of childhood sexual abuse were false (see Russell's [1999] comprehensive analysis of the "memory wars").

Therapy aside, we are not suggesting that the lack of internal criticism among many sexual assault researchers is responsible for the backlash against the studies that have found high prevalence rates of sexual assault. We *are* arguing that a lack of internal criticism is contrary to scientific principles. In addition, defective research deserves to be characterized as such because it leads to inappropriate policy decisions. Sound research that nevertheless suffers from one or more serious flaws should be criticized for these flaws, and the consequences of these flaws should be evaluated and pointed out.

Although we have some reservations about critically reviewing the research of our colleagues, we do not want to continue the tradition of failing to criticize research that is inaccurately reported or impossible to understand or that fails to include vital information for checking calculations.

THE STRUCTURE AND ORGANIZATION OF THIS VOLUME

Part I of this volume deals with rape, and Part II covers child sexual abuse. This basic organization was followed because many researchers and other interested academics and service workers tend to be interested in one or the other of these topics. However, we strongly recommend that this book be read from the beginning to the end. Four of the studies obtained prevalence data on both rape and child sexual abuse. Only the methodology that is specifically associated with child sexual abuse is described in Part II. In addition, to avoid repetition for the chronological reader, the rationales explaining why certain methodologies elevate prevalence rates whereas others reduce them are not repeated.

Chapter 2 focuses on four issues that are relevant to rape prevalence research, including the laws about rape. Chapter 3 is devoted to a description of the methodology and findings of Russell's federally funded probability sample survey on the prevalence of rape in San Francisco in 1978. Although more than 20 years have passed since Russell's research team conducted the fieldwork, this study is still worthy of attention. Not only was it the first survey focused on obtaining the prevalence of rape and child sexual abuse to be based on a large-scale community probability sample of adult women in the general population, but it also achieved a higher prevalence rate for rape than all subsequent studies. For child sexual abuse, as we shall see in Chapter 12, Russell's and Wyatt's studies obtained equally high prevalence rates when their definitions of child sexual abuse and the age range of the respondents were made comparable.

The FBI's methods for obtaining data on reported rape are described in Chapter 4, along with their most recent statistics on reported cases. These statistics are then compared with those obtained by Russell. Chapter 5 describes the methodology and findings of the high-priced annual National Crime Surveys, now renamed the National Crime Victimization Surveys, that are conducted by the Bureau of Justice Statistics at the Department of Justice. Because of the tremendous importance of these surveys in terms of resources, continuity, and influence, considerable attention is devoted to evaluating their low incidence rates and comparing them with those obtained by Russell.

Chapters 6 and 7 are devoted to descriptions of the methodologies and findings on the incidence and prevalence of rape of eight different representative surveys that meet our criteria for inclusion in this volume. Each study is also evaluated in terms of methodological soundness.

According to the official statistics, the rape rate has been declining in recent years. In Chapter 8, the validity of these findings is discussed. The data available on the trends in the rape rate over time are also included in this chapter. In addition, changes in the rape rates reported to the police over time are traced by examining the FBI's yearly statistics on reported rape. Russell's data on changes in the prevalence of rape over time are also presented; most of these cases were never reported to the police. These two ways of measuring the magnitude of the rape problem in the United States over many decades are compared.

Part II begins with Chapter 9 on the laws relating to child sexual abuse. Chapter 10 provides a description and critique of studies designed to measure the incidence of child sexual abuse in the United States. Russell's methodology and findings on the prevalence of child sexual abuse are the subject of Chapter 11. The other eight representative surveys that assessed the prevalence of child sexual abuse and that met our criteria for inclusion are described and evaluated in Chapters 12 and 13, and comparisons are made between some of these studies in Chapter 14.

Chapter 15 is devoted to an assessment and comparison of the prevalence of child rape based on the six studies that have provided data on this subject. Evaluation of these studies includes assessing the validity of the highly publicized claims of two well-known studies that most rapes are perpetrated on children and adolescent girls.

The backlash against research-based findings that rape and child sexual abuse are widespread problems in the United States is the subject of Chapter 16, authored by Russell. Because Gilbert has played, and continues to play, the key role in this backlash, this chapter focuses on his arguments to discredit studies that have found high prevalence rates of rape and child sexual abuse, particularly his criticisms of Russell's research. Russell then criticizes Gilbert's critiques of her research methodology and findings.

Chapter 17 ends with a plea to the public to treat the epidemic of rape and child sexual abuse in the United States as a national emergency.

NOTES

---

1. *The New York Times Magazine*, not *Time* magazine, ran this excerpt.

2. These authors included two of Russell's articles about the same study in their 16 references for what were supposed to be different studies (Gorey & Leslie, 1997, p. 397). This raises doubts about the validity of their analysis of these surveys.

PART I

The Scope of Rape

2

◆

RAPE LAWS AND
PREVALENCE RESEARCH

This chapter will focus on four important issues that are relevant to rape prevalence research: legal definitions of rape, definitions of rape used by researchers who study the prevalence of rape, some of the reasons for women's reluctance to disclose their rape experiences, and the methodological problem of telescoping in rape research.

THE LAW AND DEFINITIONS OF RAPE

Forcible rape is defined by the Federal Bureau of Investigation (FBI, 1998) as

> the carnal knowledge of a female forcibly and against her will. Assaults or attempts to commit rape by force or threat of force are also included; however, statutory rape (without force) and other sex offenses are excluded. (p. 25)

Children and adolescents who are forcibly raped qualify for inclusion in the FBI statistics.

The old-fashioned term *carnal knowledge* is not defined in the annual reports, but it is generally understood to refer to penile-vaginal sexual intercourse. Hence, the definition excludes oral and anal penetration as well as penetration when the woman is unable to consent because she is unconscious, drugged, or incapacitated in some way. Furthermore, it excludes forcible rape by males on males, females on females, and females on males.

21

Federal and state laws distinguish between *forcible rape* and *statutory rape*. The latter refers to *intercourse with a female who is below the age of consent*. In 1987 this age varied from a low of 13 years in two states to a high of 18 years in 14% of the states. Sixteen years was the age of consent in 61% of the states (Searles & Berger, 1987, p. 40, Table 13). In cases of statutory rape it is unnecessary for the prosecutor to prove that the victim resisted the attack or to establish that the rapist used force.

Because the inhabitants of different states are subject to rape laws at the state—not the federal—level, the FBI's definition affects only the statistics gathered on reported rape and rape attempts documented annually in the *Uniform Crime Reports*. Statistics aside, federal criminal laws on rape cover land that is owned by the federal government, such as buildings, parks, and some Native American reservations. In addition, federal law governs interstate commerce, including criminal acts such as transporting someone across state lines to commit a rape.

Clearly, a revision of the FBI's very narrow definition is long overdue. It has not kept up with the reforms that have been made at the state level. Fortunately, the feminist movement has been more successful in achieving reforms of state laws on rape. Mary Koss and Mary Harvey (1991) cite the following definition of rape formulated by Searles and Berger (1987) as exemplifying the reforms that started to be incorporated into the law in the mid-1970s:

> Rape is defined as nonconsensual sexual penetration of an adolescent or adult obtained by physical force, by threat of bodily harm, or when the victim is incapable of giving consent by virtue of mental illness, mental retardation, or intoxication. Included are attempts to commit rape by force or threat of bodily harm. (p. 26)

It took years of feminist struggle to get most states to reform their rape laws. However, even those states that did so are not in agreement about how to define rape, whether to substitute other terminology for this word, what acts to criminalize, and so on. For example, one feminist reform "redefined rape as sexual assault in order to emphasize that rape was a violent crime and not a crime of uncontrollable sexual passion" as it had often previously been considered to be (Searles & Berger, 1987, pp. 25-26). Patricia Searles and Ronald Berger (1987) noted that, "Equating rape with other assaults was intended to divert attention from questions of the victim's consent, for assault is, 'by definition, something to which the victim does not consent'" (pp. 25-26). By 1987, 26% of the states had redefined rape as sexual assault that was limited to penetration, and another 20% had redefined rape as sexual assault that included sexual touching as well as penetration (Searles & Berger, 1987, p. 31, Table 1). The difference between these laws regarding the scope of the sex acts defined as sexual assault renders statistical comparisons of sexual assault rates incomparable in these states.

Searles and Berger (1987) also note that instead of the term *sexual assault,* some states label penetration offenses as "sexual battery, criminal sexual penetration, criminal sexual conduct, gross sexual imposition, sexual abuse, or sexual intercourse without consent" (fn. 5, p. 25).

Feminist law reform also "broadened the primary offense beyond its traditional limitation to vaginal-penile intercourse, to include sexual penetration generally (i.e., vaginal, oral, and anal) as well as touching of intimate body parts" (Searles & Berger, 1987, p. 26). Penetration, however slight, qualifies the attack as completed rape, and the presence of semen is no longer required.

In addition, rape or sexual assault was redefined in sex-neutral terms. However, Koss and Harvey (1991) maintain that rape "is properly applied to men only when a penetration offense has occurred." Hence, they believe that an assault in which a woman uses a weapon to force a male into having vaginal intercourse with her should be disqualified as rape because *she* is the one to be penetrated. Koss and Harvey (1991) also note that "virtually all these incidents [of male victimization] are perpetrated by another male" (p. 5). However, we think it is important that the law include the full range of rape offenses, including male rape by men and women, regardless of how rare these acts may be.

Women, for example, can rape men anally with a finger, hand, or foreign object. And for those who disagree with Koss and Harvey's notion that women cannot rape because they are the ones to be penetrated, women can force men to penetrate them by threatening them physically or by means of a weapon. In addition, there are rare cases of women collaborating with male rapists either by helping them entrap a victim and/or by helping to immobilize her, or by actually participating in the sexual assaults. Women who act in this way are usually brutalized sex slaves of the rapists they assist. While the law typically treats the woman's predicament as an extenuating circumstance, it does not usually spare her from being charged for the crimes and sentenced to a term in prison (e.g., Canadian Karla Homolka Bernardo was incarcerated for her participation in the notorious rape/torture/sexual slavery femicides[1] of adolescent girls by her serial killer husband Paul Bernardo, despite her key role in his prosecution in 1995).

However, most cases of male rape by females are statutory rapes of underage males. There are also a few cases of statutory rape of underage females by adult women.

Although rape in marriage has been made illegal in most states, marital rape laws still treat rape by husbands as less serious than rape by other perpetrators. For example, the law in some states requires that marital rape be reported within a shorter period of time than rape by other perpetrators; it treats marital rape as a misdemeanor rather than a felony; and it disqualifies cases in which the wife was unable to consent because she was incapacitated by alcohol (Russell, 1992).

Unfortunately, even the best laws may not prevent sexist prejudices from affecting their implementation. For example, although it is no longer legal in most states to require rape survivors to testify about their sexual history, some attorneys manage to use various subterfuges to play on jurors' beliefs that women who dress provocatively or who have had multiple sex partners cannot be raped. In one controversial trial in Oxford, England, in 1993, for example, the attorney showed the jury a photograph of the rape survivor wearing a revealing dress. This ploy was considered the trump card in winning a not-guilty verdict for the rapist.

Hence, despite reforms of the rape laws, Koss and Harvey (1991) note that, "Many feminists maintain that the 'spirit' of the law has changed very little and that women continue to be treated as property, not as persons" (p. 125).

TERMINOLOGY USED BY RESEARCHERS

Several survey researchers who have obtained prevalence data on sexual crimes have opted to use the term *sexual assault* instead of, or in combination with, rape (e.g., Burt, 1980; Gordon & Riger, 1989; Largo et al., 1999; BJS, 1997; Sorenson, Stein, Siegel, Golding, & Burnam, 1987; Winfield, George, Swartz, & Blazer, 1990). There is probably even less consensus among prevalence researchers on a definition of sexual assault than there is on a definition of rape. Although sexual assault can be defined as synonymous with rape, this usually is not the case in research studies. For example, Winfield et al.'s (1990) North Carolina survey of 1,157 women 18 to 64 years old determined whether a sexual assault had occurred by asking the respondents,

> Have you ever been in a situation in which you were pressured into doing more sexually than you wanted to do, that is, a situation in which someone pressured you against your will into forced contact with the sexual parts of your body or their body? (p. 337)

This definition of sexual assault includes penetration, but it also includes much less severe nonpenetrative acts, making it a far cry from rape.

Pioneer rape researcher Martha Burt (1980) used the term *sexual assault* in her survey of public attitudes concerning this violation in Minnesota in 1977, yet she titled her article "Cultural myths and support for rape." Whether or not her respondents interpreted her three prevalence questions as being about sexual intercourse or a broader notion of sex is an empirical question that Burt did not address in this publication.

Burt's first question was: "Have you ever had anyone force sex on you against your will?"; the second asked: "Have you ever had anyone attempt to force sex on you, but unsuccessfully?"; and the third asked, "Have you ever had sex with someone only because you were afraid physical force would be used against you if you didn't go along?" (p. 221). While most women probably interpret the word *sex* in this context to mean sexual intercourse, it is quite possible that some interpreted this word more broadly. For example, if a date had attempted to forcibly touch the genitals of one of Burt's respondents, the woman may have interpreted this act as attempting to force sex on her whereas she may not have interpreted the same behavior as an attempted rape. Burt's atypical finding that the prevalence of *attempted* sexual assault (26.6%) was 3.2 times higher than the prevalence of completed sexual assault (8.4%) supports this possibility. This finding compares with Russell's (1984) and Patricia Tjaden and Nancy Thoennes's (1998b) identical survey findings that attempted rape was only 1.8 times higher than completed rape, and Dean Kilpatrick's (1985) survey finding that attempted rape was only 1.2 times higher than completed rape.

Some rape researchers lump rape together with acts of sexual assault, for example, Margaret Gordon and Stephanie Riger (1989). Furthermore, these researchers fail to define either of these concepts. Other researchers provide separate prevalence data on rape and sexual assault, but combine the terms for much of their analyses (e.g., BJS, 1997).

Robert Michael, John Gagnon, Edward Lauman, and Gina Kolata (1994) used the phrase "forced to do something sexual" in the question they asked respondents in their National Health and Social Life Survey (p. 223). While rape victims willing to disclose their victimization would no doubt answer this question in the affirmative, so too might respondents who were forced into less severe sexual acts.

While we understand and respect the reasons some feminist law reformers recommended using the concept of sexual assault in place of rape, we think there is a very telling reason to reject this approach: Focusing on the assault aspect of rape minimizes the meaning, significance, and common effects of sexual penetration on women as opposed to being assaulted elsewhere on their bodies.

Prevalence studies that use the term *sexual assault* always have data on rape, even when they include in their definition less serious forms of sexual violation. However, the latter studies rarely report separate data on sexual assault and rape. This omission prevents these researchers from being able to compare their prevalence rates and other findings with studies of rape, as well as with the official statistics on rape.

These are some of the reasons we made usage of the term *rape* a criterion for including studies in our sample. Studies that used the term *sexual assault* as well as *rape* were eligible for inclusion as long as they separated their prevalence estimates for these crimes.

SURVIVORS' RELUCTANCE TO DISCLOSE RAPE

Because rape is the most underreported violent crime in the United States, it poses a particular challenge to those who set out to measure its magnitude. For example, in the first national survey to assess the prevalence of rape, Kilpatrick, Edmunds, and Seymour (1992) found that only 16% of the incidents of completed rape were reported to the police (p. 5). This compares with only 9.5% of completed and attempted rapes in Russell's (1984) survey.

Many factors discourage women from reporting their rape experiences to the police. For example, the rape survivors interviewed in Kilpatrick et al.'s National Women's Study (NWS, 1992) were at least somewhat or extremely concerned:

1. about their families knowing they had been raped (71%);
2. about people blaming them for the attack (68%);
3. about people outside their families knowing about the rape (68%); and
4. about the news media publicizing their names (50%). (p. 4)

All of these concerns reveal rape survivors' well-grounded fear that they will be stigmatized for having been raped. In addition,

5. Many rape survivors are discouraged from reporting their rape to the police because they anticipate sexist and demeaning treatment by them.
6. Many fear being retraumatized by going through the investigation and trial.
7. Many consider their rape to be a private matter and want to keep it that way.
8. Many find it too embarrassing to contemplate having to talk explicitly and repeatedly about the sexual details of their rape experience to police and court officials.
9. Many believe that no purpose will be served by reporting the rape because they have no faith in the way the system of justice deals with this crime and because they anticipate a negative outcome.
10. Some are fearful of retribution by the rapist and his friends or by their partner; some want to try to forget the experience as soon as possible and not prolong the agony by a long drawn out trial.
11. Some choose not to report the rape for political reasons. For example, minority women may be unwilling to report attackers who belong to their ethnic group out of a sense of loyalty or guilt or fear of being "guilt-tripped" by other members of their ethnicity.
12. Minority women who are raped by white men may opt not to report because they anticipate no justice from the racist law enforcement and criminal justice systems.
13. Politically progressive middle-class white women may be unwilling to report minority men for the same reason (see Russell, 1975).

These concerns are common despite more than 20 years of feminists' efforts to change public attitudes about rape and to improve the way rape survivors are treated. Fortunately, several of the reasons that many rape victims opt not to report their victimization to the police do not apply to their willingness to disclose these experiences to survey interviewers. On the other hand, divulging their rape experience(s) to an interviewer cannot lead to certain positive outcomes such as facilitating the arrest of their rapist or obtaining victim compensation.

In conclusion: The secrecy of rape survivors about their experience(s) makes it exceedingly challenging to design effective studies of the prevalence of rape. This in turn is why all aspects of the methodology employed are of such vital importance. If a study has excellent methodology on all the important variables except one, that one negative feature can result in a poor estimate of rape prevalence. For example, unskilled interviewers can ruin an otherwise first-rate study. So can poor screen questions on rape.

Women's known reluctance to disclose their experiences of rape and child sexual abuse means that underdisclosure, not overdisclosure, is the problem that prevalence researchers have to overcome. Hence, the fabrication of rape experiences during interviews is exceedingly rare. Whatever motives a small fraction of women might have to fabricate rape in their real lives, such as avoiding blame for pregnancy or infidelity, are absent in a sociological interview.

Nevertheless, prevalence studies of rape cannot aspire to obtaining true prevalence rates. They measure the percentage of women respondents who are able to remember their experiences of rape, and whose experiences are evoked by the screen questions asked, and who are willing to disclose their experiences to survey interviewers. This is why many prevalence researchers describe the prevalence rate they obtain as an estimate.

THE TELESCOPING EFFECT

Incidence studies of rape based on interviews in which respondents are asked to specify the number of such assaults that occurred in the previous 12 months have been shown to suffer from a memory distortion called "telescoping" (Skogan, 1976; Sparks, Genn, & Dodd, 1977, p. 35f). Wesley Skogan (1976) describes *forward* telescoping as follows:

> There is a strong tendency for victims of crimes that occurred more than one year ago to misrecall the date of those events and mentally pull them forward into the suggested reference period. This "forward telescoping" leads to an overstatement of the crime rate for the reference year. (p. 114)

Forward telescoping can apparently be reduced by asking respondents to provide important landmark events such as the election of a new president or some natural catastrophe to help them place the date of the rape experience more accurately. This strategy is one way to achieve "bounded recall." According to Koss and Harvey (1991), studies using data from the federal government's National Crime Surveys have shown that unbounded recall produces rates that "are about one third higher than bounded recall" (p. 14).

Another method of reducing forward telescoping is to interview respondents periodically, as does the National Crime Surveys, so that "the respondents' previous contact with the interviewer serves as a reference point for where to begin remembering" (Koss & Harvey, 1991, p. 14). In addition, according to Richard Sparks et al. (1977), when there is more than one interview,

> The interviewer knows what items were reported by the respondent at the preceding interview, and can thus avoid recording items which have been telescoped into the latest reference period; he [*sic*] can also used [*sic*] the respondent's earlier reports to help establish the latest reference period in the respondent's mind. (p. 39)

However, we chose not to make the forward telescoping adjustment to Russell's rape incidence rate for two reasons. First, no other investigator whose incidence figures will be compared with Russell's in the following chapters made an adjustment for the telescoping phenomenon. Second, we consider many of the tables, figures, and textual descriptions of Russell's findings to be quite complex and sometimes confusing for readers to follow. Including the telescoping calculations would only aggravate this problem. Researchers and readers who think otherwise can do the arithmetic for themselves for Russell's and other investigators' studies.

In conclusion: Many problems beset even the most rigorously designed prevalence studies of rape. Women's reluctance to disclose their experiences of rape may be the most significant of these problems, as well as the difficulty of developing methods of inquiry that can overcome this reluctance. This was a particularly challenging undertaking in 1978 when Russell conducted her representative survey of the incidence and prevalence of rape and child sexual abuse. This pioneering study is the subject of the next chapter.

NOTE

1. *Femicide* refers to the killing of females by males *because* they are female, or, more briefly, sexist murders (see Radford & Russell, 1992).

3

◆

RUSSELL'S SURVEY ON THE INCIDENCE AND PREVALENCE OF RAPE IN SAN FRANCISCO

After the first few feminist books and articles about rape were published in the first half of the 1970s, including Russell's (1975), the National Institute of Mental Health formed the National Center for the Control and Prevention of Rape in 1976 especially to fund research on rape. Russell decided to apply for funding to conduct a study on the prevalence of rape because she considered this topic to be a top priority. Many feminists at that time claimed that rape was a widespread problem, whereas most other individuals believed it to be relatively rare. Russell thought it was vitally important to try to ascertain which of these views was correct by conducting a scientifically rigorous survey on the prevalence of rape. She knew this would be expensive research that would require substantial funding. Happily, the Rape Center funded her research proposal in 1976 (however, she delayed the starting date until 1977).

BACKGROUND

It is probably difficult for contemporary sexual assault researchers to imagine what it was like to embark on a probability sample survey of rape and child sexual abuse in the 1970s. Russell was told by numerous professional survey researchers with whom she consulted that 1,000 respondents would be far too few to obtain a sufficient number of rape victims to conduct meaningful analyses or to acquire an adequate basis for estimating prevalence rates. They also maintained that few women would be willing to divulge such experiences. In the face of the unanimous skepticism she encountered from professionals in the field, Russell came to realize that her assumption that many women would be willing to disclose their mostly secret experiences was a massive gamble. In 1977, Russell's first year of funding, the task she was engaged in was considered almost certain to fail.

Although Russell considered subcontracting with a survey research center to conduct her survey, as many principal investigators do, she became convinced that this would result in an underestimate of the prevalence of rape and the other kinds of sexual violations she planned to investigate. For example, she believed that her knowledge about rape and child sexual abuse, which survey research firms cannot be expected to have, would have a significant impact on the interview schedule to be constructed and the training of the interviewers.

Being a relative novice in interview schedule construction, Russell sought the help of an expert on this task who was renowned for her ability to formulate questions on taboo topics. Despite several weeks of her best efforts, this expert finally admitted that the task was beyond her capabilities. Hence, Russell decided to do the job with the help of her assistant.

After finalizing the interview schedule, Russell hired two freelance survey research interviewer supervisors and trainers to help select the interviewing staff and to train and supervise the interviewers. Russell played a major role in this important task as well as in all the other phases of the fieldwork.

It turned out that the professional survey researchers were wrong: A sample of 930 women was more than adequate to yield a sizeable group of rape and child sexual abuse survivors who were willing to talk about their experiences. Russell believes that her decision not to farm out her study to a survey research firm contributed significantly to this achievement.

OBJECTIVE

The major goal of Russell's 1978 San Francisco survey was to obtain a more accurate estimate of the prevalence of rape and child sexual abuse (including incestuous abuse), as well as other forms of sexual assault, among the general population of females.

METHODOLOGY[1]

The Sample

A probability sample of households was drawn by Field Research Associates, a well-respected public opinion polling organization in San Francisco. They selected "key addresses" from the San Francisco telephone directory. Each address served as a starting point for obtaining a cluster of household listings. Enumerators used these key addresses as starting points for listing all the addresses on the entire side of that block. They then applied another systematic randomizing procedure to select a number of addresses in each block proportional to the density of the block. Russell ended up with a sample of 2,000 addresses from which she hoped to obtain 1,000 interviews with adult women.

Carefully trained female interviewers went to each address drawn in the probability sample to determine whether a woman 18 years or older resided there. To be eligible for the study, the woman also had to understand and speak English or Spanish. If there was more than one eligible woman in a given household, a procedure was applied to randomly select the one to be interviewed.

Because of a high incidence of not-at-homes during the summer months when the interviews were conducted, and because of an unexpectedly large number of households in which no eligible woman resided (there were, and still are, an unusually high percentage of all-male households in San Francisco—the gay capital of the United States), an additional sample of 1,200 addresses had to be drawn to increase the number of respondents obtained. While budget problems prevented the completion of the second sample, a comparison between the samples yielded no significant differences between them. Fortunately, therefore, the randomness of the first sample was not jeopardized.

In-person interviews with the 930 randomly selected female residents of San Francisco were conducted throughout the summer of 1978. The average length of these interviews was 1 hour and 20 minutes.

San Francisco was selected as the location for this survey rather than Oakland, Berkeley, or other cities in California near where Russell resided because it is the largest and most prominent of these cities. While San Francisco is known to have a large population of gay men, she considered it unlikely that this would have an impact on the prevalence of heterosexual rape or the sexual abuse of female children.

Comparisons of the incidence of reported rapes for different cities are made problematic by different definitions of rape and by different reporting practices by the police. Nevertheless, it seems worth noting that the incidence rate for reported rapes per 100,000 individuals in several cities in 1978, when Russell conducted her study, were very similar to the incidence rate in San Francisco: 86 rapes per 100,000 individuals were reported in San Francisco, 83 per 100,000 in Los Angeles, 84 per 100,000 in Boston, 88 per 100,000 in Cleveland, and 91 per 100,000 in Dallas (Federal Bureau of Investigation [FBI], 1979).[2]

The Definition of Rape/Attempted Rape

Russell used the legal definition of rape and attempted rape in California in 1978 when her data were collected:

Rape is forced intercourse (i.e., penile-vaginal penetration), or intercourse obtained by threat of force, or intercourse completed when the woman was drugged, unconscious, asleep, or otherwise totally helpless and hence unable to consent. Attempted rape is an attempt at one of these same acts.

Russell chose this conservative, unreformed definition of rape in order to compare her study's rape incidence rate with the incidence rate obtained by the National Crime Surveys in 1978, and with the FBI's rate per 100,000 females for San Francisco and the nation.

Questions on Rape/Attempted Rape

Questions that are asked of respondents to elicit data on prevalence are typically referred to as screen questions. Many researchers' screen questions are formulated so that all the affirmative answers to them contribute to the prevalence rate. However, many of Russell's questions were different. In areas where denial was anticipated, the initial questions asked were very broad. For example, respondents who were, or who had been, married were asked, "Have you ever had an unwanted sexual experience with your husband?" Those respondents who answered in the affirmative were then asked follow-up questions to ascertain whether any of these experiences met the study's definition of completed or attempted rape.

Eighteen questions in Russell's study were designed to help elicit respondents' experiences of completed and/or attempted rape, as well as to trigger their memories of these experiences.

Many women do not conceptualize sexual attacks as rape even when those attacks fit the legal definition of rape. This is particularly true when the rapist is an intimate. Therefore it is crucial to include questions that avoid using the word *rape*. The following question was the only one out of the 18 questions on rape in Russell's survey that included this word: "At any time in your life, have you ever been the victim of a rape or attempted rape?"[3]

The following three questions were asked three times: the first time about strangers, the second time about acquaintances or friends, and the third time about dates, lovers, or ex-lovers. This was to allow respondents enough time to think about these different categories of potential rapists as well as to jog their memories about rape experiences they may have had with any of these six different kinds of perpetrators. The pronoun *he* was used in these questions because a prior question had asked about all unwanted sexual experiences with females.

1a. Did a stranger/acquaintance or friend/date, lover or ex-lover ever physically force you, or try to force you, to have any kind of sexual intercourse (besides anyone you've already mentioned)?

1b. IF YES: How many different people can you think of right now that that happened with? (An identifier—i.e., some name, word, or description that would enable the respondent to remember the experience later—was obtained for each experience the respondents disclosed at this time and whenever they disclosed a new experience thereafter.)

2a. Have you ever had any unwanted sexual experience, including kissing, petting, or intercourse with a stranger (etc.) because you felt physically threatened (besides anyone you've already mentioned)?

2b. IF YES: Did he (any of them) either try or succeed in having any kind of sexual intercourse with you?

2c. IF YES: Ask question 1b above.

3a. Have you ever had any kind of unwanted sexual experience with a stranger (etc.) because you were asleep, unconscious, drugged, or in some other way helpless (besides anyone you've already mentioned)?

3b. IF YES: Did he (any of them) either try or succeed in having any kind of sexual intercourse with you?

3c. IF YES: Ask question 1b above.

For every episode of rape or attempted rape disclosed, a separate questionnaire was administered. This included a description of the assault sufficiently detailed to ensure that the definition of completed or attempted rape had been met.

It was clear in a few cases that a respondent's definition of rape was broader than the one used in the study. For example, some respondents reported *feeling* forced rather than *being* forced, or having intercourse because of a threat but not a threat of physical force or bodily harm. These cases were disqualified as instances of rape or attempted rape.

After the interview, a staff supervisor examined each interview, checked to see that the questions on rape were being properly probed, and that appropriate decisions were being made about whether or not the experience qualified as rape.

Before the interviews were coded, Russell and two highly trained staff members reviewed every interview to check whether the interviewer had made the correct assessment of completed and attempted rape incidents. Whenever there was a disagreement between two of these women on this matter, the third woman made an independent assessment, then all three discussed the case until agreement was reached.

The Refusal/Nonparticipation Rate

Field Research consultant Joie Hubbert and other survey research consultants informed Russell at the outset of her study that San Francisco was a notoriously difficult city in which to conduct interviews. They reported that it was common for San Franciscans not to answer their doors unless they were expecting a caller. They also warned Russell that gates were often locked, making it impossible even to have access to doorbells. When using the most stringent standards for ascertaining refusal/nonparticipation rates, these impediments clearly contributed to this rate.

The proportion of respondents who refused to participate, knowing that the study was about rape, was 19%.

When the men as well as the women who declined to give a listing of those living in the household are included in the refusal/nonparticipation rate, it increased to 36%. When men would not reveal the household members—assuming there were others besides themselves—it was impossible to ascertain whether or not an eligible woman lived in the household.

The refusal/nonparticipation rate rose to 50% if it included:

Households in which no one was ever at home

Households made inaccessible to the interviewer by locked gates or other physical deterrents

Women who had agreed to be interviewed but were unavailable because of logistics, or because their husbands or some other person would not give the interviewer access to them

Many of the households that were inaccessible or where no one was at home or where a man refused to provide information about who lived in the house besides himself (if anyone) may have been households in which no eligible woman lived. Therefore, Russell regards *the 36% refusal/nonparticipation rate as the most valid of these three.* Indeed, some prevalence researchers limit their participation rates to refusals by known eligible women. Had Russell excluded households in which males or females whose eligibility was unclear, declined to report who else, if anyone, lived in the house, her refusal/nonparticipation rate would have been lower than 36%. Unfortunately, Russell did not record what percentage of men and women declined to provide enumeration data. To try to ascertain this information now would take an inordinate amount of time.

Many researchers now calculate participation or response rates instead of refusal rates, presumably because some or many of those who do not participate in the survey also do not refuse to participate. Russell's 36% refusal/nonparticipation rate translates into a 64% participation rate. Although this participation rate is lower than Russell hoped it would be, Peters, Wyatt, and Finkelhor (1986) have noted that participation rates for surveys on child sexual abuse are typically lower than surveys on other topics, including other sensitive topics. Presumably, this applies to surveys on rape as well.[4]

Quantitative and Qualitative Data

As well as quantitative data, Russell obtained substantial amounts of qualitative data. This made it possible to find out how respondents understood the questions. In addition, it enabled staff members to do careful cleaning of the data—particularly the data on prevalence—to ensure that there was no double counting of victimizations. Finally, it also made it possible to verify that respondents' answers properly fitted the study's definitions of rape and child sexual abuse.

FINDINGS

The Incidence Rate for Rape

In order to obtain an incidence rate for rape, Russell's survey interviewers asked each survivor of completed or attempted rape if the assault had occurred in the 12 months prior to the interview. All cases of wife rape[5] were excluded in this first comparison because rape in marriage was not illegal in California or most other states in 1978.

The Incidence Rate Excluding Wife Rape. Thirty-four of the completed and attempted nonmarital rapes disclosed by Russell's 930 respondents occurred during the 12 months prior to the interview (i.e., from mid-1977 to mid-1978). Since women had to be 18 years old to be eligible for the survey, these 34 rapes were confined to women who were at least 17 years old at the time of the rape. Hence, *the incidence rate for completed and attempted nonmarital rape was 37 per 1,000 females 17 years and older residing in San Francisco in 1977-1978* (or 3.7%; 34/930 × 1,000 = 37).

Just over half of the 34 rapes that had occurred within the 12 months prior to the interview were completed (51%) and just under half of them were attempted (49%).

The Incidence Rate Including Wife Rape. Since Russell's incidence rate will be compared in the following chapters with other studies that include wife rape, a second incidence rate was calculated based on the 36 cases of completed and attempted rape that include the two wife rapes that had occurred in the prior 12 months. Hence, *the incidence rate for completed and attempted rape including wife rapes was 40 per 1,000 females 17 years and older residing in San Francisco in 1977-1978* (or 4.0%; 37/930 × 1,000 = 40).

The Prevalence Rate for Rape

Of the 930 women in Russell's sample, *24% (223) disclosed at least one completed rape, and 31% (291) disclosed at least one attempted rape.* (Some respondents were included in both these categories, which is why their numbers add up to 514 instead of 407; see below.) When completed and attempted rapes are combined, as they are in the official statistics, *44% (407) of*

TABLE 3.1 Number of Women Victimized by Completed and/or Attempted Rape Once or More by Different Rapists

Number of Rapes by Different Rapists	Number of Women Raped	Number of Incidents (Number of Attacks × Number of Women Attacked)
1	205	205
2	112	224
3	47	141
4	27	108
5	7	35
6	2	12
7	3	21
8	2	16
9	2	18
Total	407	780

the respondents in Russell's survey disclosed at least one completed or attempted rape.

It is important to mention that all the completed and attempted rapes contributing to these prevalence rates were committed by different rapists. Multiple rapes by one perpetrator were counted as only one rape.

When wife rape was excluded from the total number of rapes to bring the statistics in line with the failure of the rape laws in California and most other states in 1978 to criminalize marital rape, the prevalence estimates are as follows: 19% of the 930 women (175) disclosed at least one completed nonmarital rape, and 31% (284) disclosed at least one attempted nonmarital rape. When the survivors of attempted nonmarital rape who had *also* been victimized by completed nonmarital rape were excluded, the prevalence rate for attempted nonmarital rape dropped to 22% (204). When the categories of rape and attempted rape are combined, 379 (41%) disclosed at least one completed or attempted nonmarital rape.

Because Russell's prevalence rates for completed and attempted rape, as well as the percentage of these incidents that were reported to the police, will be compared in Chapters 5, 6, and 7 with other studies that include wife rape, further analyses will include wife rape unless otherwise stated.

Exactly half (50%) of the 407 women who disclosed an experience of completed or attempted rape had been raped more than once. As may be seen in Table 3.1, these rape survivors were attacked from one to nine times by different rapists (a pair or group rape is counted as one attack). Of those women who were attacked, the average number of incidents with different rapists was close to two (1.92).

EVALUATION[6]

Russell's shockingly high prevalence rates of 24% for completed rape and 44% for completed and attempted rape raise the question of whether some respondents fabricated their experiences.

Fabrication of rape experiences is very rare because of the stigma of being a rape victim. And, as we mentioned in Chapter 2, fabrication of rape during a research interview is likely to be even more rare. Assuming that attitudes toward rape were more victim-blaming in 1978 (when Russell's survey was conducted) than they are today, the stigma of rape was likely to have been even greater then than now. Following are three other factors that make fabrication especially unlikely in Russell's study:

- The interviewers were instructed to convey to respondents that the contribution to the study by women with no experiences of sexual victimization was as valuable as those who had been sexually victimized.
- Interviewers were asked to try to assess the honesty and reliability of respondents' answers. The consensus among them was that underdisclosure, not fabrication, was a significant problem.
- A few respondents admitted on a self-administered questionnaire they completed at the end of the interview that they had been unwilling to disclose some of their sexually abusive experiences. However, no respondent admitted on this questionnaire to fabricating or embellishing an experience of rape.

Factors Contributing to Russell's Study Obtaining a High Prevalence of Rape

Because prior surveys suffered from severe underdisclosure of rape experiences (e.g., Ennis, 1967; National Crime Panel Surveys [the original name for the National Crime Victimization Surveys]), Russell made a concerted effort to minimize this problem in her survey. Following are some of the methodological features of her study that we consider relevant to the high rape rates her study obtained.

Russell uses the terms *rape-appropriate* and *child sexual abuse-appropriate* methodological features to refer to those that were designed specifically to elicit disclosures of these taboo experiences. She selected 10 of the methodological features of her study that she considers to be rape-appropriate and rape-sensitive. We believe that their inclusion contributed greatly to her respondents' ability (e.g., by triggering their recall of these experiences) and willingness to disclose these forms of sexual victimization. Several of these methodological characteristics are unique to Russell's study.

Rape-Appropriate Methodology

Opting for Face-to-Face Interviews. Although there is no consensus about the relative efficacy of face-to-face interviews, telephone interviews, and self-administered questionnaires for obtaining prevalence data on rape and child sexual abuse, Peters et al. (1986) found that face-to-face interviews were associated with higher child sexual abuse prevalence rates in their comparative study of 19 prevalence surveys (pp. 37-40). After mentioning a number of advantages to this mode of collecting data (e.g., the opportunity to develop good rapport and to motivate the respondent to be truthful by asking explicit questions forthrightly and by modeling comfort with the material), Peters et al. (1986) concluded that the advantages of face-to-face interviews (FFI) may be due to "the possibility of using well-selected and trained interviewers to enhance candor." However, "Without this special component, FFI may be no different from the other modes" (p. 40). We agree with this conclusion.

Engaging in Extensive Pretesting of the Interview Schedule. During the year Russell took to develop her interview schedule, it was repeatedly pretested. The final test involved respondents whose histories of remembered sexual assault experiences were already known to Russell. When the prevalence questions yielded disclosures by these respondents of all these incidents, Russell considered her interview schedule ready to be used in her survey.

Fieldwork Not Farmed Out to Other Professionals. Except for the drawing of the sample, all facets of the study were undertaken by Russell and her staff, not subcontracted out to professional survey researchers with no particular knowledge or sensitivity about rape and/or child sexual abuse.

To our knowledge, no systematic study has yet been undertaken to determine whether interviewers who are trained and supervised by survey research centers hired to do the job are as successful in obtaining realistic disclosures of rape or child sexual abuse as are interviewers who are trained and supervised by the principal investigator and her staff. Nevertheless, we suspect that, other things being equal, in-house training of interviewers by qualified project staff is likely to be more successful in prevalence research on taboo topics like rape and child sexual abuse than farming the job out to a survey research organization.

Rejecting Victim-Blaming Interviewer Applicants. Russell required her interviewer applicants to take a test on their rape myth beliefs. Those who did poorly on this test were not hired for the job.

Providing Additional Education About Rape and Child Sexual Abuse. The 33 interviewers who were hired received an intensive 65-hour training over a period of 2 weeks. It included education about rape and child sexual abuse, desensitization to sexual words, and rigorous training in administering the interview schedule.

Matching Interviewers and Respondents. Interviewers and respondents were matched by gender, and also by race/ethnicity whenever possible. We believe that such matching is particularly important in a study of sexual assault about which most survivors are very secretive.

Ensuring Complete Privacy and Confidentiality. The need for absolute privacy for the interview was stressed. If a respondent was unable to obtain this at her home, the interview was conducted at the study's office. Before starting the interview, the respondent was required to complete a consent form on which confidentiality was promised. She was told that this form would be locked up in the office and that her name and address would be erased from all the other records. We consider privacy to be a particularly crucial variable in overcoming victims' reluctance to disclose, and we consider confidentiality to be particularly important in building trust.

Constructing Questions to Engender Trust in Survivors of Sexual Assault. Respondents were asked how strongly they agreed or disagreed with several questions that were deliberately formulated to convey a non-victim-blaming attitude by the interviewers. For example, "Any woman could be a victim of rape or sexual assault," and, "Rape victims are not responsible for having been raped." Russell deliberately avoided framing the latter question as "Rape victims *are* responsible for having been raped." Another question: "Sexual assault within families is very common," was designed to convey to incest survivors that they were far from alone. A similar question for survivors in general was: "Most women experience some kind of sexual assault at least once in their lives."

Postponing Questions About the Details of Each Victimization. Interviewers were instructed to go through all the prevalence questions before completing a mini-interview schedule for each incident of rape or child sexual abuse that qualified as sufficiently serious to contribute to the prevalence rate. Respondents were asked to choose an "identifier" that would remind them of each experience. This rule was implemented after discovering during the pretest that completing a mini-interview schedule right after the first mention of an incident that qualified as a rape or a case of child sexual abuse resulted in many respondents failing to disclose all their experiences because of their reluctance to complete a mini-interview schedule for each one.

Avoiding Words Like Incest, Molestation, and Rape. Because many respondents do not perceive themselves as victims of incest, molestation, or rape, these terms were not used in the interview schedule except for one question that included the word *rape*. (There were many more questions about rape that avoided using this word.)

Formulating Many Screen Questions About Rape (18) and Child Sexual Abuse (14) That Are Behavior- and Relationship-Specific. Extensive pretesting of the interview schedule revealed that the number of different experiences of sexual victimization that respondents were able to recall was facilitated by asking many questions that were behaviorally and relationship specific.

A meta-analysis conducted by Bolen and Scannapieco (1999) found that the number of screen questions was the strongest methodological feature to predict the prevalence of child sexual abuse (p. 291). These researchers compared studies with screen questions ranging from 1 to 14 in number, and found that the more screen questions there were, the higher the prevalence rate. Similarly, when Peters et al. (1986) examined the prevalence rates obtained in 14 different studies of child sexual abuse, they found "a definite connection between the number of questions asked and the prevalence rates reported" (p. 40). They explained this finding by noting that many questions provide respondents with "more cues regarding the various kinds of experiences that the study was asking about and . . . they gave the respondents a longer time and more opportunities to overcome embarrassment and hesitation about making a disclosure" (cited in Finkelhor, 1994, p. 37). Presumably, these findings are equally applicable to rape.

Devising Inverted Funnel Questions. Rape-appropriate methodology requires devising "inverted funnel questions" as opposed to "broad funnel-type questions." Each of the latter type of questions requires subjects "to recall, order, and evaluate their experiences" at the same time (Wyatt & Peters, 1986b, p. 248)—which is too taxing to facilitate success in respondents' efforts to recall their experiences. As an example of the broad funnel-type question, Wyatt and Peters (1986b) cited one asked by Finkelhor (1979):

> Now we want to ask you to think of three sexual experiences—or however many up to three—that you had *before the age of 12 with an adult* (a person over 16) including strangers, friends, or family members like cousins, aunts, uncles, brothers, sisters, mother, or father. Pick the three most important to you and answer the following questions. (cited by Wyatt & Peters, 1986b, p. 248)

This question asked the respondents to recall far too much information at one time.

On the other hand, Russell's questions pertained "to narrowly delimited sub-areas regarding the types of child sexual abuse, regardless of the subjects' responses to previous questions" (Wyatt & Peters, 1986b, p. 248). Hence respondents had the opportunity to respond to a number of questions about different types of abuse, rather than to only one question about many of them.

Repeating the Same Question About Different Perpetrators. For example, Russell's interviewers asked respondents the same question about forced intercourse three times, first by strangers, second by acquaintances or friends, and third by dates, lovers, or ex-lovers. This gave respondents the opportunity to focus on these different kinds of perpetrators, thereby facilitating their ability to recall these experiences if they had had them. Mentioning these six types of perpetrators ranging from the least intimate (strangers) to the most intimate (lovers) also communicated to the respondents that the interviewer was interested in their experiences with nonstereotypic types of rape.

Requiring Interviewers to Probe. Interviewers were required to probe respondents' answers to several questions as well when they obtained a description of each incident of rape or child sexual abuse that qualified for inclusion in the prevalence rates. For example, the following probes were suggested in the mini-interview schedules about each experience recalled:

> Did any other kind(s) of unwanted sexual experience(s) ever happen with this person (these people)?
>
> Besides what you've described, what else exactly did he/she/they do to you or force you to do to him/her/them?
>
> Is there anything else he/she/they *tried* to do to you or tried to force you to do to him/her/them?

Interviewers were instructed to continue probing the respondents' descriptions of the attack until they were satisfied that the definitions of rape or child sexual abuse had been met. They were also encouraged to diverge from the interview schedule in order to probe answers that were unclear to them, or if the respondent needed help in overcoming her distress. This made the interview more informal and humane, and allowed the interviewer to use her skills more freely.

Having a Relatively Long Duration for the Interview. Russell's interviews took an average of 1 hour and 20 minutes each. This is substantially longer than in most other prevalence studies. It allowed time to develop good rapport between interviewers and respondents and for respondents to recall additional experiences of rape and child sexual abuse as the interview proceeded.

Other Methodological Features That Were Not Specifically Designed to Facilitate Disclosures of Rape and Child Sexual Abuse That We Believe Contributed to Russell's High Prevalence of Rape

Making Prevalence the Major Focus of the Study. Russell's study is, to our knowledge, the only one whose essential objective was to ascertain the prevalence of rape and child sexual abuse. We believe this contributed significantly to her high prevalence rates for rape and child sexual abuse because it made it possible to explore this difficult task in great depth. John Murphy (1991) also maintains that studies with a limited focus "that concentrate solely on sexual abuse or related issues tend to report higher prevalence rates than do studies that investigate child sexual abuse along with a variety of other topics"

(p. 86). Murphy speculates that "this may be due to the notion that child sexual abuse studies may give the respondent time to adjust to the subject matter along with the oppotunity to recall information they might not have remembered in a less focused interview" (p. 86). Murphy's reasoning applies to Russell's even narrower focus on the prevalence and incidence of rape and child sexual abuse.

Paying Interviewers by the Hour, Not by the Interview. This policy avoided rewarding interviewers for brief interviews with minimal disclosure and punishing those who did lengthy interviews and obtained high disclosure.

Payment of a Fee of $10 for the Interview. Obviously, the value of $10 was much higher in 1978 than it is now. This payment increased respondents' motivation to cooperate and likely made it more difficult for them to break off the interview. Not one of them did so.

On the other hand, the exclusion of populations of women from Russell's sample who are most vulnerable to rape and child sexual abuse is undoubtedly a major factor that contributed to lowering her study's prevalence rates. This unfortunate consequence applies to all prevalence studies based exclusively on household samples because they exclude women in institutions such as prisons, mental hospitals, half-way houses, brothels, and the military, as well as runaways and homeless women. These women are likely to have been subject to particularly high rates of rape and child sexual abuse.

Methodological Limitations of Russell's Survey

1. The most obvious limitation of Russell's survey is the fact that it was confined to one city. Therefore her findings cannot be generalized beyond San Francisco.

2. Russell's 64% participation rate diminishes the representativeness of her sample. Surprisingly, research on participation rates in studies of child sexual abuse shows that they have no predictable impact on its prevalence (Bolen & Scannapieco, 1999; Peters et al., 1986). However, comparable research on rape studies has not, to our knowledge, been undertaken.

3. Russell's study is extremely difficult to replicate because the interview schedule was not designed to be self-explanatory. Nor is a clear set of written instructions still available.[7] Although a few researchers have sought to replicate Russell's survey, Dutch researcher Nel Draijer, who investigated the prevalence

of incestuous abuse in the Netherlands, is the only one of them to complete her study. However, her study was by no means an exact replication of Russell's methods, although it was greatly influenced by them.[8]

4. Russell's data also proved exceedingly difficult to analyze. Survey research firms had advised her to simplify her analysis by restricting the number of sexual abuse experiences per respondent to the most recent incident, the most upsetting incident, the first incident, and/or some combination of these. While this approach would enable a researcher to calculate a valid prevalence rate (i.e., the percentage of women who have ever experienced rape or child sexual abuse), it would have precluded the calculation of an incidence rate and undermined the validity of the analyses of the characteristics of different types of sexual assault. Hence, Russell ignored this advice despite the considerable challenge involved in finding a way to analyze data in which the number of victims' experiences of sexual assault ranged from none to more than 20 with different perpetrators. Fortunately, Bill Wells, a brilliant consultant at UC Berkeley, solved this analytical problem.

5. Finally, Russell's sample size of 930 women was too small to obtain sufficiently large numbers of respondents in minority racial/ethnic groups to do anything beyond simple analyses. This was particularly the case for Native American women.

Some researchers have assumed that Russell's very high rate of rape in San Francisco was due to that city's reputation for being a center of sexual deviance and libertarian sexual views. However, others have assumed the opposite: that the more permissive the attitudes to sex, the lower the rape rate will be. No sound data are available to shed light on which, if any, of these views is correct. (The relationship between the prevalence of child sexual abuse found and the region in which the study was conducted will be discussed in Chapter 14.)

CONCLUSION

We think that the strengths of Russell's study far outweigh the shortcomings. Russell succeeded in creating a methodology that was uniquely geared to encourage respondents to disclose their taboo experiences. The many ways in which Russell's methodology is exemplary is all the more commendable because hers was the first probability survey ever undertaken that focused on ascertaining the prevalence of these forms of sexual victimization. It continues to demonstrate to the scholarly community that rape-appropriate and child sexual abuse-appropriate methodology can enable many women to share their most private experiences of sexual violation with women interviewers.

The findings and innovative methodology of Russell's study have stood up well over time. Many aspects of the methodology that she pioneered still qualify as exemplary for conducting prevalence research today.

NOTES

1. For much more detailed information on all aspects of Russell's methodology, see Russell (1986), Chapter 2.

2. The rape rate per 100,000 individuals in San Francisco in 1978 was higher than in other major cities, for example, New York, 55; Washington, D.C., 70; and Chicago, 45, but lower than in others, for example, Detroit, 107; Atlanta, 139; and Memphis, 103 (FBI, 1979).

3. Twenty-two percent of the respondents answered this question in the affirmative and offered descriptions that met the study's definition of rape or attempted rape.

4. Russell conducted several analyses to try to assess the bias introduced by the nonparticipants. The representativeness of the sample was also assessed by comparing the characteristics of those who were interviewed with the characteristics of the population from which the sample was drawn—that is, women residents of San Francisco. These analyses are available elsewhere (see Russell, 1990, pp. 27-41).

5. The term *wife rape* is preferred over *marital rape* because it reveals the gender of the victim. All terms relating to sexual and nonsexual violence that conceal the fact that women are typically the ones targeted are avoided when possible.

6. Child sexual abuse will be referred to from time to time in this chapter because many features of the methodology described here apply to estimating its prevalence as well as the prevalence of rape. This will save us from having to repeat these points in Chapter 11.

7. Numerous interviewer instruction memos were handed out as needed during the fieldwork period. However, several of these memos cannot be located.

8. Interestingly, Draijer (1990) obtained a prevalence rate for incestuous abuse that was very similar to Russell's. Although it was also considered very high, it revolutionized Dutch people's understanding of this form of sexual victimization in their country.

4

◆

RAPES REPORTED TO THE POLICE: A COMPARISON OF THE FBI'S AND RUSSELL'S DATA

THE FBI STATISTICS ON RAPE

The FBI coordinates the yearly gathering of statistics on eight offenses known to the police: four violent crimes against individuals (murder, rape, aggravated assault, and robbery) and four property crimes (burglary, larceny-theft, motor vehicle theft, and arson; FBI, 1996, p. 1). The purpose of this program is to generate "a reliable set of criminal statistics" (FBI, 1996, p. 1). The statistics on the eight offenses were chosen "as an Index for gauging fluctuations in the overall volume and rate of crime" (FBI, 1996, p. 1). These statistics are published annually in the *Uniform Crime Reports* (*UCR*). No statistics are obtained on the annual prevalence of these crimes (i.e., the percentage of individuals who are victimized by each of these crimes during a 12-month period).

Unfounding

A number of reported rapes are "unfounded" by the police every year. "Unfounding" refers to the "percentage of complaints determined through investigation to be false" (*UCR*, 1993, p. 24). These complaints are excluded from the crime counts. Eight percent of the rape complaints made in 1995 were "unfounded" because the police considered them to be "false or baseless," as compared to only 2% of the other Index crimes (murder, robbery, aggravated assault, burglary, larceny-theft, motor vehicle theft, and arson; FBI,

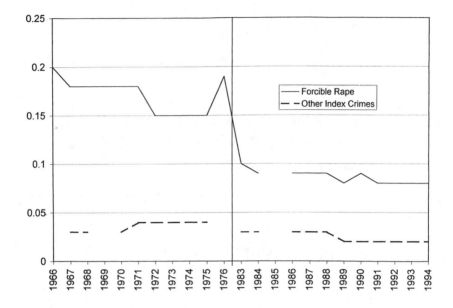

Figure 4.1. The *Uniform Crime Reports'* Unfounded Rates for Forcible Rape and Other Index Crimes: 1966-1976 and 1983-1994

NOTE: For reasons unknown, considerable data on the percentages of unfounded Index crimes are missing from the *UCR*. The vertical line indicates missing data from 1977 to 1982; the blanks in both graphs also reflect missing data.

1996, p. 24). The criteria used by the police to determine which complaints are false or baseless are not explained in the *Uniform Crime Reports*.

Figure 4.1 compares the fluctuations in the percentages of unfounded rapes between 1966 (the year in which these percentages were first published) and 1994 with the fluctuations in the percentages of all the other Index crimes during this period (see Table A1.8.1 in Appendix 1 for the figures on which Figure 4.1 is based). Table A1.8.1 shows that the fluctuations in the percentages of unfounded rapes ranged from a low of 8% to a high of 20% compared to a low of 2% and a high of 4% for all the other Index crimes combined.

No explanation is provided for why so many more reported rape cases are unfounded by the police than other major crimes of violence. Nor is any explanation given for the fluctuations in the percentage of unfounded cases over time or why there were periods when the percentages of unfounded cases were not published. In a recent study of rape myth acceptance among the male clients of female prostitutes, "23% agreed that half or more of the women who report a rape are lying because they want to punish the man they accuse, and 21% believed that half or more of reported rapes are invented by women who want to protect their reputation" (Monto & Hotaling, 1998, p. 9). Since these myths are also widespread in the general population (Burt, 1980), it is likely that some percentage of policemen also subscribe to them. In short, sexism seems a likely explanation for why so many more cases of rape than other violent crimes are considered to be false or baseless by the police.

One thing is clear: It is inaccurate to describe the official statistics on rape published in the *UCR* as reported cases is inaccurate because they represent only those cases that the police find credible.

THE VOLUME AND RATE OF REPORTED RAPES (MINUS THE UNFOUNDED CASES) IN THE UNITED STATES IN 1997

According to the *UCR* for 1997, 96,122 cases of forcible completed and attempted rape (excluding unfounded cases) were reported to law enforcement agencies throughout the nation during that year (FBI, 1998, p. 25; these are the most recent statistics available). Eighty-eight percent of these rapes were completed and 12% were attempted. The *UCR*'s *rate* of *reported rape for 1997 was 70 per 100,000 females (or 0.7 per 1,000 females;* p. 26).

METHODOLOGY

Data Collection

While the UCR Program was started in 1929 (FBI, 1996, p. 378), the data on trends in the FBI's rape rates over time started in 1932 (see Table A1.8.1 in Appendix 1). The *UCR* Program is "a nationwide, cooperative statistical effort of over 16,000 city, county, and state law enforcement agencies voluntarily reporting data on crimes brought to their attention" (FBI, 1996, p. 1). The statistics "are compiled from monthly law enforcement reports or individual crime incident records transmitted directly to the FBI or to centralized state agencies that then report to the FBI" (FBI, 1996, p. 378). By 1995, "law enforcement agencies active in the *UCR* Program represented approximately 251 million United States inhabitants—95% of the U.S. population" (FBI, 1996, p. 378).

Definition of Rape

As mentioned in Chapter 2, the *UCR* continues to define forcible rape as

the carnal knowledge of a female forcibly and against her will. Assaults or attempts to commit rape by force or threat of force are also included; however, statutory rape (without force) and other sex offenses are excluded. (FBI, 1998, p. 25)

This narrow definition of rape means that the following acts are excluded from the FBI's statistics published in the *UCR:* oral and anal penetration; penetration when the female is unable to consent because she is unconscious, drugged, or incapacitated in some way; forcible rape by males on males, females on females, and females on males. Although wife rape meets the FBI's definition of rape, these assaults would presumably only have been included in their statistics as they became illegal in different states.

The FBI counts both pair and gang rape as one forcible rape (*Uniform Crime Reporting Handbook,* 1984).

UNIFORM CRIME REPORT
FINDINGS FOR 1978

It is important to remember that the FBI's *UCR* statistics on reported rapes always exclude the unfounded cases. However, in the interest of readability, we will not repeatedly qualify the term "reported rapes" by adding (and not unfounded).

According to the *UCR* (FBI, 1979), 583 forcible rapes and attempted rapes of females were reported in San Francisco in 1978 (p. 89). Based on the estimated population of 343,552 females in San Francisco in July 1978 ("Population Projections," 1978), 583 rapes constitutes *a rape rate of 1.7 per 1,000 females* (583/343,552 × 1,000 = 1.7).

The national *UCR* (FBI, 1979) rate for reported rapes in 1978 was even lower than the rate for San Francisco—*0.6 per 1,000 females* (p. 15). While there was no information on the *UCR*'s percentage of completed rapes in San Francisco in 1978, 75% of the rapes recorded nationwide that year were completed rapes (p. 15).

EVALUATION:
THE *UCR*'S RATE OF REPORTED RAPE
VERSUS THE ACTUAL RAPE RATE

Even the compilers of the *UCR* provide several examples of their failure to achieve their goal of providing reliable statistics on crime. For example, they point out that "not all law enforcement agencies provide data for complete reporting periods," thus necessitating the estimation of crime counts (FBI, 1996, p. 367). These estimates are combined with the crime statistics that are reported. Modified recording procedures and incomplete reporting are also noted as problems (1996, p. 378).

With regard to rape in particular, the compilers of the *UCR* (1996) acknowledge "the inability of some state *UCR* Programs to provide forcible rape figures in accordance with *UCR* guidelines" (p. 367). No explanation is given for why these guidelines are not followed, how often this is the case, and if this is a more serious problem for rape than for the other Index crimes. The compilers also refer to other problems at the state level that have required "unique estimation procedures" (p. 367). They note, for example, that the *UCR* Programs in Illinois (from 1985 to 1995) and in Michigan and Minnesota (in 1993) were unable to provide acceptable forcible rape statistics to the FBI (1996, p. 367).

Since the laws on rape vary by state, and since it is reasonable to assume that there is considerable variety in how seriously different law enforcement agencies take their responsibility to ensure that these statistics are carefully and consistently compiled, uniformity in the acquisition of the statistics on reported rape in the United States is an impossible goal. In addition to these sources of inaccuracy in the FBI's statistics on rape, it is important to remember that the vast majority of rape victims do not report their victimizations to the police.

TABLE 4.1 Comparison of FBI's and Russell's 1978 Incidence Rates per 1,000 Women for Completed and/or Attempted Rapes That Occurred Within the 12 Months Prior to the Interviews

Study/Source	Incidence Rate	Number of Rapes	Number of Respondents	Number of Times Russell's Rate Is Higher Than FBI's
Russell, San Francisco, 1978	36.7	(34)	930	
FBI, San Francisco, 1978ᵃ	1.7	—		21.6
FBI, National, 1978bᵇ	0.6	—		61.2

SOURCES: a. *UCR,* 1979, p. 79
         b. *UCR,* 1979, p. 15

A COMPARISON OF THE *UCR*'S
AND RUSSELL'S RAPE STATISTICS
IN SAN FRANCISCO IN 1978

Rape Incidence Rates

As previously mentioned, the incidence rate for completed and attempted nonmarital rapes in Russell's survey was 36.7 per 1,000 females 17 years and older residing in San Francisco in 1977-1978 (see Chapter 3). In contrast, the *UCR*'s (1979) 1978 incidence rate for San Francisco was only 1.7 per 1,000 females of all ages. Hence, *Russell's rape incidence rate for this city was 21.6 times higher than the UCR's.* Furthermore, as shown in Table 4.1, *Russell's rape incidence rate was 61.2 times higher than the UCR's national incidence rate of 0.6 for completed and attempted rapes* per 1,000 females.

In addition, the *UCR* statistics include women who live in institutions, women who are homeless, and women who are raped in San Francisco but who do not reside there, whereas Russell's survey excluded all these categories of women. Homeless women and women who live in institutions are at particularly high risk of having been raped. Hence, the 1977-1978 disparities between the rape incidence rates of the *UCR* and Russell's survey would have been even greater but for this methodological difference.[1]

This comparison leaves no reasonable doubt that the FBI's statistics on reported rape grossly understated the true rape rate in 1978. It is crystal clear that the official statistics on reported rapes only represented the tip of the iceberg.

The Number of Incidents of Completed and Attempted Rape

The *UCR* (FBI, 1979) recorded 583 incidents of completed and attempted forcible rapes in San Francisco in 1978. Had the *UCR* obtained the same incidence rate of 36.7 per 1,000 females for San Francisco as Russell did, their 583 incidents of completed and attempted rape would have increased to 12,593 incidents (583 × 21.6).

Russell's Report Rate for All Completed and Attempted Rapes

As previously mentioned, *only 9.5% (66) of the incidents of completed and attempted rape (excluding wife rape) in Russell's survey were reported to the police* (see Table 4.2). Table 4.2 also shows that Russell's reported rate for completed rape was higher than her reported rate for attempted rape (12.9% and 8%, respectively). However, this difference only approached significance at the $p < .05$ level. In addition, Table 4.2 shows that more completed and attempted rapes were reported in the prior 12 months than rapes that occurred at any time in the victims' lives (13.5% vs. 9.5%, respectively).

A COMPARISON OF REPORTED AND UNREPORTED RAPES DISCLOSED IN RUSSELL'S SURVEY

How do cases of rape or attempted rape that are reported to the police differ from those that are not reported? This question is critical because a great deal of knowledge about rape is based only on reported cases. Since only a small percentage of rapes is ever reported to the police, the similarities and differences between reported and unreported cases have enormous implications. To show that they are very different is to show that studies based

TABLE 4.2 Completed and/or Attempted Rapes Reported to Police in Russell's Survey

	Rapes Reported to Police		
Type of Rape	Percentage	Number [1]	Sample Size
Excluding wife rape			
Completed/attempted	9.5	66	672 [2,3]
Completed	12.9	32	249
Attempted	8.0	34	423
Completed/attempted in past 12 months [4]	13.5	5	37
Including wife rape [4]			
Completed/attempted	8.6	66	740 [2]

NOTES: 1. Multiple attacks by the same perpetrator counts as one only; rape/attempted rape involving multiple perpetrators is also counted as only one experience.

2. Missing observations on whether or not the rape attacks were reported to the police: 40.

3. Sixty-eight cases of wife rape have been subtracted from this number.

4. Wife rape was still legal in California in 1978; therefore respondents could not report these attacks.

on reported cases, such as the *UCR*, have little relevance to the rape issue in general. To begin this analysis, we take a closer look at the reported and unreported rapes in Russell's sample (see Table 4.3).

While only 9.5% of all completed and attempted rapes disclosed in Russell's survey were reported to the police, the third column of Table 4.3 shows that close to one third (30%) of all the stranger rapes divulged by respondents were reported to the police. This percentage is far higher than reports of rape by any other type of rapist. For example, the report rate for stranger rape is more than twice as high as the report rate for authority figures (13%)—the category with the next highest report rate. Table 4.3 also reveals that the closer the relationship between the victim and rapist, the less likely that the rape was reported to the police.

In 1978, date rape and rape by lovers still had little credibility with the police and the public at large. Why a much higher percentage of women who were raped by boyfriends rather than by dates, lovers, or ex-lovers reported their experiences of rape to the police is difficult to comprehend.

A comparison between the fifth and seventh columns in Table 4.3 further illustrates how focusing solely on reported rapes distorts the reality of the true frequency of rape. For example, although 55% of all rapes that were reported

TABLE 4.3 Perpetrators of Completed and/or Attempted Rape in
Russell's Survey and Reporting to Police by Type of Rapist

Rapist/Victim Relationship[1]	Total Rapes[2]	Rapes Reported to Police		Reported Rapes by Perpetrator Compared to All Reported Rapes		Rapes by Perpetrator Compared to All Rapes	
Column numbers	1 (N)	2 (N)	3[3] (%)	4 (N)	5 (%)	6 (N)	7 (%)
Stranger	115	35	30	35/64	55	115/672	17
Acquaintance	173	12	7	12/64	19	173/672	26
Friend of family	17	1	6	1/64	2	17/672	3
Friend of victim	62	1	2	1/64	2	62/672	9
Date[4]	124	1	1	1/64	2	124/672	18
Boyfriend[4]	31	3	10	3/64	5	31/672	5
Lover or ex-lover	63	2	3	2/64	3	63/672	9
Relative (not husband)	31	2	6	2/64	3	31/672	5
Authority figure (not relative)	56	7	13	7/64	11	56/672	8
Total	(672)	(64)			102[5]		100

NOTES: Missing observations: 33.

1. Husbands are excluded because there was no law against wife rape in California in 1978, so none of the victims of wife rape reported being raped at that time.
2. In cases of pair or group rape, only the primary perpetrator is included here.
3. These figures were obtained by calculating the number of rapes reported in column 2 for each type of rapist/victim relationship as a percentage of the total number of rapes by each type of rapist (col. 6) (e.g., for stranger rape, 35/115 × 100 = 30%).
4. The term *date* includes relationships where there has been very little contact (e.g., one date), whereas the term *boyfriend* has more long-term connotations. However, these terms were not defined for our respondents; we merely accepted their usage of them.
5. This total does not add up to 100% due to rounding.

to the police involved strangers (column 5), stranger rapes were only *17%* of the total number of reported and unreported rapes (column 7). Another disparity was found in rapes by acquaintances, which constituted 19% of the reported cases (column 5) but 26% of the total number of rapes (column 7). Only 2% of the reported cases involved date rapists (column 5), whereas 18% of the total number of cases were date rapes (column 7).

Separation of the rapes that were reported to the police from the rapes that were not reported to the police in Russell's survey yields the following interesting findings:

1. More completed than attempted rapes were reported to the police—13% and 8%, respectively (significant at $p < .05$ level).

2. Just over one fifth of the reported rapes (22%) involved more than one rapist, compared to only 7% of the unreported cases (significant at $p < .001$ level).

3. Victims who were raped on more than one occasion by the same rapist were less likely to report any of the rapes to the police than victims who were raped only once (this finding reached a significance level of only $p = .07$).

4. Victims who were physically threatened with a weapon in connection with being raped were more likely to report the rape to the police than those who were not so threatened: 24% and 7%, respectively (significant at the $p < .01$ level).

5. When the rapist was armed with some kind of weapon, whether or not he actually used it or threatened to use it, the victim was much more likely to report the rape to the police than when the rapist was unarmed: 33% and 7%, respectively (significant at the $p < .001$ level).

6. The greater the degree of physical violence used, the more likely the rape was to be reported. Thirty-eight percent of the victims who were beaten or slugged, 18% of those who were hit or slapped, and only 5% of those who were pushed or pinned reported the rape to the police (significant at the $p < .001$ level).

7. Victims who were living with their parents at the time of the rape were less likely to report the rape to the police than women who did not live with their parents: 7% and 12%, respectively (significant at the $p < .05$ level).

8. There was a highly significant relationship between how upset the victim said she was as a result of the rape and whether or not she reported the rape to the police. Fifteen percent of those who described themselves as having been "extremely upset" reported the rape to the police, compared with only 8% of those who said they had been "very upset," 5% of those who said they had been "somewhat upset," and none of those who said they had been "not very upset" or "not at all upset" (significant at the $p < .001$ level).

9. Similarly, 16% of the victims who described having suffered great long-term effects reported the rape to the police. This compares with 10% of those who described having experienced some long-term effects, and only 4% of those who described having experienced few or no long-term effects (significant at the $p < .001$ level).

A number of factors were unrelated to the reporting of rape victimization, for example: (a) whether or not the victim was married at the time of the rape; (b) the victim's household income at the time of the rape; (c) the age difference between the victim and the rapist; (d) the victim's religious upbringing or religious preference at the time of the interview; and (e) whether or not the rape or attempted rape involved more than one female victim.

THE OUTCOME OF REPORTED RAPES
IN RUSSELL'S SURVEY

Of the 670 cases of rape and attempted rape in Russell's survey where information on both the rapist and the outcome of the victim's police report were available, only 2% (13 cases) resulted in arrests, and only 1% (6 cases) culminated in convictions. However, if the conviction rate for rape and attempted rape is calculated on the basis of reported cases only, it increases to 9%.

Although stranger rape was by far the most likely form of rape to be reported (see Table 4.3), not one of the 35 reported cases of stranger rape ended with a conviction. However, there was also only one arrest for stranger rape, whereas there were three arrests of acquaintance rapists. Presumably, stranger rapists are the most difficult rapists to catch and identify, despite the fact that stranger rapes are the most likely to be believed by the police.

In summary: This analysis of the differences between the reported and unreported cases in Russell's survey shows that reported rapes were most often perpetrated by strangers, and were more violent, traumatic, and life-threatening than rapes that were not reported. This certainly makes intuitive sense. It follows that the rapes that are reported (and founded) by the police are very unrepresentative of unreported rapes.

THE NATIONAL INCIDENT-BASED
REPORTING SYSTEM (NIBRS)

In 1982, the Bureau of Justice Statistics (BJS) and the FBI sponsored a study of the *UCR* Program "with the objective of revising it to meet law enforcement needs into the 21st century" (BJS, National Incident-Based Reporting System [NIBRS]; http://www.ojp.usdoj.gov/bjs/nibrs.htm). A 5-year redesign effort was undertaken to develop a statistics-gathering program to provide more comprehensive and detailed crime statistics than those obtained by the FBI. This redesign effort resulted in the formation of the National Incident-Based Reporting System, which will "replace the nearly

70-year-old UCR program" (Greenfeld, 1997, p. 11). NIBRS has expanded the offenses that law enforcement agencies track from 8 crimes to 57 crimes. NIBRS also revised the FBI's definition of rape as follows:

> *Forcible rape* is the carnal knowledge of a person forcibly and/or against that person's will; or not forcibly or against the person's will where the victim is incapable of giving consent because of his/her youth or because of his/her temporary or permanent mental or physical incapacity. This offense includes both male and female victims and threats and attempts. (Greenfeld, 1997, p. 31)

In addition, NIBRS provided separate definitions for:

1. statutory rape
2. forcible sodomy (which includes "oral or anal sexual intercourse")
3. sexual assault with an object (use of "an instrument or object to . . . penetrate the genital or anal opening")
4. forcible fondling
5. incest ("nonforcible sexual intercourse between persons who are related to each other within the degrees wherein marriage is prohibited by law") (Greenfeld, 1997, pp. 31-32)

It is surprising that NIBRS's definition of rape still uses the old-fashioned term carnal knowledge instead of penile-vaginal sexual intercourse. Nevertheless, these definitions are an enormous improvement on the FBI's *UCR* definition of rape. Instead of combining rape, forcible sodomy, and sexual assault with an object—as rape researchers and state statutes are increasingly doing—NIBRS separates them. This makes it possible for researchers to analyze them separately or in combination. This is a great advantage for researchers, who continue to define rape in different ways, because it will enable them to make more precise comparisons between their data and NIBRS's data.

The BJS has received data from Alabama, North Dakota, and South Carolina—"the first NIBRS-participating States for . . . 1991" (Greenfeld, 1997, p. 11). Among other findings, the data on gender and rape revealed that 90.3% of all rapes involved female victims and male perpetrators; 8.7% involved male victims (their perpetrators are not reported); 0.8% involved victims and perpetrators who were both female; and 0.2% involved male victims and female perpetrators (Greenfeld, 1997, p. 11).

It is important to remember that all NIBRS's statistics are based on reported cases. Thus the gender of rapists and rape victims may well be different in the entire universe of rape crimes from those reported by NIBRS.

We hope that NIBRS will find a way of gathering much more reliable statistics from law enforcement agencies in the United States than the FBI has managed to do. Currently, there is a very low participation rate with NIBRS by police departments. This undermines the validity of their findings. Clearly, the participation of police departments must be drastically increased in order for NIBRS's statistics to become useful. In addition, they should address unfounding rates, which are higher for rape complaints than for other crimes. They should also ensure that women staff and people of color are well represented at all levels of the work involved. (Only one female out of 12 members was listed as a member of the Steering Committee, and only one female out of seven was mentioned as a member of the Technical Working Group. This is totally unacceptable.)

The UCR Program is currently being converted to NIBRS, and a BJS study is being conducted to identify the best ways to encourage a "wider and more rapid adoption of full NIBRS" by law enforcement agencies (BJS, National Incident-Based Reporting System [NIBRS], http://www.ojp.usdoj.gov/bjs/nibrs.htm).

There is a NIBRS (April 1998) Web site (http://www.nibrs.search.org/frmain.htm) on which a discussion forum is being planned to

> enable justice agency professionals and NIBRS experts nationwide to ask questions and share information and experiences. . . . In addition, the What's New section lists the newest information available on this project, particularly new documents from the FBI (Implementing the National Incident-Based Reporting System; no page number provided).

Presumably, individuals can write to this Web site with questions and suggestions. Those working on NIBRS will hopefully be open to input from rape researchers. If this is not the case, we must work together to ensure that they become receptive to our questions and concerns.

A RADICAL REFORM IN THE COMPILATION OF RAPE STATISTICS[2]

According to *The Philadelphia Inquirer* reporters Mark Fazlollah, Craig McCoy and Robert Moran (March 21, 2000), "for many years, sex-crime investigators deliberately mislabeled rapes and other offenses to make the city appear safer" (p. A9). Regarding rape specifically, "Current and former investigators said they dumped cases to cope with an overwhelming workload and pressure from commanders to generate favorable statistics" (p. A9). In addition, Fazlollah et al. (2000) maintain that:

> The sex-crimes unit, founded in 1981, buried nearly a third of its caseload over the next 17 years. Rapes, attempted rapes and other reported acts were given administrative labels such as "investigation of person" or were rejected as unfounded. Either way, they did not show up in crime statistics. (p. A9)

Consequently, "many of the thousands of cases misclassified by the sex-crimes unit over the last two decades received little or no investigation" (p. A9).

To ameliorate the crisis in confidence in the rape statistics that resulted from these shocking revelations by the staff of *The Philadelphia Inquirer,* Police Commissioner John Timoney announced that a committee of women will be appointed from Women Organized Against Rape, the Women's Law Project, the Pennsylvania chapter of the National Organization for Women (NOW), and the Penn Women's Center "to help police decide when to believe sexual-assault complaints and how to classify them" (p. A9). In cases of disagreement between the women and the police, Timoney reported that the women will "quite literally" have "the final say on our classification" (p. A9).

This radical innovative plan to allow women advocates "to review the department's handling of sexual assaults 'from start to finish'" is unique to Philadelphia (quotation of Carol Tracy, the executive director of the Women's Law Project in Philadelphia, in Fazlollah, et al., 2000, p. A9). Barbara DiTullio, president of the Pennsylvania chapter of NOW, suggests that this plan "could make Philadelphia a model for police departments across the country" (Fazlollah, et al., 2000, p. A9).

Women must organize to put strong pressure on their state legislatures throughout the country to implement similar reforms.

NOTES

1. It is difficult to know the precise impact of another methodological difference on the incidence rates of reported rape: Whereas the FBI's incidence rate is based on females of all ages, Russell's was based on females who were 17 years and older. Since the *UCR* does not provide information on the ages of rape survivors, it is impossible to make Russell's and the FBI's databases more comparable with regard to age.

2. Thanks to Laura X for bringing the following information to our attention.

5
◆

THE FEDERAL GOVERNMENT'S ESTIMATES OF THE INCIDENCE OF RAPE

Rather than being revealed, the true incidence of rape is covered up by these [the National Crime Survey] data.

Koss & Harvey, 1991, p. 22

The first step in facing the reality of sexual violence in the United States is to take the blinders off official data-collection activities.

Koss & Harvey, 1991, p. 22

In recognition of the fact that most crimes are never reported to the police, the federal government instituted the National Crime Panel Surveys (NCPS) in 1972 "to assess the extent and character of criminal victimization" in the United States (Law Enforcement Assistance Administration [LEAA], 1975, p. iii). The surveys were conducted yearly to document the incidence of eight categories of reported and unreported crimes (i.e., rape, robbery, aggravated assault, simple assault, personal theft, household theft, burglary, and motor vehicle theft), as well as to provide extensive descriptive statistics about them.

These victimization surveys were initially conducted by the U.S. Bureau of the Census for the National Criminal Justice Information and Statistics Service of the Law Enforcement Assistance Administration (LEAA) in the U.S. Department of Justice (BJS, 1996, p. vii). In 1979, the Bureau of Justice Statistics (BJS) took over this responsibility and the surveys were renamed the National Crime Surveys (NCS). These surveys obtained information about crimes from a nationally representative sample of male and female household residents aged 12 or older in the United States. Approximately 50,000 households and 100,000 individuals are interviewed for the survey annually (Bachman & Saltzman, 1995, p. 6).

The information recorded by these national surveys is based on *incidents*. An incident was defined as "a specific criminal act involving one or more victims and one or more offenders" (LEAA, 1975, p. iii). These surveys have never attempted to assess the *prevalence* of the Index crimes, that is, what percentage of individuals had been victimized for each crime during the year under investigation.

The National Crime Surveys were also carried out in particular cities from time to time in the early years. In 1974, San Francisco was 1 of 13 cities surveyed (the only time). Interviews were conducted with 18,410 San Francisco residents (both female and male) aged 12 years and over who were living in approximately 9,900 households (LEAA, 1975, p. iii). Respondents were asked about criminal acts that had occurred within the prior 12 months (i.e., in 1973).

The National Crime Surveys are the second largest and most expensive ongoing surveys sponsored by the U.S. government. Only the Census is larger and more costly.

THE INCIDENCE OF RAPE IN
SAN FRANCISCO IN THE 1970s

Employing the FBI's definition of rape as "carnal knowledge of a female forcibly and against her will," as well as "assaults or attempts to commit rape by force or threat of force," the NCS reported a *rape rate for San Francisco in 1974 of 5 per 1,000 females* (FBI, 1979, p. 14). This compares with Russell's incidence rate of 36.7 per 1,000 female residents of San Francisco in 1978 (see Figure 5.1). Hence, Russell's incidence rate for rape is *more than seven times higher than the NCS's rate.*

As may be seen in Figure 5.1, the NCS's rape incidence rate for the entire United States in 1978 was even lower than its incidence rate for San Francisco in 1974, that is, *only 1.7 per 1,000 females* as compared with 5 per 1,000 females, respectively. Hence, Russell's incidence rate of 36.7 per 1,000

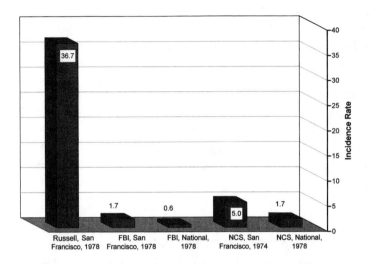

Figure 5.1. A Comparison of the Incidence Rates for Completed and/or Attempted Rape in the 1970s for the FBI, the National Crime Surveys, and Russell's Study

women in San Francisco is *22 times higher than the NCS's national incidence rate* of 1.7.

One of the purposes of the National Crime Surveys was to correct for the fact that the FBI's crime statistics are necessarily confined to crimes that are reported to, and "founded" by, the police (from here on, crimes reported to the police should be assumed to be limited to "founded" cases). However, Figure 5.1 demonstrates that the NCS's rape rate in San Francisco in 1974 was less than three times greater than the FBI's rate of rapes reported to the police (5/ 1.7). In addition, Figure 5.1 shows that the NCS's *national* rape rate was less than three times greater than the FBI's national rate of rape reported to the police (1.7/0.6). This small difference between the FBI's statistics on reported rape and the NCS's statistics on both unreported *and* reported rape hardly justifies the enormous cost of administering these annual surveys.

This comparison indicates that the NCS's methodology for assessing the incidence of rape was seriously inadequate. Some of the methodological shortcomings of the NCS were thoroughly documented by Russell (1984), and subsequently by several other researchers and experts on survey methodology and rape, particularly rape researcher Mary Koss (Koss, 1992, 1996; Koss & Harvey, 1991; also see Biderman & Lynch, 1991; Eigenberg, 1990; Kilpatrick et al., 1985). Yet despite these articulate, well-reasoned criticisms of the NCS's methodology, the NCS decision makers did not complete the implementation of their methodological changes until 1992.

The name of the National Crime Surveys was changed in 1992 to the National Crime Victimization Surveys (NCVS) to coincide with the revised methodology. Throughout the remainder of this book the surveys prior to 1992 will be referred to as the NCS and those after 1992 as the NCVS. The following section will evaluate the impact of the NCVS's revised methodology on female respondents' disclosures of rape and the methodology used to obtain them.

THE NATIONAL CRIME VICTIMIZATION SURVEYS' (NCVS) ASSESSMENT OF THE NATIONAL INCIDENCE OF RAPE IN THE 1990s

According to Helen Eigenberg (1990), an extensive evaluation of the NCS was published by the National Academy of Sciences in 1976 (p. 666). This led to a "decade-long effort to improve its ability to measure victimization, particularly certain difficult-to-measure crimes like rape and sexual assault" (BJS, 1996, p. vii). These efforts included

> a consortium of experts in criminology, survey design, and statistics [who] conducted a detailed study and testing of the survey during 1979-85 to design an improved NCVS. This work received guidance from an advisory panel that included criminal justice practitioners, policymakers, and representatives from victims' groups. (BJS, 1996, p. 149)

In addition, a panel of experts on sexual assault recommended ways to improve measures of these crimes.

Following is the NCVS's procedure for selecting the survey participants:

> Each month the U.S. Bureau of the Census selects respondents for the NCVS using a "rotating panel" design. Households are randomly selected, and all age-eligible individuals [12 years and older] in a selected household become part of the

panel. Once in the sample, respondents are interviewed every 6 months for a total of seven interviews over a 3-year period. (BJS, 1996, p. 3)

After the NCVS's revised methodology was field-tested, most of the revisions, including those relating to rape, were incorporated into the design in three stages beginning in 1989 (BJS, 1996, p. 2). The revised rape questions were phased into the interview schedule and administered to half of the households sampled in 1992. By June 1993, all of the revisions were incorporated into the interview schedule and administered to all the households in the sample (BJS, 1996, p. 152). The first annual criminal victimization report reflecting all the revisions was published in 1996. (The revised questions can be found in BJS, 1996, p. 153.) According to Ronet Bachman and Bruce Taylor (1994), the NCVS "has drastically changed the way it estimates the incidence of rape" (p. 499). They have also drastically changed their definition of rape.

DEFINITIONS OF RAPE

The National Crime Surveys continued to use the FBI's (1995) definition of forcible rape as "carnal knowledge of a female forcibly and against her will" (p. 23) from 1973 to 1992 (Bachman & Saltzman, 1995, p. 6). As with the FBI, the NCS always combined completed and attempted rape (attempted rape was defined as "assaults or attempts to commit rape by force or threat of force" [FBI, 1995, p. 23]). Koss (1996) expresses puzzlement that the NCVS maintained virtually the same definition of rape from 1973 until 1992 "given the range of reforms that were occurring statutorily" (p. 57). Be this as it may, in 1992, rape was defined for the revised NCVS as

> carnal knowledge through the use of force or threat of force, including attempts; attempted rape may consist of verbal threats of rape. It includes male as well as female victims. (Bachman & Saltzman, 1995, p. 6)

According to the BJS (1997), the term rape also includes "both heterosexual and homosexual rape"[1] (p. 149). Since "carnal knowledge" has traditionally referred to penile-vaginal penetration, use of this terminology contradicts the inclusion of same-sex rapes. On the other hand, since attempted rape includes verbal threats of rape, females can qualify as perpetrators of attempted rape by this revised definition.

Further confusing the matter, a different definition of rape is provided in the NCVS's interview manual:

> Rape is forced sexual intercourse and includes *both psychological coercion as well as physical force.* Forced sexual intercourse means vaginal, anal or oral penetration by the offender(s). This category also includes incidents where the penetration is from a foreign object such as a bottle. (Bachman & Saltzman, 1995, p. 6)

These definitions barely overlap. Furthermore, the inclusion of a broader concept of sexual intercourse in the second definition is inconsistent with the first definition's use of the term "carnal knowledge."

It is unfortunate that the NCVS's revised definition(s) of rape continues to exclude acts that are defined as rape in many states—"intercourse with girls below the statutory age of consent" and "nonforcible rapes of persons incapable of consent by virtue of unconsciousness, sleep, intoxication, or mental impairment" (Koss, 1996, p. 58).

On the other hand, by including psychological coercion and verbal threats of rape, the definitions of completed and attempted rape include acts that are not even illegal. For example, verbal threats of rape are not, to our knowledge, against the law anywhere in the United States. The law has consistently refused to effectively protect women who are subject to threats of death (restraining orders often prove worthless), let alone threats of rape, particularly if the perpetrator is a woman's husband.[2]

Consider how appalled the public would be if it were legal for women to report and charge as rape all their experiences of verbal threats to rape. Failing to distinguish between threats and acts of rape could easily result in the trivialization of the prevalence of rape.

The NCVS also fails to define psychological coercion. If it is defined subjectively (i.e., women who report *feeling* coerced), then rape would be even more endemic than it already is. Many women feel coerced to have sex by boyfriends, lovers, partners, or husbands who, for example, threaten to get sex elsewhere if the women decline the men's advances. Many women also feel threatened by dates who refuse to take them home if they resist having sex and/or by partners who show them pornography to bolster their demand to have vaginal, oral, or anal intercourse. Koss (1996) observes that the term *psychological coercion*

> may suggest to respondents situations involving false promises, threats to end the relationship, continual nagging and pressuring, and other verbal strategies to coerce sexual intercourse, which are undesirable but not crimes. (p. 60)

Koss (1996) cites her finding that 25% of women in her national sample of college students said that "they had engaged in sexual intercourse after being overwhelmed by a man's continual arguments and pressure" (p. 60). Koss did not include these kinds of psychological coercion in her counts of completed or attempted rape because they did not meet her definition of rape.

It is ironic that some researchers, including Russell, chose to define rape in narrow legal terms in order to be able to compare their rape rates with those obtained by the FBI and the NCS. While broadening the definition of rape in keeping with the expansion of many legal statutes[3] is certainly desirable, the NCVS's inclusion of psychological coercion and threats of rape as attempted rape makes this definition significantly broader than the definitions used by other researchers whose studies will be described in the following chapters. Why the NCVS researchers chose to substitute their very narrow definition for one that is so broad that it includes relatively nonserious forms of victimization is a mystery.

Other things being equal, the NCVS's broader definitions *should* result in their rape rate being considerably higher than Russell's, but as we will shortly see, it fails to get anywhere close to it.

RAPE INCIDENCE RATES

As may be seen in Table 5.1, *the NCVS's national rape incidence rate was only 0.8 per 1,000 females 12 years and older* in 1992 for those residing in half of the sampled households where the old interview schedule was administered, whereas it was *2.9 per 1,000 females* for the respondents residing in the other half of the sampled households who received the revised instrument. The latter 2.9 per 1,000 figure applies to 1992 and 1993 combined, that is, half the households in 1992, and all of them in 1993.

Table 5.1 shows that the NCS's 0.8 rape rate per 1,000 females is *46 times lower than Russell's 36.7 per 1,000 rate,* and the NCVS's 2.9 rape rate per 1,000 females is *13 times lower than Russell's 36.7 per 1,000 rate*. This comparison is visually depicted in Figure 5.2.

Although the NCVS rape rates are still unrealistically low, it is nevertheless evident that the revised methodology did obtain a higher rape rate than the old methodology. Specifically, *NCVS's 2.9 rape rate per 1,000 females for 1992/1993 is 3.6 times greater than the NCS's 0.8 per 1,000 females rape rate for 1992.*

TABLE 5.1 Comparison of Completed and/or Attempted Rape Incidence Rates: Russell, the FBI, and the National Crime Victimization Survey (per 1,000 females)

Source	Incidence Rate	(N)	Number of Times Russell's Rate Is Higher
Russell, San Francisco, 1978	36.7	(34)	—
FBI, National, 1995	0.7[a]		49
NCS, National, 1991	1.4[b]		25
NCS, National, 1992	0.8[b]	(old methodology)	46
NCVS, National, 1992/3	2.9[c]	(revised methodology)	13
NCVS, National, 1994	2.7[d]		13

SOURCES: a. UCR, 1996, p. 15
b. Table 6, BJS, 1994, p. 19
c. Table 7, BJS, 1995
d. Table 2, BJS, 1997, p. 7

When the NCS's rape rates are examined over time, however, we see that the 0.8 per 1,000 females figure is the lowest rate on record (see Table A1.8.2 in Appendix 1). Michael Rand, Chief of the BJS Victimization Statistics Unit, informed Russell that this rate was "an anomaly" because 45% of the rape victims who disclosed their victimization in 1992 were male, an atypically high percentage for male cases. In addition, because the old methodology was used in only half of the sample, there were even fewer actual rapes than usual on which to base the incidence rate (Rand, personal communication, July 17, 1997).

Hence, it is more appropriate to compare NCVS's 1992/1993 rape rate with the NCS's *mean* rape rate from 1987 to 1991, that is, 1.22 rapes per 1,000 females. Following this procedure, *the NCVS's 1992/1993 rape rate of 2.9 per 1,000 females is 2.4 times higher than the NCS's mean rape rate of 1.2 per 1,000 females for 1987 to 1991* (see Table A1.8.2 in Appendix 1). Although more than doubling the incidence rate for rape may sound like a considerable achievement, this is not the case because the lower the rate is, the smaller the increase that is required to double it.

The NCVS's rape rate of 2.7 per 1,000 females for 1994 is the most recent estimate available at this time. Russell's rape rate of 36.7 per 1,000 females is *approximately 14 times higher* than the NCVS's 1994 rape rate estimate despite the fact that the NCVS includes victimizations disclosed by

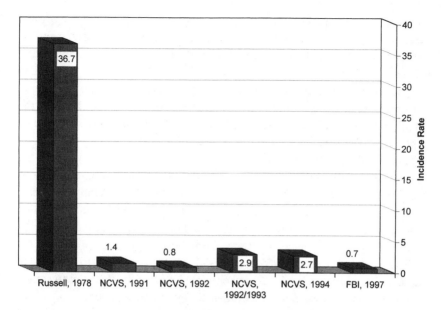

Figure 5.2. A Comparison of Russell's Incidence Rate for Completed and/
or Attempted Rape With the Incidence Rates of the FBI and the National
Crime Victimization Surveys in the 1990s

females 12 years and older whereas Russell's were limited to women 17 years
and older.[4]

THE NUMBER OF ACTUAL RAPES
DISCLOSED TO THE NCVS

There is no information on the actual number of rapes represented
by the rape rates in the NCVS reports. However, BJS statistician Rand informed Russell that *typically, the approximately 50,000 females who were
regularly interviewed for the NCS and who are now being interviewed for the
NCVS, yield only from 60 to 100 actual rape cases* (personal communication,
July 17, 1997).

The NCVS's exceptionally low 2.7 per 1,000 females rate of completed
and attempted rape demonstrates the failure of the revised methodology

to provide anything even close to a sound estimate of the incidence of rape (Figure 7.1 in Chapter 7 reveals that Russell's incidence rate for rape and attempted rape is more than 13 times higher than the NCVS's incidence rate; Tjaden and Thoennes's incidence rate is more than three times higher, and Kilpatrick et al.'s National Women's Study's incidence rate for completed rape only is more than double the incidence rate of the NCVS). Nor can the small number of rapes disclosed to the NCVS interviewers be assumed to be representative of the numerous undisclosed rapes.

The small numbers of identified rape survivors interviewed by the NCVS also make it unfeasible for their researchers to conduct useful analyses of their rape data. This may be the reason why the NCVS frequently combines their findings on rape and sexual assault. However, this unfortunate practice makes it impossible for rape researchers and other interested individuals to learn much of significance about rape from these surveys.

There are public use NCVS data tapes[5] that "allow incidents to be coded in more than 15 different ways, from completed rape with a weapon to sexual verbal threats of harassment" (Bachman & Taylor, 1994, p. 508, fn. 7). However, "rape (completed, attempted, verbal) and sexual attack (completed, attempted, verbal) will continue to be used in BJS publications" (Bachman & Taylor, 1994, p. 508, fn. 7). Researchers should not have to go to such lengths to obtain the NCVS's data on rape.

THE NCVS'S LOW DISCLOSURE OF RAPE: SOME EXPLANATORY HYPOTHESES

The NCVS's revised methodology will now be examined to try to ascertain why its disclosure rate for rape is so low. (Perhaps the term *rape disclosure rate* should replace the term *rape rate* in recognition that the true incidence of rape is, and will always be, unknown.) First, we will consider whether the NCVS's questions may discourage women from disclosing their rape experiences.

The Questions

The NCVS's questions on rape underwent a radical revision, although they are still asked in the context of other types of physical assault. There are six "screeners," defined by the NCVS as the questions "that ascertain whether the respondent has been a crime victim" (BJS, 1996, p. 152). If the respondent replies in the affirmative to any of the screen questions, the interviewer completes an incident report about the crime. Following is the first violent crime screen question asked of all respondents:

Has anyone attacked or threatened you in any one of these ways:

a) With any weapon, for instance, a gun or knife?
b) With anything like a baseball bat, frying pan, scissors, or stick?
c) By something thrown, such as a rock or bottle?
d) [Did the attack] include any grabbing, punching, or choking?
e) *Any rape, attempted rape or other type of sexual assault?*
f) Any face to face threats?

OR

g) Any attack or threat or use of force by anyone at all?
   (Emphasis added; *BJS,* 1996, p. 153)

The NCVS designers anticipated that rapes may be disclosed in response to all of these questions.

It is certainly reasonable to expect that some rape victims will reveal their victimization in answer to question (e), but many will not, particularly those who were raped by intimates. In Russell's (1984) survey, for example, only half the experiences of rape and attempted rape were disclosed in answer to the one question that included the word *rape.* In Koss's national student survey, 55% of the women raped by strangers defined the victimization as rape whereas only 23% of those raped by acquaintances described the assault as rape.

The NCVS's questions (b) and (c) are completely inappropriate for rape, and questions (a), (d), and (f) are relevant only to violent rapes. While question (e) is more appropriate to rape, its usefulness may be undermined by its inclusion in a set of questions that are far more related to violent nonsexual crimes than to rape.

The NCVS's second violent crime screen question is a great improvement on the first. It starts out by addressing sexual assault victims' reluctance to disclose:

Incidents involving forced or unwanted sexual acts are often difficult to talk about. Have you been forced or coerced to engage in unwanted sexual activity by

a) someone you didn't know before? b) a casual acquaintance? or c) someone you know well? (BJS, 1996, p. 153)

The fact that this screen question asks about a broad range of sexually assaultive experiences (being forced or coerced to engage in unwanted sexual activity) is also a good strategy for eliciting disclosures about rape. Then, when the interviewer completes the incident form, she can probe for whether the experience meets the definition of rape, attempted rape, or sexual assault. However, this depends on how good the interviewers are at probing for these crimes. In addition, restricting the question to strangers, casual acquaintances, and "someone you know well" may prompt respondents to overlook rape by other perpetrators such as family members, distant relatives, dates, and authority figures.

There are also four more screen questions about crime, none of which mention the words *sex, sexual assault,* or *rape.* The first two have multiple subquestions designed to jog respondents' memories about all types of crimes. Like the first screen question, they both ask respondents whether they were "attacked or threatened"; one screen question mentions possible locations of the attacks while the other asks about different types of "known attackers" (BJS, 1996, p. 154). The third and fourth screen questions are about reporting crimes to the police.

A problem with the term "known attackers" is that it is unlikely to prompt respondents to think about rapes by husbands, lovers, dates, family members, and/or authority figures. Many men who rape females with whom they have close or intimate relationships use force, not violence (e.g., holding the victim down as opposed to beating her up). More to the point, many rape survivors in these situations do not conceptualize their experiences as attacks.

For example, the third screen question asks: "Were you attacked or threatened OR did you have something stolen from you—a) At home including the porch or yard—" (BJS, 1996, p. 154). Asking about theft takes the focus off the beginning attack and threat portion of this question. This diversion is exacerbated by the follow-up probe's reference to the porch and the yard. These are not places that rapes typically happen. Something like, "At your home, on the street, or in the offender's home" would be far more likely to yield disclosures about rape.

To determine whether or not an incident should be recorded as a rape, the interviewer asks: "Do you mean forced or coerced sexual intercourse?" If the respondent requests clarification of the terms *rape* or *sexual intercourse,* interviewers read them the definitions of these terms in the interviewer's manual (Bachman & Saltzman, 1995, pp. 6-7). There is no comparable instruction to assist respondents who have trouble differentiating the terms *forced* and *coerced*. If the sexual assault described by the respondent does *not* meet the NCVS's definition of completed or attempted rape, the case will likely be reclassified as a sexual assault.

Bachman and Taylor (1994) note that the NCVS has been criticized for the "'crime context' in which questions are administered. It is believed," they continue, "that this context causes some rates of victimization to be underestimated primarily because respondents may not interpret their victimization as 'crimes'" (pp. 509-510). For example, Koss (1992) found that half of her national student sample "did not think their experience qualified as any type of crime" (p. 66). She concluded that this finding "strongly suggests that underdetection will occur if identification hinges on the respondent conceptualizing her victimization as a crime" (p. 66).

Bachman and Taylor (1994) counter Koss's conclusion by pointing out that the NCVS interviewers were required to ask respondents to mention "any attack or threat or use of force . . . even if you were not certain it was a crime" (p. 153). How effective this statement was in muting the impact of the crime context, we do not know.

However, the failure to include terms that connote rape (e.g., *forced intercourse*) in this and the other three screen questions, as well as the use of general terms like *attack* that apply to sexual and nonsexual crimes, makes it likely that these factors lower the rape disclosure rate. According to Eigenberg (1990), for example,

> Respondents may refuse to reveal that they have been raped when they are presented with vague questions, in view of the stigmatization that often accompanies rape. This indirect method of soliciting information may make it more difficult for embarrassed respondents to reveal their victimization. Respondents also may infer that they are not supposed to talk about rape or that the researcher is not interested in that type of crime because it is not mentioned directly. In this respect they are given a message that talking about rape is unacceptable. (p. 664)

Although Eigenberg was commenting here on the questions asked in the NCS, her observations also apply to the NCVS.

If it is impossible for some reason for the NCVS to administer a separate interview schedule or survey on violence against women, at the very least there should be a separate section of the survey devoted to asking about women's experiences of rape and sexual assault, and possibly woman battering as well.

In conclusion: Although we think the NCVS's revised questions have increased the rape disclosure rate, this is hardly a great accomplishment given how ineffective the old questions were. Furthermore, we believe that the revised questions continue to play a significant role in the NCVS's failure to obtain realistic levels of rape disclosure by women. Koss (1996) points out that a combination of multiple, behaviorally specific, and culturally sensitive questions that "jog respondents' recall about the variety of guises in which rape may appear" are the most successful in obtaining disclosures of rape (pp. 63-64). The NCVS's revised questions are a far cry from meeting Koss's standards for the most suitable questions to ask about rape.

The Interviews

Method of Interviewing. As previously mentioned, once individuals are in the NCVS sample, they are interviewed "every 6 months for a total of seven interviews over a 3-year period" (BJS, 1996, p. 3). Two of these interviews are generally conducted face-to-face while five are conducted over the telephone. Just under a third (30%) of the NCVS interviews utilize computer-assisted telephone interviewing (CATI) in which "interviewers in centralized telephone facilities read questions from a computer screen and enter responses directly into a computer" (BJS, 1996, p. 151).

In Chapter 3, Russell agreed with Peters, Wyatt, and Finkelhor's (1986) research-based conclusion that face-to-face interviews are the best method for obtaining disclosures on child sexual abuse *if* the study has "well-selected and trained interviewers to enhance candor" (p. 40). We also noted that privacy for telephone interviews is more difficult to achieve. Hence, the fact that five out of seven of the NCVS's interviews are conducted over the telephone probably contributes to their underestimate of the prevalence for rape.

Although CATI has much to commend it, including the improvement in the interviewers' adherence to the interview schedule because of the monitoring that it permits, this method of interviewing cannot change a poorly designed instrument into an effective one, nor transform an interviewer who does not invite disclosure into one who does.

Privacy. A major disadvantage of telephone over face-to-face interviewing is the lack of control the interviewer has over whether or not the respondent has privacy for the interview. Absolute privacy that ensures confidentiality for respondents without fear of interruption is of vital importance for interviews on sensitive topics like rape. Telephones are typically located in a central place in households to give easy access for household members, particularly in homes that cannot afford more than one telephone. In middle-class homes where call waiting is now a popular feature, the interview is subject to interruption from this source as well as from other household members. In some poor homes, "crowded living conditions . . . may not provide sufficient privacy to discuss intimate matters" (Koss, 1996, p. 61). The NCVS (BJS, 1996) researchers address this issue in the following way:

> Many NCVS items can be answered with a simple "yes" or "no." These two features [it is not clear what the first is] make it difficult for anyone overhearing a phone interview to follow what is being described, thereby giving the respondent *a measure of privacy.* (p. 150; emphasis added)

However, a "measure of privacy" is not good enough.

The NCVS researchers also note that their respondents "are allowed to break off and reschedule, if their privacy is violated during an interview" (BJS, 1996, p. 150). However, it is unwise to place the responsibility on respondents to decide whether or not they will tolerate a lack of privacy. Furthermore, some respondents may rarely or never be able to count on having privacy in their homes. In these cases, there may be little point in rescheduling the interview.

In addition, rape survivors who prefer not to disclose their experiences would probably not be motivated to reschedule the interview when their privacy is violated. The interviewer should be the one who insists on privacy and the need to reschedule the interview if necessary to obtain it.

The NCVS researchers appear to recognize the importance of privacy when it comes to face-to-face interviewing in the respondents' homes. BJS information analyst Felicia Hobbs reports that, "Part of the procedure for conducting an interview is for the interviewer to be alone with the respondent" (personal communication, March 5, 1999). However, the failure to insist on absolute privacy for the telephone interviews on rape is unacceptable. If respondents do not have confidence that they will have privacy for the duration of their interviews, their willingness to disclose rape experiences is likely to be undermined.

Proxy Respondents. The NCVS interviewers obtain information from "proxy respondents," that is, "other household members," in three circumstances: when knowledgeable household members insist that 12- or 13-year-olds not

be interviewed directly; when respondents are "physically or mentally incapable of granting interviews"; and/or when respondents are absent from the
household during the study's interviewing period (BJS, 1997, p. 139). Non-
household members may also provide information about incapacitated persons "in certain situations" (which are not specified) (1997, p. 139).

The practice of interviewing proxy respondents is totally inappropriate in
rape research. Adults cannot be presumed to be knowledgeable about children's experiences of rape. Nor can it be assumed that proxies will know
about the rape experiences of individuals who are absent from the household
or those who are incapacitated. Incapacitated and absent individuals should
be considered ineligible for the study, while children who are not permitted to
be interviewed should be included in the nonparticipation rate. Unfortunately, no information on the number of proxy respondents is available in the
NCVS's report for 1994.

The Interviewers and Their Training

According to Bachman and Taylor (1994),

> Before implementation of the redesigned survey instrument, all NCVS interview-
> ers assigned to the redesign underwent extensive retraining, including practice
> sessions that involved role-playing the interview situation with the new question-
> naire. During these training sessions, particular emphasis was placed on new ques-
> tions that respondents might perceive as "sensitive" (e.g., those regarding sexual
> assault). (p. 509)

There is nothing in this description to suggest that the training included educating the interviewers about rape. It seems unlikely that this occurred, since
rape constituted a relatively small segment of the interview. When interviewers do not demonstrate that they understand and empathize with rape survivors, verbally or nonverbally, the disclosure rate will certainly reflect this.

The Attitudes About Rape in the NCVS Report

The attitudes about rape portrayed in the NCS and the NCVS reports are a
major reason for our skepticism about how well the NCVS's interviewers
were likely trained to ask about rape. Consider the following statement in
BJS's (1996) NCVS Report for 1993, for example:

At the inception of the NCS in the early 1970's, *it was deemed inappropriate for a government-sponsored survey to ask respondents directly about rape.* Reports of rape and attempted rape were obtained only if the respondent volunteered this information in response to questions about assault and attacks. (p. 150; emphasis added)

Such Victorian attitudes could hardly have been more counterproductive for yielding disclosures about rape. Readers may need reminding that these interview questions remained unchanged until 1992.

As recently as 1996 the NCVS report states that, "Public attitudes toward victims have changed, permitting more direct questioning about sexual assaults" (BJS, 1996, p. 2). However, direct questions on rape and other sexual assault have been used successfully since Russell's survey in 1978 (although, as we have emphasized, it is important to combine such questions with other behaviorally specific questions that avoid using words like *rape*). Judging from the NCVS's interview questions, there continues to be a lack of clear, direct, and explicit language about rape in all but one question. This serious flaw undermines the redesigners' goal of questioning women more directly about their rape experiences, if any.

When Russell developed her interview schedule in 1977, just five years after the NCS researchers embarked on their survey, she used sexually explicit language like *forced intercourse, anal intercourse,* and *sexual contact* with particular relatives such as fathers, brothers, uncles, and grandfathers. Even though later researchers have generated successful results by adopting this style of interviewing, the NCVS appears to be reluctant to learn from other researchers who have been much more successful at measuring the magnitude of the rape problem.

Furthermore, the NCVS's focus on violent rapes at the expense of rapes by intimates perpetuates and reinforces the "stranger-in-the-bushes" rape myth—an inexcusable stereotype in this day and age. In addition, the fact that the revised NCVS still requires some interviews to be done with proxy respondents reveals the researchers' failure to understand that many rape survivors do not reveal their experiences to anyone.

That the NCVS continues to indicate that rape is an infrequent crime, particularly in light of all the studies that show otherwise, misleads and misinforms the public. As Koss (1996) points out, "The statistics are interpreted for the public as attesting to the rarity of rape victimization" (p. 66; Eigenberg, 1990, makes the same point numerous times). As an example, Koss (1996) cites a table on family violence published in a BJS report that indicates zero cases of rape perpetrated by spouses and ex-spouses, with no explanation, leaving journalists, legislators, policymakers, and the public to conclude that the problem is nonexistent (see BJS, 1994, p. 150). (p. 66)

In sum, the NCVS, with its poorly worded questions and outdated methodology, continues to propagate archaic myths about rape: for example, that a high percentage of rapes are reported to the police; that proxy respondents are likely to know about the rape experiences of other members of the household; and that rape of females is a rare phenomenon. Such grossly misleading and inaccurate information minimizes this horrific crime.

Matching of Interviewers and Respondents

The NCVS does not have a policy of matching interviewers and respondents for gender or race/ethnicity (Rand, personal communication, March 22, 1999). However, 90% of the NCVS interviewers are female. This large percentage is not explained, but it is fortunate for obtaining disclosures from female rape victims. However, since there is no way that interviewers can know ahead of time when they will be encountering a rape survivor, this presumably means that up to 10% of female respondents will be interviewed by men. This is likely to lower the rape disclosure rate for female respondents.

Brief Interviews

According to Rand, interviews with respondents who report some victimization during the previous 6 months last, on average, about 22 minutes, whereas interviews with respondents who do *not* report any victimization during this period "take about 5-6 minutes" (personal communication, March 22, 1999). Given that the interviews focus on many crimes besides rape, their brevity leaves little time for respondents to reflect on their experiences during the interview. A brief period of only 5 to 6 minutes likely undermines the interviewer's ability to elicit unintended disclosures from respondents, as well as for the respondents to reconceptualize some experiences as rape.[6]

OTHER DEFECTS OF THE
REVISED NCVS METHODOLOGY

Failure to Separate Data on the Rape of Females

The NCVS gathers data on the rape and sexual assault of males as well as females. Yet there are generally "about 10 or fewer" victims of male rape or sexual assault even when completed and attempted rapes are combined. In many tables, the NCVS combines the information on male and female rape victims and/or rape and sexual assault (BJS, 1997). Consequently, separate information on the rape of females is largely missing.

The failure of the NCVS to provide information on the true numbers of rapes represented by their incidence rates makes it impossible for interested researchers to recalculate the NCVS's findings in order to separate rape survivors by gender or to distinguish rape and sexual assault of females. In this era of high awareness and concern about rape as a major problem for women in the United States, it is shocking that the NCVS's methods of reporting their statistics give the public a bare minimum of information about female rape victims.

Failure to Respond to Criticism by Other Researchers

The investigators of the BJS's victimization surveys have not addressed the disparity between their finding on the infrequency of rape and those of numerous others studies. They have also failed to address the criticisms made by several experts on rape and survey research methodology concerning the many defects that characterize the methodology of both the NCS and NCVS (e.g., Biderman & Lynch, 1991; Eigenberg, 1990; Kilpatrick et al., 1985; Koss, 1992, 1996, p. 61; Russell, 1984). Many of these criticisms were available prior to the redesign of the NCS's methodology in 1991.

The many defects in the NCVS that we have pointed out in this chapter have undoubtedly been critical factors in the absurdly low rape rates they continue to report.

Lack of Self-Criticism

The NCVS researchers have frequently drawn misleading inferences from their survey findings. Instead of admitting that their rape rate may be low "due to poor detection of rape" (Koss, 1996, p. 66), their findings are instead interpreted "as attesting to the rarity of rape victimization" (p. 66). This lack of acknowledgment that their low incidence rate may simply be due to methodological limitations is a breach in responsible scientific practice.

Failure to Consult Researchers Who Have Obtained More Realistic Assessments of the Incidence of Rape

The NCVS's disregard for the progress made by other researchers in assessing the magnitude of the rape problem in the United States is another breach in responsible scientific practice. Koss (1996) notes, for example, that the revisions made by the NCVS researchers "were undertaken without consultation with diverse groups with expertise on violence against women," many of whom have a deep understanding about rape and the methodological issues surrounding it (p. 67). Since several rape researchers have been more successful than the NCS and the NCVS researchers in assessing the incidence and prevalence of rape, these researchers should have been invited to assist the NCVS with the revisions in their methodology.

Omission of Individuals at High Risk of Rape

Because the NCVS's rape statistics are based on the disclosures of those who live in households, these surveys exclude women who live in institutions and women who are homeless. As we have already noted, these women are at very high risk of rape. While this problem is shared by all other studies based on household samples, this does not invalidate the importance of this factor in lowering the true incidence of rape. Furthermore, the enormous funds available for the NCVS surveys would presumably enable these surveys to include these populations in their samples.

Misleading Statements

Documentation of misleading statements in the NCVS reports will be confined to two examples. Although marital rape is not specifically mentioned when the term *rape* is defined in the NCVS, it is reasonable to suppose that it qualifies as rape. However, Koss (1996) refers to a 1994 BJS report in which a table was published indicating *zero* cases of rape by husbands or ex-husbands (p. 66). Koss notes that no explanation is provided for the absence of such rapes. This is particularly odd since the BJS staff have claimed that wife rape "is and *always* has been coded as such [rape] if a victim was raped by his or her spouse or partner" (Bachman & Taylor, 1994, p. 508, emphasis in the original; Koss, 1996, p. 58). "If this statement is true," Koss (1996) argues,

> then the BJS rape estimates were including marital rapes . . . in their reports before these acts were included in many state statutes and prior to modification of federal rape law. (p. 58)

This seems exceedingly unlikely. Furthermore, since Russell's survey reveals that 14% of the women who had ever been married in her San Francisco sample disclosed an experience of wife rape, the finding of zero cases of wife rape in 1996 makes it reasonable to infer that the NCS's and NCVS's methodologies for obtaining such information are woefully inadequate.

In a column titled "Highlights" in BJS's *NCVS* report (1997), the claim is made that there were 430,000 rapes and sex assaults in 1994 (p. v). Note that the word *estimate* is not used, despite the fact that it *is* an estimate. We also noted earlier that the very small number of actual rapes is never revealed in the NCVS reports.

Conflict of Interest

Koss is quoted as saying that there is an inherent "conflict of interest" in the Justice Department's providing the NCS/NCVS statistics because these findings are used to formulate the president's crime policy. Therefore, the BJS has "a motive to give us figures to suggest the present crime policy is working" (Koss quoted by Allen, 1997, p. C9). Hence, the lower the incidence of rape found (as well as the incidence of other crimes), the better they look.

This conflict of interest may help to account for BJS researchers' reluctance to revise their methodology to make it more suitable for rape, their failure to learn from the findings of other researchers, and their stubborn insistence that rape is an infrequent crime. Eigenberg (1990) pointed out that "the very agency responsible for gathering seriously deficient data legitimizes the subsequent findings by assuring us that rape is an infrequent crime" (p. 665).

CONCLUSION: TO REVISE OR QUIT

Because of the large sample size of the NCVS, the information it provides on rape could be extremely valuable if their methodology were sound and rape-appropriate. Instead, their survey methods result in a massive underestimation of the incidence of rape, thus resurrecting the old myth "that rape is a rare occurrence" (Eigenberg, 1990, p. 656) (documented in Table 5.1 and visually portrayed in Figure 5.2).

Speaking about the NCS, Eigenberg (1990) criticizes the fact that "the problems associated with the NCS are rarely mentioned in the literature on rape, and [that] there appears to be widespread ignorance of this critical deficiency" (p. 656). For example, she cites 12 researchers and research teams, "including some of the most prestigious [researchers] in criminology," who failed to discuss the NCS's "idiosyncratic screen questions" (p. 665).

Large numbers of individuals and institutions rely on the NCS/NCVS's statistics on rape in the belief that they must be the soundest because they are sponsored by the federal government, they are available on a yearly basis, and they include tens of thousands of respondents. In addition, no independent researcher has the resources to provide annual statistics on rape, and the American public has little interest in any but the most recent figures. According to the BJS for 1994, for example,

> Researchers at academic, government, private, and nonprofit research institutions use NCVS data to prepare reports, policy recommendations, scholarly publications, testimony before Congress, and documentation for use in courts. Community groups and government agencies use the data to develop neighborhood watch and victim assistance and compensation programs. Law enforcement agencies use NCVS findings for training. The data appear in public service announcements on crime prevention and crime documentaries. Finally, print and broadcast media regularly cite NCVS findings when reporting on a host of crime-related topics. (reported in BJS, 1997, p. 3)

Koss (1996) also points out that, sadly, "because most international victimization surveys have been modeled on the NCVS, the effects of inadequate measurement have rippled around the world" (p. 56).

The NCVS's researchers spent more than 10 years trying to rectify some of the glaring methodological problems present since the NCS's inception in 1972. Imagine the hue and cry if it had taken equally long to revise a survey designed to measure the incidence of AIDS in the population.

Eigenberg (1990) notes that, "Feminists' critiques of science challenge the value-neutral assumptions of science and argue that science has been used to maintain sexist, racist, classist, and heterosexist values" (p. 668). Does a sexist bias account for the fact that those responsible for revising the NCVS have made it virtually impossible to glean more than the most minimal information about the rape of females from their reports? By failing on this most elementary task, the NCVS has displayed a profound lack of disquiet about the tremendous popular concern about the rape of females in the United States.

Koss (1996) has noted that "flawed data blunt social concern for rape victims, feed illusions that rape is relatively rare, and fuel the backlash against rape victims" (p. 66). Indeed, we believe that the NCS and the NCVS have functioned as the scientific arm of the backlash against the relatively recent discoveries that have occurred since the 1970s concerning the prevalence of rape, child sexual abuse, and other forms of violence against women. The NCS's and the NCVS's claim that rape is an infrequent crime has fueled the attack on researchers who have documented the high prevalence of rape in the United States, particularly Koss. Gilbert (1991c), for example, specifically used the NCS data that documents the infrequency of rape to attack the rape rates found by Koss and by Russell (see Chapter 16 on the backlash).

When writing about the NCS, Eigenberg (1990) urged that, "We must do a better job of advertising the fact that NCS does not measure rape effectively" (p. 668). The more people who become aware that this statement also applies to the NCVS, the more pressure will hopefully be brought to bear on those responsible for the NCVS's poor methodology and their totally inaccurate findings about the rape rate. This could lead to more and better revisions than those that were implemented in 1992.

Currently, the NCVS's massive underestimate of the incidence of rape is not only useless, but dangerous, because it misinforms the public regarding the magnitude of the rape problem. We would actually be far better off without these surveys. Hence, unless their methodology is repeatedly revised until it yields more realistic assessments of the incidence of rape, it would be preferable for them to discontinue their questions on rape.

The NCS's and NCVS's misleading rape statistics have been an ongoing insult to the millions of rape survivors in the United States, as well as to women in general, so many of whom live in fear of rape and the sometimes accompanying crimes of mutilation and femicide.[7]

NOTES

1. The term *male-on-male rape* is preferable to the term *homosexual rape* because the latter is likely to be interpreted as rape by homosexuals. Studies of men in prison have documented that many of the rapists are heterosexual.

2. Exceptionally, when Stephen Spielberg was the target of a rape threat by a man, his would-be attacker was arrested and convicted. This is but one of many examples of the sexist application of the law.

3. By 1987, some degree of law reform had been enacted in every state (Searles & Berger, 1987).

4. Although Russell's respondents were 18 years and older, the question on incidence includes the previous 12 months.

5. These data tapes are housed at the National Archive of Criminal Justice Data (NACJD) at the University of Michigan. They can be found at http://www.icpsr. umich.edu/NACJD/home.html. (personal communication to Russell's research assistant, Roberta Harmes, by Felicia Hobbs, BJS Information Analyst, March 5, 1999).

6. British feminist researcher Liz Kelly (1988) found that multiple interviews with time in between for respondents to reflect on the questions they were asked about sexual violence yielded several additional experiences after the first interview.

7. As previously mentioned, femicide refers to the killing of females by males *because* they are female. The National Women's Study found that almost half of all the rape survivors in their national probability sample described being fearful of serious injury or death during their rape experience (Kilpatrick et al., 1992, p. 4).

6
◆

THE PREVALENCE OF RAPE: OTHER REPRESENTATIVE SAMPLES, PART 1

The main purpose of this book is to review studies that have attempted to ascertain the incidence and/or prevalence of rape and/or the prevalence of child sexual abuse in order to try to arrive at the soundest estimates of the prevalence of these crimes in the United States. We will be reviewing only the 10 surveys that meet our criteria (listed in Chapter 1), two of which are confined to child rape (to be analyzed separately in Chapter 15) and two of which have already been described and evaluated (Russell and the NCVS in Chapters 3 and 5). Table A1.6.1 in Appendix 1 compares the methodological characteristics of the eight studies that include incidence and/or prevalence data on the rape of adult women. The following three studies are reviewed in this chapter (the dates apply to fieldwork):

1. Gail Wyatt, Los Angeles County, California, 1981-1984
2. Dean Kilpatrick, Connie Best, Lois Veronen, Angelynne Amick, Lorenz Villeponteaux, and Gary Ruff, Charleston County Survey, South Carolina, 1983
3. Dean Kilpatrick and Crime Victim Center Co-investigators Connie Best, Julie Lipovsky, Heidi Resnick, and Benjamin Saunders's National Women's Study, 1989-1991

These studies were all conducted after Russell's 1978 survey (Russell, 1982, 1983b, 1984) described in Chapter 3. They are presented in chronological order according to when the fieldwork was done.[1]

The omission of women who reside in institutions or who are homeless from the samples of all eight of these surveys contributes to the underestimation of their prevalence rates. This limitation has already been discussed in connection with Russell's survey and the NCVS, so it will not be repeated in the evaluations of other studies.

GAIL WYATT'S SURVEY, LOS ANGELES COUNTY, 1981-1984

Gail Wyatt (1985) conducted a study in Los Angeles County that was primarily about the child sexual abuse experiences of African American[2] and white women aged 18 to 36 years. She also gathered data on the prevalence of rape.

Wyatt (1992) described her sampling method as a "multistage stratified probability sample . . . with quotas to recruit comparable samples of African American and white American women 18-36 years of age in Los Angeles County" (pp. 80-81). She used random digit dialing to obtain her samples of 126 African American and 122 white American women between the ages of 18 and 36 years ($N = 248$ respondents; Wyatt, 1985, p. 509). Wyatt (1985) reports that "the quotas set for white women were selected to match those for African American women" (p. 510) "with various levels of education, marital status, and numbers of children" (1992, p. 81). By this method, considerable comparability in the educational levels of these two groups was achieved (Table 1, 1985, p. 509). However, there were considerable differences in age, number of children, and marital status.

Wyatt reported three different refusal rates as follows:

1. 27% if the 335 women who terminated before eligibility was determined are excluded (Wyatt, Newcomb, & Notgrass, 1991, p. 49, note 2).
2. 33% if, of the 335 women who terminated, only the estimated number of eligible women are included.
3. 45% if all of the 335 women who terminated contact before eligibility was determined were included (Wyatt et al., 1991, pp. 49-50, note 2).

There were four interviewers, all of whom were female. They underwent an intensive 3-month training program. The gender and ethnicity of respondents and interviewers were matched—an unusual accomplishment in a study of rape and child sexual abuse (Wyatt, 1992, p. 81).

Respondents were interviewed face-to-face for 3 to 8 hours. The interviewers administered Wyatt's Sex History Questionnaire (a 478-item structured interview schedule) "to obtain both retrospective and current data regarding women's consensual and abusive sexual experiences, and the effects on their intimate relationships, and psychological and sexual functioning" (Wyatt, 1992, p. 81).

At the end of the sex history, respondents were asked about nonconsensual sexual experiences that may have occurred since they were 18, and which may have involved a friend, a relative, or a stranger (Wyatt, 1992, p. 82). The following definition of rape was read to the respondents: *rape is "the involuntary penetration of the vagina or anus by the penis or another object"* (Wyatt et al., 1991, p. 36). They were then asked:

1. Since the age of 18, have you ever been raped? and,
2. Since the age of 18, has anyone ever tried to rape you? (Wyatt et al., 1991, p. 37).

When the respondent answered in the affirmative to either of these questions, the interviewer asked other questions to ascertain the details of each incident.

Findings

Twenty-five percent of the African American women and 20% of the white American women in Wyatt's sample reported at least one incident of completed or attempted rape (Wyatt, 1992). This difference was not, however, statistically significant. When these two ethnic groups are combined, 22% of the respondents disclosed at least one incident of completed or attempted rape (see Table A1.6.1 and Figure 6.1). Unfortunately, Wyatt does not provide separate prevalence rates for completed and attempted rape.

The 55 rape survivors in Wyatt's (1985) study disclosed 146 incidents of attempted or completed rape, that is, an average of close to three rapes each. Fifty-five percent of the 146 incidents were disclosed by African American women and 45% by white American women (whether or not this difference is statistically significant was not indicated).

Evaluation

In contrast to Wyatt, most prior and subsequent prevalence research with multiethnic samples has not matched the socioeconomic status of whites and other ethnic groups, thereby confounding the respondents' ethnicity and

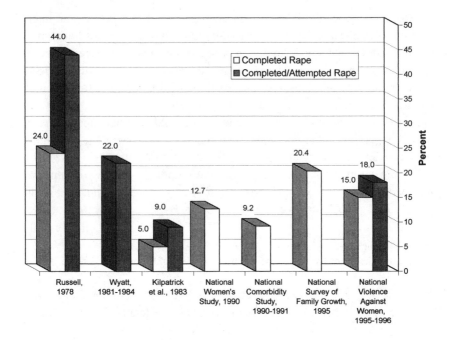

Figure 6.1. A Comparison of Prevalence Rates for Completed and/or Attempted Rape Obtained by Seven Representative Samples

social class. Hence, this aspect of Wyatt's research has been especially valuable, as also is her finding of no statistically significant differences in the prevalence of rape for African American and white American women. On the other hand, the latter finding may be due to the small size of Wyatt's sample ($N = 248$). The sample size is smaller than desirable for a prevalence study, particularly since Wyatt was interested in focusing on ethnic differences. In addition, the study's small size limited the complexity of the analyses that she was able to conduct and also her ability to generalize her findings.

Wyatt's Refusal/Nonparticipation Rate

It appears that Wyatt's calculation of her refusal rates may not be accurate. Her random-digit dialing process, beginning with 11,834 telephone numbers, yielded 5,272 usable numbers, which "eventuated to 1,348 households in which a woman resided" (Wyatt, 1985, p. 509). Wyatt does not account for the 3,924 remaining households. This makes it impossible to know whether or not these households should be included in her nonparticipation rate.

Within the 1,348 households in which a woman resided, there were 335 women who terminated before eligibility was determined, 266 eligible women who refused to participate, and 709 eligible women who agreed to participate. These figures total to 1,310, leaving 38 households unaccounted for. Wyatt offers no explanation for this discrepancy. Depending on how Wyatt handled these 38 households in her calculations, all three of the refusal rates she reported may be slightly incorrect.

With regard to her second refusal rate of 33% ("if, of the 335 women who terminated, only the estimated number of eligible women are included" [Wyatt et al., 1991, pp. 49-50]), Wyatt does not explain how she estimated how many of the 335 women would have been eligible for the study. In addition, because Wyatt does not provide enough information regarding how she calculated the 33% refusal rate, it is impossible for the reader to understand her calculations.

Comparison of Wyatt's Rape Prevalence Rate With Other Studies

Wyatt's 22% prevalence rate for completed and attempted rape of women between the ages of 18 and 36 years is difficult to compare with the majority of studies that report prevalence figures for completed rape only (see Table A1.6.1). Of the two other studies that report the prevalence of completed and attempted rape combined, Russell's 44% is exactly double Wyatt's prevalence rate, and Wyatt's rate is more than double Kilpatrick et al.'s (1985) 9% prevalence rate. (As will be evident shortly, this survey by Kilpatrick et al. has serious methodological problems with regard to estimating the prevalence of rape.)

Wyatt's 18- to 36-year age range for respondents also makes it difficult to compare with other studies. When Russell recalculated her prevalence rate for respondents aged 18 to 36 years, her prevalence rate rose from 44% for completed and attempted rape to 52%. This is not surprising since research has shown that young women report more experiences than older women. Russell's recalculated assessment of the prevalence of completed and attempted rape is close to two-and-a-half times higher than Wyatt's.

Had Russell been able to make her definition of rape comparable to Wyatt's (Wyatt included anal intercourse and penetration with a foreign object, whereas Russell did not), the discrepancy between these two prevalence rates would have been even higher.

Explanations for Wyatt's Prevalence Rate

Unlike Wyatt's prevalence rate for *child sexual abuse,* which is the highest ever reported (see Chapter 12), her prevalence of rape is almost certainly too low. Her use of only two screen questions is the most likely explanation for this discrepancy.[3] Although Wyatt used the word *rape* in her screen questions, we have already noted that this normally prevalence-lowering practice was mitigated by the interviewers being required to read the definition of rape to the respondents. While this definition is behaviorally specific ("the involuntary penetration of the vagina or anus by the penis or another object" [Wyatt et al., 1991, p. 36]), the language is very technical and probably inaccessible to many of Wyatt's less educated respondents. It also would have been helpful to provide one or more examples of objects.

In conclusion: Many people would consider a prevalence rate of 22% for completed and attempted rape to be very high. However, it would have been significantly lower had Wyatt's study not been limited to women between the ages of 18 and 36, who are at greater risk of rape than their older sisters. On the other hand, it would have been higher had she used more than two screen questions.

DEAN KILPATRICK, CONNIE BEST, LOIS VERONEN, ANGELYNNE AMICK, LORENZ VILLEPONTEAUX, AND GARY RUFF'S CHARLESTON COUNTY SURVEY, SOUTH CAROLINA, 1983

Dean Kilpatrick, Director of the Crime Victims Research and Treatment Center in Charleston County, South Carolina, together with five of his colleagues (1985), used random digit dialing to obtain a probability sample of 2,004 women household residents aged 18 and over in Charleston County, South Carolina. In addition to questions about the prevalence of rape and child molestation, these researchers explored a number of topics including robbery and aggravated assault as well as the mental health consequences for the victims of these crimes.

Three-thousand-ninety-three households were contacted, yielding 2,383 eligible women, 2,004 of whom participated in the study. According to Kilpatrick et al. (1985), the refusal and termination rate was 15.9%, yielding a completion rate of 84.1%. When the households with "unavailable designated respondents" are included, the completion rate drops to 78.2% (p. 867). Women employed by Louis Harris and Associates conducted the interviews by telephone in April 1983 (see Table A1.6.1 for these and other methodological features of this study).

To qualify as a rape victim in Kilpatrick et al.'s (1985) study,

> the woman must have had an experience in which someone used force or threat of force to make her have sexual relations against her will, and that sexual activity had to include forced sexual intercourse and/or forced oral or anal sex. (p. 868)

With attempted rape, on the other hand, "victims were classified on the basis of their labeling the incident as an attempted rape" (p. 868).

Only two screen questions about rape were used:

1. Has anyone ever tried to make you have sexual relations against your will?
2. Has anyone ever attempted to rape you or actually raped you? (Kilpatrick & Amick, 1984, p. 6)

According to Kilpatrick et al. (1985), "Respondents were classified into one of eight mutually exclusive victimization groups: completed forcible rape ($n = 100$), attempted forcible rape ($n = 79$), completed sexual molestation ($n = 55$), attempted sexual molestation ($n = 37$)," and comparable classifications for robbery and aggravated assault (p. 867).

Findings

Only 4.9% ($n = 100$) of the respondents revealed that they had been victims of completed forcible rape, and another 3.9% ($n = 79$) revealed that they had been victims of attempted forcible rape.[4] Assuming the numbers in these two groups of women were mutually exclusive, as Kilpatrick et al. maintained, the prevalence of rape was 8.9% (Kilpatrick et al., 1985, p. 867).

Evaluation

Clearly, Kilpatrick et al.'s (1985) finding of a 9% prevalence of rape is extremely low and, we believe, a gross underestimate of the percentage of women who are victimized by this crime. As may be seen in Figure 6.1 (in the section on Wyatt's findings, above) and Table A1.6.1, this assessment of the prevalence of rape is by far the lowest of all the studies to be compared in this and the next chapter.

Underestimates of rape are problematic for a few reasons. First, the lower the rape disclosure rate, the more likely it is that the rapes that are divulged by respondents will have been perpetrated by strangers, will have been violent, will have caused injury to the victim, will have involved the use of a weapon, will have been reported to the police, and, most important of all, will have had severe and long-lasting consequences (e.g., having to move, quitting a job, dropping out of school, changing lifestyles, as well as detrimental psychological effects). (See Chapter 4 for documentation of these findings.) In addition, studies with low disclosure rates cannot adequately assess the effects of rape because some portion of the nondisclosing respondents can be assumed to have also been victims of rape. Thus, the lower the disclosure rate, the less valid comparisons become between rape disclosers and nondisclosers.

Factors Reducing the Prevalence of Rape

The following factors probably contribute to the failure of Kilpatrick et al.'s methodology to yield a more realistic assessment of rape prevalence.

First, as noted above, Kilpatrick et al. (1985) state that they classified their 290 victimized respondents "into one of eight mutually exclusive victimization groups." However, these researchers fail to explain how they achieved this. For example, it is virtually certain that some of the 100 victims of completed rape in Kilpatrick et al.'s study would also have been victimized by attempted rape. How did they decide in which category to place these women's experiences? Furthermore, how did they decide into which group to place a respondent who was the victim of completed rape, robbery, and attempted molestation? A large number of cases of completed and attempted rape, as well as the other crimes that Kilpatrick et al. included in their study, must have been discounted by their method of classifying them.

In addition, because of Kilpatrick et al.'s (1985) unfortunate decision to lump together all eight of the crimes listed above, there is considerable missing information about rape separate from these other crimes. All subsequent analyses were based on this highly disparate assortment of victims.

Next, two screen questions on rape are likely to result in a serious underestimate of the prevalence rate (see section on "Rape-Appropriate Methodology" in Chapter 3 for our rationale for this observation).

Fourth, the use of the word *rape* in one of the two screen questions is highly problematic.

Kilpatrick is now among the researchers who emphasize the importance of avoiding use of the word *rape* in screen questions. Heidi Resnick and her colleagues (1993)—including Kilpatrick—point out that the use of the word *rape* to identify sexual assault leads to vast underestimations of true rape rates (p. 985). In addition, Kilpatrick, Resnick, Saunders, and Best (1998) conclude that "it is possible that at least two-thirds of all adult cases may be missed by using such a screen approach" (p. 169). For example, Naomi Breslau, Glenn Davis, Patricia Andreski, Belle Federman, and James Anthony (1991) obtained a prevalence rate for completed rape of only 2.6% in their random sample survey of 21- to 30-year-old female members of health organizations in southeast Michigan. The only screen question in this study used the term rape.

Obviously, much can be gained by using the word *rape* in a screen question when there are several other well-crafted screen questions that do not use this term. Inclusion of the term *rape* in a question can make it possible to compare the percentage of respondents who conceptualize their rape experience(s) in this way with those who do not. For example, Russell, who used the word *rape* in one of her screen questions but not in 17 additional questions, found that only 50% of the women who disclosed rape experiences made their disclosures in answer to the screen question that asked them if they had ever been a victim of rape or attempted rape (the other 50% came from some of the other 17 questions).

Fifth, Kilpatrick et al.'s (1985) method of ascertaining women's experiences of attempted rape required respondents to label assaults as such (p. 868). Hence, once again, in order to contribute to the prevalence of attempted rape, respondents had to conceptualize their experiences in a way that many such victims fail to do. As Koss and her colleagues (Koss, Gidycz, & Wisniewski, 1987) point out: "the assumption that the word rape is used by victims of sexual assault to conceptualize their experiences" is a poor one (p. 162). This is particularly the case when women are raped by their husbands and other intimates (see Russell, 1982).

Sixth, invariably, there are many more *incidents* of crime victimization than there are *victims* of crime. Not only did Kilpatrick et al. (1985) discard all their respondents' second, third, or fourth rape experiences, but their goal of mutual exclusivity may have resulted in their discarding many one-time experiences of completed or attempted rape as well. No rationale is offered for this decision, nor is any attempt made to analyze the consequences of it for their prevalence assessments.

Seventh, despite Kilpatrick et al.'s (1985) inclusion of oral and anal rape in their definition, these acts are not mentioned in their screen questions. Therefore, many respondents probably failed to report such experiences. If the definition of rape is not routinely read to the respondents during the interview, then the questions become the operational definers of this crime.

In conclusion: This study by Kilpatrick and his colleagues suffers from many serious methodological shortcomings that explain why they obtained such an unsatisfactorily low prevalence rate. Nor are the defects in this study ever acknowledged in future publications. In providing a rationale for a follow-up study (conducted by Kilpatrick, Benjamin Saunders, Lois Veronen, Connie Best, and Judith Von [1987]) in which a subsample of the 2,004 women in the parent study were interviewed, these researchers said that they had designed it "to overcome the . . . limitations of *others'* research"—not their own (emphasis added; p. 489). Their sole acknowledgment of a methodological problem related to the need to "employ more sensitive screen questions" (p. 489).

Kilpatrick et al.'s (1987) follow-up study, which was conducted 2 years after the parent study, is not included in our sample of surveys because it does not qualify as representative. Of the 2,004 women in the parent sample, only 933 were recontacted (47%), and only 399 (43%) of these women agreed to be reinterviewed (Kilpatrick et al., 1987, p. 481). This means that the respondents in the subsample constituted only 20% of the original 2,004 women in the parent sample.

DEAN KILPATRICK AND CRIME VICTIM CENTER CO-INVESTIGATORS CONNIE BEST, JULIE LIPOVSKY, HEIDI RESNICK, AND BENJAMIN SAUNDERS' NATIONAL WOMEN'S STUDY, 1989-1991

Kilpatrick and another team of colleagues had the opportunity to learn from the mistakes of Kilpatrick et al.'s two earlier studies (1985; Kilpatrick et al., 1987) when designing the first national survey of the lifetime prevalence of completed rape in the United States. They refer to this survey as the "The National Women's Study (NWS)." A few of the results of this groundbreaking survey were published in a brief 16-page report titled *Rape in*

America: A Report to the Nation, coauthored by Kilpatrick, Christine Edmunds, and Anne Seymour (1992). Only six pages of this report are devoted to rape statistics. Additional information about this survey finally became available in 1998 (Saunders, Kilpatrick, Hanson, Resnick, & Walker, 1999).[5]

Methodology

Kilpatrick et al. hired Schulman, Ronca, and Bucuvalas, Inc. (SRBI)—a survey research firm in New York—to conduct their study and write a lengthy report about its methodology (Boyle, 1992). However, this report is still an unpublished draft "not for citation" (permission to cite was obtained 3/23/2000). SRBI used random digit dialing to obtain a national household probability sample of 4,008 English-speaking adult American women 18 years and older. Two thousand eight of these women represented a cross section of all adult women, and 2,000 were obtained by an oversampling of younger women between the ages of 18 and 34 (Kilpatrick et al., 1998, p. 164).

The methodology required that the interviewers attempt to interview each of the 4,008 women three times at 1-year intervals referred to as Waves 1, 2, and 3 (Kilpatrick et al., 1992, p. 15). The statistics on the lifetime prevalence of rape were obtained from the Wave 1 survey.

Eighty-five percent of the respondents completed the interviews in Wave 1 (Kilpatrick et al., 1998, p. 164). After 1 year (Wave 2), 81% of the 3,220 NWS participants were located and reinterviewed (Kilpatrick et al., 1992, p. 1). The incidence rates were derived from these Wave 2 interviews by finding out "how many women were raped in the one year between Wave One and Wave Two" (Kilpatrick et al., 1992, p. 15).

To correct for the oversample of 2,000 younger women between the ages of 18 and 34, "the data was [*sic*] weighted by age and race to 1989 estimates of the distribution of these characteristics in the U.S. population of adult women" (Kilpatrick et al., 1998, p. 164).

Definition

The National Women's Study's definition of completed rape was

any nonconsensual sexual penetration of the victim's vagina, anus, or mouth by an object or a perpetrator's penis, finger, or tongue that involved the use of force, the threat of force, or coercion. (Saunders et al., 1999, pp. 189-190)[6]

It was left to the respondent to interpret the meaning of "force, threat of force, or coercion" (Saunders et al., 1999, pp. 189-190). Note that rape by peers is not excluded in this study. However, no data on attempted rape were gathered. For respondents who had been raped more than once, "incident characteristics were obtained for up to three rape incidents: the first rape, the most recent rape, and the rape deemed most subjectively distressing by the victim, other than the first or most recent rapes" (Saunders et al., 1999, p. 190).

Questions

The following preamble plus questions were designed to determine whether or not a woman had experienced rape:

> Another type of stressful event that many women have experienced is unwanted sexual advances. Women do not always report such experiences to the police or discuss them with family or friends. The person making the advances[7] isn't always a stranger, but can be a friend, boyfriend, or even a family member. Such experiences can occur anytime in a woman's life, even as a child. Regardless of how long ago it happened or who made the advances,
>
> Has a man or boy ever made you have sex by *using force* or threatening to harm you or someone close to you? Just so there is no mistake, by sex we mean putting a penis in your vagina.
>
> Has anyone ever made you have oral sex by force or threat of harm? Just so there is no mistake, by oral sex, we mean that a man or boy put his penis in your mouth or someone penetrated your vagina or anus with his mouth or tongue.
>
> Has anyone ever made you have anal sex by force or threat of harm?
>
> Has anyone ever put fingers or objects in your vagina or anus against your will by using force or threats? (Kilpatrick et al., 1992, p. 15)

Women who answered in the affirmative to any of these four questions were considered victims of completed rape.

Interviews

Interviewers from the survey research firm conducted highly structured interviews on the telephone that lasted approximately 35 minutes. The interviews were conducted using the Computer Assisted Telephone Interview (CATI) system, which "insures that the interview schedule, with its built-in skip and fill patterns, is followed exactly" (Saunders et al., 1999, p. 191). This procedure significantly reduces the chance of errors. In addition, "supervisors randomly checked each interviewer to insure that they are following the interview schedule and performing correctly and appropriately" (Saunders et al., 1999, p. 191).

Participation Rate

Eighty-five percent of women contacted agreed to participate and completed the initial (Wave 1) telephone interview. At the 1-year follow-up (Wave 2), 81% of the participants ($n = 3,220$) were located and reinterviewed (Kilpatrick et al., 1992, p. 1).

Findings

Kilpatrick et al. (1992) did not report an incidence rate for rape, and it is not possible to extrapolate this measure from the data they provide. However, they reported a prevalence rate of 0.7% for respondents who had experienced a completed forcible rape in the previous year (p. 2). These researchers use this 0.7% prevalence rate as the basis for stating that "this equates to an estimated 683,000 adult American women who were raped during a twelve-month period" (p. 2). However, their Figure 2 (p. 3), to which they refer the reader, reports data on "the *number* of forcible rapes per year," *not* the number of *women* raped in a year. Furthermore, Figure 2 compares the 683,000 *incidents* of rape BJS's National Crime Survey obtained in 1990 and the FBI's statistics on reported rapes in the same year. Hence, it appears that they became confused about which unit of analysis they were using—rape incidents or rape victims.

Kilpatrick et al.'s (1992) lifetime prevalence of completed rape is 12.7%, that is *12.7% of the women interviewed reported having been victims of at least one completed rape in their lifetimes.* Thirty-nine percent of the women who had been raped reported being raped more than once (p. 2). Another way of expressing this finding is to say that the average number of completed rapes per victim was 1.4 (714 rapes/507 rape victims = 1.4; see Table A1.6.1).

Evaluation

A national survey of the incidence and prevalence of rape has been greatly needed, especially because the NCVS has proved to be so inadequate in its assessments of the incidence of rape (see Chapter 5), and because no other satisfactory national incidence or prevalence studies of the general population (as opposed to students) had ever been conducted before.[8] Hence, Kilpatrick et al.'s (1992) national survey was a groundbreaking achievement.

The NWS achieved an excellent participation rate of 85% for its Wave 1 respondents and 81% for its Wave 2 respondents. The findings on the prevalence (but not the incidence) of completed rape is a tremendous advance on Kilpatrick et al.'s (1985) earlier study in 1983. The behaviorally specific screen questions about rape are also a great improvement on those he and Amick devised in 1983.

The NWS must also be commended for doing a thorough analysis of child rape, including its prevalence rate (Saunders et al., 1999). This research is described and evaluated in Chapter 15 on child rape. The rape of children is typically obscured by being lumped together with less serious forms of child sexual abuse. We recommend that future rape and child sexual abuse research provide information on child rape—including its prevalence.

Groundbreaking as the NWS is, we have already pointed out Kilpatrick et al.'s failure to report an incidence rate for rape, even though they presumably have the data to do so. We also believe that their 12.7% prevalence rate for the completed rape of females substantially underestimates the magnitude of this crime in the United States.

Factors Reducing the Prevalence of Completed Rape

1. Although the screen questions in the NWS were well-formulated, behaviorally-specific questions, and although four screen questions are more than the number used in many other studies, the prevalence rate for this study would almost certainly have been higher had it included more screen questions (see the rationale for this statement in Chapter 3 under "Rape-Appropriate Methodology").

2. Interviews were quite short, averaging 35 minutes each. This left little time for interviewers to develop good rapport with respondents or time for respondents to pause, to think, and to try to recall sometimes long-buried rape experiences. It also left little time for them to get over their embarrassment or habitual secrecy about these crimes.

3. The interviewing was done by interviewers who were employed by a survey research company (the possible relevance of this factor was discussed in Chapter 3).

4. The use of random-digit dialing to obtain the sample eliminates women without telephones from the study—that is, mostly poor women who are more at risk of being raped than more affluent women (e.g., see Russell, 1984, pp. 84-85).

5. The degree of privacy for the interview is more often jeopardized by telephone interviews than with face-to-face interviews (see Chapter 5 for the arguments supporting this conclusion). Privacy is one of the most crucial requirements for frank disclosures about rape.

6. Matching the gender and race/ethnicity of interviewers and respondents is advisable when conducting research on rape, because there appear to be good grounds for believing that it increases respondents' disclosures of rape. However, Kilpatrick and his colleagues did not report whether such matching was done for the NWS. Hence, the role of this factor is unknown.

7. The NWS's definition of rape does not include rapes that occur when women are unable to consent because they are incapacitated in some way. The practice of deliberately drugging women to incapacitate and rape them has become a much-publicized issue in recent years because the use of a drug called "roofies" (Rohypnol, a brand name for flunitrazepam) has become more widespread, particularly in date rape situations. How widespread this practice is will never be known, since victims of roofies-related rape typically do not remember what happened to them. These experiences would not qualify as rape in Kilpatrick et al.'s study.

In conclusion: Conducting the first national study of the prevalence of rape is a groundbreaking achievement by Kilpatrick and his colleagues. Their methodology, which yielded a 12.7% prevalence rate for completed rape, is a vast improvement over the methodology of the National Crime Victimization Surveys as well as Kilpatrick et al.'s (1985) earlier study of the prevalence of rape. However, we have shown that the NWS's 12.7% prevalence rate was substantially lowered by numerous methodological factors.

NOTES

1. Most researchers who compare prevalence survey data focus on the year of publication rather than the year during which the fieldwork was undertaken. We consider the fieldwork year to be more appropriate from a historical point of view. In

addition, it seems reasonable to expect the more recent studies to benefit from the strengths and weaknesses of earlier studies.

2. By African American, Wyatt is referring to individuals "of African descent whose parentage also includes a variety of other ethnic and racial groups found in America" (Wyatt et al., 1991, p. 49, endnote 1).

3. For information about the positive relationship between prevalence and the number of screen questions, see Chapter 3, "Rape-Appropriate Methodology."

4. Kilpatrick and his colleagues report only the *numbers* of completed rapes, attempted rapes, and other crimes, leaving it to interested readers to calculate the prevalence of rape and other crimes.

5. A very small amount of additional information about the methodology and prevalence findings of this survey was also published in Resnick et al. (1993) and Kilpatrick et al. (1998).

6. For a slightly different definition, see Kilpatrick et al. (1992, inside back cover).

7. The word *advances* seems a poor choice for a question about rape. Although advances can culminate in rape, the word doesn't connote being taken by surprise—a very common feature of rape and assaults on children. Nor does it seem appropriate for the typical rape experiences of wives and other intimates.

8. The National Opinion Research Center (NORC) conducted a national survey of 10,000 households in 1967 to ascertain the incidence of crime victimization, including rape, in the prior 12 months. Some of the methodological problems with this survey are discussed in Russell, 1984, pp. 31-32.

7

◆
_____

THE PREVALENCE OF RAPE: OTHER REPRESENTATIVE SAMPLES, PART 2

_____

In this chapter we will describe and evaluate the methodologies of another three representative samples in which the investigators sought to ascertain the prevalence of rape (the dates apply to fieldwork):

4. Ronald Kessler, Amanda Sonnega, Evelyn Bromet, and Michael Hughes, National Comorbidity Survey, 1990-1992
5. The National Center for Health Statistics, the Fifth National Survey of Family Growth, 1995
6. Patricia Tjaden and Nancy Thoennes, Center for Policy Research, National Violence Against Women Survey, 1995-1996

RONALD KESSLER, AMANDA SONNEGA, EVELYN BROMET, AND MICHAEL HUGHES, NATIONAL COMORBIDITY SURVEY, 1990-1992

_____

Kessler et al. (1995) report findings on the prevalence of posttraumatic stress disorder (PTSD) in the United States population and the kinds of traumas most strongly associated with it, including completed rape and child molestation. Their data were obtained from the National Comorbidity Survey,[1] which Kessler et al. (1995) described as "the first nationally representative face-to-face general population survey to assess a broad range of *DSM-III-R* disorders" (p. 1048).

The National Comorbidity Survey was based on "a stratified, multistage area probability sample" of 8,098 individuals between the ages of 15 and 54 years in the noninstitutionalized U.S. population (Kessler et al., 1995, p. 1049). This survey was administered in two parts, each of which took somewhat more than one hour to complete. The question relating to the prevalence of rape was asked in part 2 of the study.

Because of budgetary constraints, part 2 was administered to "only a subsample of respondents consisting of all those aged 15 to 24 years . . ., all others who screened positive for any lifetime diagnosis [of a disorder] in part 1 . . ., and a random subsample of other respondents" (Kessler et al., 1995, p. 1049). The participation rates for these subsamples were 99.4%, 98.1%, and 99%, respectively, and for part 1 the participation rate was 82.4%. Kessler et al. note that, "A special nonresponse survey was carried out to ascertain and then statistically adjust for nonresponse bias" (p. 1049).

While 8,098 respondents participated in part 1 of the National Comorbidity Survey, only 5,877 respondents participated in part 2 (i.e., 72.5% of part 1 respondents), including 3,065 women (Kessler et al., 1995, p. 1049). Kessler et al. believe that the adjustments that they were compelled to make to part 2 of the sample did not jeopardize its representativeness (p. 1048). Weighting procedures were used to adjust for differential participation to make the sample representative of the total population and to approximate the national population distributions for age, sex, race/ethnicity, marital status, education, living arrangements, region, and urbanity.

The 12 traumatic experiences investigated, including rape and child sexual abuse, were presented to respondents in booklets to avoid embarrassment (Kessler et al., 1995, p. 1050). Interviewers asked respondents about these experiences by number, for example, "Did you ever experience event number 5 on the list?" Number 5 read as follows: "You were raped (someone had sexual intercourse with you when you did not want to by threatening you or using some degree of force)" (p. 1051). This is the only screen question on rape. The parenthetical clarification of the word rape embedded in the question constitutes the National Comorbidity Survey's definition of this crime. Note that attempted rape was not included.

The 158 interviewers who participated in the National Comorbidity Survey had worked for an average of five years as interviewers for the survey research center that conducted this study. They were also given "a 7-day study-specific training program in the use of the Composite International Diagnostic Interview (CIDI)" (Kessler et al., 1995, p. 1049).

Findings

Kessler et al. (1995) report that 281 of the 3,065 female respondents aged 15 to 54 were victimized by completed rape. *This constitutes a prevalence rate of 9.2%.*

Evaluation

Clearly, Kessler et al.'s (1995) methodology for part 2 of the study is far from ideal. Nor is it possible to evaluate how successful the weighting procedures are for maintaining its representativeness.

Factors Reducing the Prevalence of Rape

1. We would expect one screen question on rape to yield a very low prevalence rate. It is virtually certain that more screen questions would have increased this survey's disclosure rate, particularly if the questions were behaviorally specific and designed to include nonstereotypic rapes such as those perpetrated by husbands, partners, other relatives, authority figures, and other intimates.

2. Although the only question on rape specifically used the word rape, the prevalence-lowering effect of this was probably somewhat mitigated by providing respondents with a definition that did not use this word. Whether or not the interviewers referring to rape as "event number 5" encouraged or discouraged disclosure by respondents is a question that deserves further research. It could be that this demonstration that rape is too taboo for the interviewer to mention would discourage some survivors from breaking their silence. On the other hand, the fact that the same procedure was used for all of the traumatic experiences may nullify this effect. In addition, any myths about rape that the interviewers may hold are less likely to be conveyed to respondents by a question on "event number 5."

3. Kessler et al.'s definition of rape excludes types of rape that, if included, would clearly have raised the prevalence rate, for example, oral and anal penetration, rape with a foreign object, and rape when the victim is unable to consent because she is incapacitated.

4. The central focus of Kessler et al.'s survey was on PTSD and the co-morbidity of the *Diagnostic and Statistical Manual of Mental Disorders (DSM-III-R)*—not on the prevalence of rape. A study focused on sexual assault in general is more likely, other things being equal, to obtain higher disclosure rates than one that is focused on another subject and in which there is minimal coverage of rape.

5. Kessler et al.'s survey used interviewers from a survey research center. Although they received a 7-day training program, Kessler et al. described it as "study-specific." Since a basic tenet of survey research requires that interviewers not be given substantive training about the issue(s) being studied, it seems very unlikely that this survey provided training to rid the interviewers of conventional rape myths and/or to educate them about the widespread prevalence of this crime.

For all these reasons, we feel bound to conclude that the methodological defects of the National Comorbidity Survey make it a poor study for ascertaining a sound prevalence rate for rape.

THE NATIONAL CENTER FOR HEALTH STATISTICS, THE FIFTH NATIONAL SURVEY OF FAMILY GROWTH, 1995

The fifth National Survey of Family Growth (NSFG) was conducted in 1995. It was jointly planned and funded primarily by the National Center for Health Statistics (NCHS), the National Institute for Child Health and Human Development, and the Office of Population Affairs, with additional support from the Administration for Children and Families (Abma, Chandra, Mosher, Peterson, & Piccinino, 1997, fn. p. 1). No principal investigator is mentioned in this report. Joyce Abma, Anjani Chandra, William Mosher, Linda Peterson, and Linda Piccinino (1997), the authors of the NSFG report, describe the goal of this survey as the collection of data "on factors affecting pregnancy and women's health" in the United States (p. 1). In 1995, this survey included two questions on the prevalence of rape for the first time.

The NSFG (Abma et al., 1997) was based on a national probability sample of 14,000 women aged 15 to 44 years. The sample was selected from among households that responded to the 1993 National Health Interview Survey (NHIS). The NHIS is a continuous multistage household survey conducted by NCHS that covers the U.S. civilian noninstitutionalized population. Data are collected on each household member. (p. 2)

In order to obtain a sufficient number of African American and Latina women, the NSFG (Abma et al., 1997) oversampled these two ethnic groups. Weighting was used to correct for refusals and for different sampling rates and to engender agreement with control totals by age, race, maternal and marital status provided by the U.S. Bureau of the Census (p. 2).

Of the sample of 14,000 women aged 15 to 44 years, 10,847 agreed to participate in the 1995 NSFG, yielding a participation rate of 79%.

Female interviewers received a week of training in Computer-Assisted Personal Interviewing (CAPI), after which they conducted in-person interviews in the homes of the respondents and recorded their answers on laptop computers. About 10 minutes of the approximately 100-minute interview

was conducted with a self-administered technique called Audio Computer-Assisted Self-Interviewing, or Audio CASI, in which the woman hears the questions over headphones and enters her answers directly into the computer. This meant that neither the interviewer nor anyone in the household could hear the questions or the answers in this section. (Abma et al., 1997, p. 2)

Although there is no explicit statement about who conducted the interviewers' training, it appears that they were trained by NSFG staff. Since all the interviewers were female, clearly interviewers and respondents were matched by gender.

No definition of rape is mentioned in the NSFG report. Hence the following two questions on rape constitute the operational definitions of this crime.

1. The interviewer asked the respondents "whether their first intercourse was 'voluntary or not voluntary.'"
2. Respondents were asked in the [10-minute] self-administered segment of the interview "whether they had *ever* been forced by a man to have sexual intercourse against their will." (Abma et al., 1997, p. 5)

According to William Mosher, a statistician at the Centers for Disease Control, the privacy provided for the main screening question on rape "helped them [respondents] open up about these devastating incidents" (Bovsun, 1997, p. 1).

No data were obtained on attempted rape.

Findings

A fifth (20%) of the women respondents reported that their first sexual intercourse had been nonvoluntary and/or that they had been forced by a man to have intercourse against their will at some time in their lives (Abma et al., 1997, p. 33, Table 22).[2] Hence, the lifetime prevalence for completed rape was 20%.

Evaluation

First, we will address the question of what enabled the NSFG survey to achieve the remarkably high 20% prevalence for completed rape. Then we will explore why the prevalence rate was not higher, or, to put it another way, what methodological features would have likely increased the prevalence rate.

Factors Elevating the Prevalence of Rape

1. The NSFG's combination of data collection methods may be the best so far devised for obtaining disclosures about experiences of rape. BJS found that Computer-Assisted Telephone Interviewing (CATI) obtained significantly higher disclosure rates than when they used a combination of face-to-face interviewing and telephone interviews.[3] Although we do not know whether tests have been done on the relative efficacy of CATI as compared with *personal* computer-assisted interviewing (CAPI), the improvement in these methods of data collection over other more traditional methods seems clear. For example:

   a. "The CATI system ensures that the interview schedule, with its built-in skip and fill patterns, is followed exactly." (Saunders et al., 1999, p. 191)
   b. It is easier to ensure privacy for in-person interviews than telephone interviews (the difficulty of achieving privacy with telephone interviews was discussed at some length in Chapter 3).
   c. The longer the time required to complete the interview (about 100 minutes for the NSFG), the more likely the respondent is to break off the call. Most households typically have only one telephone line. Blocking incoming calls and preventing other household members from being able to make calls typically become more difficult the longer the duration of the interview. With the growing popularity of call-waiting, telephone interviewing is likely to become increasingly difficult.

d. All the advantages of CAPI over regular telephone or face-to-face interviewing also apply to CATI. For example, both of these methods enable a supervisor to randomly check each interviewer to insure that they are following the interview schedule and are "performing correctly and appropriately" (Saunders et al., 1999, p. 191). This can prevent interviewers from repeating the same inadvertent errors in several interviews. It can discourage them from making deliberate errors because they feel awkward asking certain questions and/or because they consider some questions inappropriate and/or because they simply want to keep the interview short for their own convenience.

e. The quality of the interviews conducted by interviewers who consistently fail to obtain any disclosures of rape can be evaluated to try to ascertain whether the interviewer's interviewing skills or attitudes about rape may be responsible. Disclosure rates are greatly affected by the quality of the interviewing, so the sooner poor interviewers are identified and removed, the more accurate the prevalence rates are likely to be.

f. Using computer-assisted self-administered questions (the Audio CASI technique) to ask the second question on rape (about forced intercourse) may well have increased the respondents' disclosures about this crime. A few questions about the respondents' sexual partners and experiences of abortion were asked in both the Audio-CASI and the interviewer-administered sections of the interview to enable a comparison to be made regarding which method obtained the higher disclosure rate. Since the 1995 NSFG report is only a preliminary one, the results of this experiment have still to be ascertained.

g. Abma and her colleagues (1997) offer additional reasons for how CAPI improved the quality of the data the NSFG obtained:

> It reduced design errors and ambiguities in the questionnaire by requiring detailed specification of the questionnaire.
>
> It reduced interviewer error by automatically skipping to the next appropriate question.
>
> It reduced respondent error by automatically performing consistency checks during the interview. (p. 2)

Other factors that likely contributed to NSFG's relatively high prevalence of completed rape include the following:

2. The NSFG respondents were women aged 15 to 44 years. Research has established that older women report significantly fewer incidents of rape (e.g., see Siegel et al., 1987, pp. 1147-1148, and Chapter 8).

3. The term *nonvoluntary intercourse* was used as a synonym for rape. However, this term is broader than the NSFG's definition of rape as forced sexual intercourse against a woman's will. "Nonvoluntary intercourse" could include

unwanted but nonforceful intercourse that the respondent did not resist physically or verbally. Not only would such acts not qualify as rape by NSFG's definition of rape, it would also not qualify by the definitions used in the other surveys evaluated in this chapter and Chapter 6.

On the other hand, only 7.8% of the NSFG's respondents answered "yes" to the question on whether or not they had experienced nonvoluntary intercourse. Furthermore, some of these respondents were probably also subjected to one or more experiences of forceful intercourse. Hence the 7.8% of affirmative answers to this question likely contributed only a fraction to the overall prevalence rate.

4. The interviewers were all female.

5. The interviewers received in-house training rather than being trained by an outside agency.

6. Respondents were given $20 to complete their interviews. A large pretest had shown the NSFG researchers that this financial incentive "increased response rates, reduced costs, and improved the reporting of sensitive items" (Abma et al., 1997, p. 2).

Factors Reducing the Prevalence of Rape

1. Rape disclosure would almost certainly have been higher if the NSFG had used more than two questions to elicit respondents' rape experiences.

2. If the context of the questions on rape had been sexual assault or sexual violence against women rather than fertility, family planning, and women's health, the disclosure rate may have been higher.

3. Few respondents asked about their experiences of "forced sexual intercourse" are likely to interpret this to include experiences of oral, anal, and digital penetration, and/or sexual intercourse obtained by threat of force and/or sexual intercourse obtained when the victim was incapacitated in some way. Other studies in this chapter vary in which of these sex acts they include. Clearly, the more sex acts that are included, the higher the disclosure rate is likely to be.

4. When discussing the advantages of using the Audio CASI technique, Abma et al. (1997) noted that "this meant that neither the interviewer *nor anyone in the household* could hear the questions or the answers in this section" (i.e., the 10-minute self-administered section) (p. 2; emphasis added). This description suggests that some members of the household *could* sometimes hear the inter-

view during the 90-minute interviewer-administered portion of the interview. This in turn implies that the interviewers were not required to insist on total privacy. If this conclusion is correct, it seems reasonable to assume that some of the respondents who did not have total privacy would not disclose their experiences of rape.

In conclusion: The 20% prevalence rate for completed rape obtained by the NSFG in 1995 appears to be astoundingly high, particularly given the factors outlined above that likely served to lower it. As Figure 6.1 in Chapter 6 shows, except for Russell's 1978 survey, the NSFG's prevalence rate for completed rape is higher than those obtained by all the other studies described in Chapters 6 and 7. Moreover, it is only 15% lower than Russell's 24% prevalence rate for completed rape (20.4% / 24% = .85; 1 − .85 = 15%). This is all the more remarkable since the researchers involved are not rape researchers.

However, we have also pointed out that the NSFG's prevalence rate for completed rape may have been somewhat lower had the forced intercourse definition of rape been used in place of the term *involuntary intercourse.*

PATRICIA TJADEN AND NANCY THOENNES, NATIONAL SURVEY, SPONSORED BY THE NATIONAL INSTITUTE OF JUSTICE AND THE CENTERS FOR DISEASE CONTROL AND PREVENTION (CDC), 1995/1996

Patricia Tjaden and Nancy Thoennes were the principal investigators of the National Violence Against Women (NVAW) Survey conducted in 1995 and 1996. The National Institute of Justice (NIJ) and the Centers for Disease Control and Prevention (CDC) jointly sponsored and funded this research on stalking and rape through the Center for Policy Research in Denver, Colorado.

Besides ascertaining the incidence and prevalence of rape, the NVAW (Tjaden & Thoennes, 1998b) also obtained data on their respondents' experiences as children of physical assaults by adult caretakers, physical assault in adulthood by all kinds of perpetrators, and stalking at any time in their lives—also by all kinds of perpetrators. The respondents who were victims of any of these crimes "were asked detailed questions about the characteristics and consequences of their victimization" (p. 1).

John Boyle, senior vice president and director of the Government and Social Research Division at Schulman, Ronca, and Bucuvalas, Inc. (SRBI)—the national research organization that also administered the National Women's Study—designed the survey, analyzed the data, and coauthored with Tjaden (Tjaden & Boyle, 1998b) a lengthy unpublished report on the methodology of this survey.

Sampling Method

A national sample of 8,000 women and 8,000 men 18 years and older was drawn in 50 states and the District of Columbia. SRBI generated the sample "using a random digit dialing approach" (Tjaden & Boyle, 1998, p. 5). "In households with more than one eligible adult, the adult with the most recent birthday was selected as the designated respondent" (Tjaden & Thoennes, 1998a, p. 14). Some of the NVAW survey's basic demographic characteristics were compared with those of the general population "as measured by the U.S. Census Bureau's 1995 Current Population Survey" (Tjaden & Thoennes, 1998a, p. 14). However, sample weighting was not found to be necessary.

Interviewers

Tjaden chose SRBI to conduct the NVAW survey because of their "considerable experience conducting surveys of women on sensitive issues, as well as surveys on crime and victimization" (Tjaden & Boyle, 1998, p. 5). SRBI noted that they take special care in the identification and selection of their interviewers in recognition of the fact that "the quality of the interviewing staff used in a survey is one of the most important factors affecting the validity, [and] reliability of the data collected" (Tjaden & Boyle, 1998, p. 34). Furthermore, their most experienced interviewers were used on this survey.

The interviewers used CATI, the computer-assisted telephone interviewing system. Female respondents were interviewed by female interviewers, and Spanish-speaking interviewers conducted the interviews with Spanish-speaking respondents.

Definition

Tjaden and Thoennes (1998a) defined rape "as an event that occurred without the victim's consent, that involved the use or threat of force to penetrate the victim's vagina or anus by penis, tongue, fingers, or object, or the victim's mouth by penis" (p. 13).

Screen Questions

The NVAW investigators adapted the first four of the following screen questions that had been used by the National Women's Study.

1. Has a man or boy made you have sex by using force or threatening to harm you or someone close to you? Just so there is no mistake, by sex we mean putting a penis in your vagina.
2. Has anyone, male or female, ever made you have oral sex by using force or threat of force? Just so there is no mistake, by oral sex we mean that a man or boy put his penis in your mouth or someone, male or female, penetrated your vagina or anus with their mouth.
3. Has anyone ever made you have anal sex by using force or threat of harm? Just so there is no mistake, by anal sex we mean that a man or boy put his penis in your anus.
4. Has anyone, male or female, ever put fingers or objects in your vagina or anus against your will or by using force or threats?
5. Has anyone, male or female, ever *attempted* to make you have vaginal, oral, or anal sex against your will, but intercourse or penetration did not occur? (Tjaden & Thoennes, 1998a, p. 13)

Questionnaire

Tjaden and Boyle (1998) used "a modified version of a questionnaire developed and implemented by Statistics Canada for their Violence Against Women Survey" (p. 2).

Participation Rate

According to Tjaden and Thoennes (1998b), the NVAW survey's participation rate for households was 72%, and for respondents it was 97% (p. 15). The participation rate was calculated by applying the formula established by the Council of Applied Survey Research Organizations (CASRO) as follows: the total number of interviews completed plus the total number of cases screened out of the interview "because there were not any adults or women [*sic*] in the household,"[4] divided by the total number of interviews completed plus the total number of cases screened out of the interview plus the number of refusals plus the number of terminations of the interview, that is (8,000 + 4,829)/(8,000 + 4,829 + 4,608 + 351) = 72.1% (Tjaden & Boyle, 1988, pp. 53, 54). However, the 97% participation rate for NVAW's respondents needs to be included in the overall participation rate. This lowers the participation rate slightly to 69.8% (97% × 72%).

The participation rate was computed in such a complex manner to take account of the individuals who refused *before* their eligibility could be determined. More typically, the participation rate is determined by dividing those who participate by those who are approached to participate but do not do so. This procedure assumes that those household members who do not participate are *eligible* to participate. This is a poor assumption in surveys in which only adult women are surveyed. Certainly, some of these households contain no females. Tjaden and Boyle counteracted this problem by adding to the formula's denominator and numerator those individuals who were screened out because they were ineligible to participate. In other words, by leaving these individuals out of the equation, it is as if Tjaden and Boyle automatically assumed that all these households contained *no* eligible participants. Had all the studies reviewed in this book used this formula, some of their participation rates would have been higher than they were reported to be.

Duration of Interview

The average duration of interviews was approximately 35 to 40 minutes.

Findings

Tjaden and Thoennes do not report the NVAW survey's incidence rate for rape in the prior 12 months; instead, they report obtaining a 0.3% prevalence rate for completed and attempted rape in the prior year. These victims averaged 2.9 rapes each. This very high average is probably due to the NVAW survey's rule that in cases of multiple rapes of a victim by the same perpetrator, each rape was counted as a separate incident. In addition, one victim reported that she had been raped approximately twice a month during the previous year (Tjaden, personal communication, November 1998).

To calculate the number of actual victims in the NVAW sample who had been raped in the previous year, we multiplied the total number of women in the sample (8,000) by the percentage of those who had been raped in the past year (0.3%). This calculation yielded 24 victims of rape in the prior year (8,000 × 0.3 = 24). Based on an average of 2.9 rapes for each of these 24 women, an estimated 876,064 women in the United States have been raped annually. From this and other information Tjaden and Thoennes provided, we were able to extrapolate an incidence rate of 8.7 completed and attempted rapes per 1,000 women.[5]

The NVAW survey's lifetime prevalence of completed and attempted rape was 18%. According to Tjaden and Thoennes, their prevalence of completed rape alone was 15%, while attempted rape was only 3%. (The prevalence of attempted rape is almost certainly incorrect, as will shortly be explained.)

Evaluation

The methodology of the NVAW survey appears to have been modeled in part on the National Women's Study (Kilpatrick, Edmunds, & Seymour, 1992). For example, their definitions of rape are very similar, including the failure to include rapes perpetrated on incapacitated women. In addition, Boyle adapted the NWS's screen questions for the NVAW survey, merely adding one question on attempted rape. While Boyle coauthored with Tjaden the unpublished report on the methodology of the NVAW survey, he is the sole author of a similar unpublished report on the NWS's methodology (Boyle, 1992). Both surveys used CATI, both were quite brief in duration (25 minutes for the NVAW Survey and 35-40 minutes for NWS), and both used interviewers from SRBI. Perhaps this explains why the national prevalence of completed rape for these two studies is so close: 12.7% for the NWS and 15% for the NVAW survey.

The NVAW survey's large sample size of 8,000 women permits complex analyses to be made without fear of the numbers in different categories becoming too few to analyze. This advantage makes it all the more surprising that there is little information about rape in Tjaden and Thoennes's (1998a) report. These researchers have combined their data on rape and physical assault in some instances (e.g., their analysis of victim-perpetrator relationships, the sex of perpetrators, and the injuries and types of medical care received [pp. 8-9]). It is hoped that further reports will provide more information.

Comparison of Incidence Rates: The NVAW and NCVS

Tjaden and Thoennes (1998a/b) compared the 876,064 rape incidents that they estimated had occurred in the United States in the previous year with the 432,100 rapes and sexual assaults estimated by the National Criminal Victimization Survey for 1994 (the most recent year for which estimates were

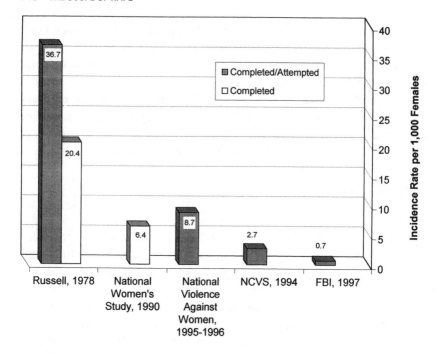

Figure 7.1. A Comparison of Incidence Rates for Completed and/or Attempted Rape per 1,000 Women Obtained by Five Surveys

NOTE: The rates of the National Women's Study and the National Violence Against Women Study are estimated. Calculations are explained in the text.

available). This comparison reveals that their estimate of the number of rape incidents is almost exactly double the number estimated by the NCVS, despite the fact that the NCVS includes the far less serious crime of sexual assault in their count, uses a substantially broader definition of rape, and includes rapes of females over 11 years old in contrast to rapes of females over 18—as did the NVAW study (see Chapter 5).

When we compare NVAW's 8.7 incidence rate for completed and attempted rapes per 1,000 women with the NCVS's 2.7 incidence rate per 1,000 women for the same crimes, we see that *the NVAW's incidence rate is more than three times higher than the NCVS's incidence rate* (see Figure 7.1). This measure of incidence is more meaningful than Tjaden and Thoennes's comparison of the number of rape incidents obtained by these two surveys.

On the other hand, the NVAW's incidence rate is distorted by one respondent's report of approximately 24 rapes by her spouse (Tjaden, personal communication, November 1998). The fewer the actual number of rapes on which incidence rates are based, the more subject they are to such distortions. If the woman reporting 24 rapes is excluded from the calculation because of her distorting effect, then the 23 remaining women who were raped in the preceding year would have experienced an average of 2 rapes each.[6] The resulting incidence rate would be 6/1,000 (i.e., the original incidence rate of 3/1,000 × 2 = 6/1,000). This rate is still more than double the incidence rate obtained by the NCVS.

The Prevalence of Rape

The NCVS is the only study with which Tjaden and Thoennes compare their findings and methodology, even though the NCVS does not measure prevalence and most researchers on the magnitude of the rape problem consider prevalence to be a much more appropriate measure than the incidence rate.

The NVAW survey's 18% prevalence for completed and attempted rapes is less than half the comparable prevalence rate obtained by Russell, and significantly lower than Wyatt's 22% prevalence rate (see Figure 6.1 in Chapter 6 and Table A1.6.1 in Appendix 1).

Figure 6.1 (in Chapter 6) reveals that the 3% contribution of attempted rape to the combined prevalence of completed and attempted rape is lower than the comparable prevalence rates obtained by Russell (1984) and Kilpatrick et al. (1985). More specifically, the NVAW's 3% prevalence for attempted rape compares with Russell's 20% prevalence for attempted rape, whereas the disparity between the NVAW's and Russell's prevalence rates for completed *and* attempted rape combined is much smaller, that is 18% and 24%, respectively. Perhaps the fact that four of the NVAW's screen questions ask about completed rape while only one asks about attempted rape may explain this.

Factors Reducing the Prevalence of Rape

Although Bolen and Scannapieco's (1999) research is about the prevalence of child sexual abuse, it is noteworthy that their comparison of the methodology and findings of 22 random sample surveys yielded the finding that the greater the number of respondents, the lower the prevalence estimates were (p. 293). As these researchers note, this finding is counterintuitive "because one would expect that sampling more individuals would give a better estimate of the prevalence of child sexual abuse" (p. 294). The explanation they suggest is that greater attention can be paid to respondents in smaller samples.

Finally, the NVAW study's low prevalence of attempted rape may be partially responsible for lowering its combined rate of completed and attempted rape.

In conclusion: The NVAW survey is a very solid achievement. Although we have noted that Tjaden and Thoennes did not calculate an incidence rate for rape, this oversight can be corrected. In addition, they presumably can provide more comprehensive information on rape than they reported in their 1998 report.

However, there appears to be a problem with Tjaden and Thoennes's unusually low prevalence of attempted rape that may be related to their asking only one question about it.

COMPARISONS BETWEEN REPRESENTATIVE SURVEYS

Incidence Rates

Figure 7.1 compares the four surveys described in this and the previous chapter that obtained an incidence rate for rape per 1,000 females, or for which such an incidence rate could be extrapolated, as well as the FBI's incidence rate per 100,000 females for reported rapes. With the exception of Russell's study, the other four studies were all conducted in the 1990s. The NWS and Russell's study are the only two that reported an incidence rate for completed rape (see Figure 7.1). Russell's 20.4 per 1,000 incidence rate is more than three times greater than the NWS's incidence rate of 6.4 per 1,000 females.

As may be seen in Figure 7.1, Russell's incidence rate of 36.7 per 1,000 females for completed and attempted rape is more than four times higher than the NVAW study's 8.7 incidence rate (when the woman reporting 24 rapes is included). Furthermore, in contrast to Tjaden and Thoennes's method of calculating the number of rape incidents, Russell counted multiple rapes by one perpetrator as only one incident; that is, her incidence rate was based on the number of rapes perpetrated by different rapists. Had Tjaden and Thoennes used this method, their incidence rate would have been substantially lower; just how much lower would depend on how many other victims of rape by a single perpetrator during the particular year in question were counted more than once.

Prevalence Rates

The prevalence rates for rape obtained by the seven studies that calculated them are difficult to compare because of the different combinations of completed and/or attempted rape they obtained (see Figure 6.1, Chapter 6, and Table A1.6.1 in Appendix 1).

For the six studies that reported a separate prevalence rate for completed rape, prevalence ranged from a low of 5% (Kilpatrick et al., 1985) to a high of 24% (Russell, 1984), with a mean prevalence rate of 14%.

Only three studies reported a separate prevalence rate for attempted rape, and we have argued that both the NVAW's 3% estimate and Kilpatrick et al.'s 4% estimates are inaccurate. This leaves only Russell's 31% prevalence for attempted rape.

The four studies reporting a combined prevalence rate for completed and attempted rape range from a low of 9% (Kilpatrick et al., 1985) to a high of 44% (Russell, 1984), and a mean of 23%.

A few critics have dismissed Russell's high prevalence of rape as unrealistically high (e.g., Gilbert, 1991c). Some early critics suggested that the reason it was so high may be due to the idiosyncratic character of San Francisco. However, it is evident from a comparison of the prevalence rates for completed rape obtained by the studies analyzed in Chapters 6 and 7 that some other studies obtained quite high prevalence rates, particularly the 20% rate obtained by the NSFG (Abma et al., 1997). Nevertheless, when looking at the combined rate of completed and attempted rape, Russell's 44% prevalence rate is still much higher than those obtained by all the other studies. It is exactly double Wyatt's 22% rate—the next highest after Russell's. However, in our analysis of Russell's study, we offered many reasons for the high level of disclosure Russell attained.

Since the statistics published by the *Uniform Crime Reports* and the National Crime Victimization Surveys routinely combine attempted and completed rapes, we recommend that future prevalence studies provide separate data on completed and attempted rape, as well as combining them. All three of the national surveys described in this chapter have failed to obtain data on attempted rape.

We also recommend that future prevalence researchers obtain data on the incidence rates of rape. This will enable them to compare their findings to those of the NCVS as well as to the UCR's reported rape rate.

Most important of all, we recommend that rape prevalence researchers include rape-appropriate features in their methodologies. Russell's study offers several examples of such methods (described in Chapter 3). This recommendation is based on our assumption that the myths about rape that are prevalent in American culture will be shared by many interviewers, and that interviewers who subscribe to these myths will be less likely to gain the trust necessary for respondents to disclose their rape experiences. Hence, rejection of such myths should be one of the criteria for selecting interviewers, and their training should also include education about the spuriousness of these myths.

We believe that Russell's methods of selecting and educating interviewers for her study may be a key factor in the high disclosure rate she obtained for rape. While no research has yet been done to substantiate our reasoning here, we believe that future research will confirm that rape-sensitive methodology will, other things being equal, be found to be related to high disclosures of these crimes.

CONCLUSION: THE SOUNDEST ESTIMATE OF PREVALENCE

Although we calculated the mean prevalence rates for completed rape, and completed and attempted rape combined, for all the studies that had obtained these statistics, we do not believe this is the soundest way to estimate the prevalence of rape. As previously mentioned, we believe the best method is to discard the findings of inferior studies of prevalence, and either to select the prevalence rate obtained by the soundest study, or to calculate the mean prevalence rates of more than one study if there are two or more that qualify as comparatively sound.

Four of the seven prevalence of rape studies evaluated in Chapters 3, 6, and 7, are national in scope: the National Women's Study, the National Comorbidity Study, the National Survey of Family Growth, and the National Violence Against Women Study. Of these four surveys, all suffer from serious methodological problems for assessing prevalence. Although the 20.4%

prevalence rate obtained by the NSFG is almost certainly superior to those obtained by the other three national surveys, its methodology suffers from several serious weaknesses. Most conspicuous of these is that there were only two screen questions, one on "nonvoluntary intercourse" which may have yielded answers that do not qualify by most definitions of rape. In addition, respondents were limited to females aged 15 to 44, thus excluding the age groups with the lowest rates of rape. Although the NSFG obtained the second highest prevalence rate for rape, we believe that it significantly underestimates the scope of this problem.

Given that the three remaining studies that we evaluated are all confined to a very limited region of the United States, none of their estimates can be generalized beyond these locations. Furthermore, the generalizability of all of the studies, including the national ones, are limited to the dates when their field work was conducted. While bearing these limitations in mind, we decided to base our evaluation of the soundest estimate of the prevalence of rape on the study (or studies) with the soundest methodology for arriving at such an estimate. The criteria we used for ascertaining the soundness of studies includes the appropriateness of the methodology for measuring prevalence, the rigor with which the methodology was administered, and the sensitivity and appropriateness of the methodology for obtaining disclosures on rape.

Application of these criteria resulted in our selection of Russell's prevalence rates of 24% for completed rape and 44% for both completed and attempted rape as the most sound of all the studies examined. A low participation rate is the most significant shortcoming of her study (aside from its confinement to the city of San Francisco). Nevertheless, Russell's methodology was generally very sound and rigorously executed. Her creation of rape-appropriate methods appears to have been particularly effective at eliciting disclosures of these usually secret experiences. This enabled Russell to develop an unusually rape-sensitive interview schedule, an innovative method of selecting interviewers, and rape-appropriate training for the interviewers.

The other prevalence-of-rape studies that are sufficiently sound to qualify as worthy of consideration are Wyatt's (1985) study in Los Angeles, Kilpatrick et al.'s National Women's Study (Kilpatrick et al., 1992), the National Survey of Family Growth (Abma et al., 1997), and Tjaden and Thoennes's (1998a) National Violence Against Women study. In our evaluations of each of these studies, however, we noted various methodological flaws that we consider to be responsible for their underestimation of the prevalence of rape in the United States.

The prevalence of rape obtained by these four studies ranged from Kilpatrick et al.'s low of 12.7% for completed rape, Tjaden and Thoennes's 18% prevalence for completed and attempted rape, Wyatt's 24% for completed and attempted rape, and the National Survey of Family Growth's 20% prevalence for completed rape. Russell's 44% for completed and attempted rape is clearly by far the highest (see Table A1.6.1). However, *all* these studies show that rape does indeed qualify as a serious epidemic in the United States.

NOTES

1. Since the abbreviation NCS has been used to describe the National Crime Surveys, the National Comorbidity Survey will not be similarly abbreviated.

2. Although 20.4% is given as the total percentage of women who were ever subjected to forced intercourse, a breakdown of the ages when the rapes occurred adds to only 20% (Abma et al., 1997, Table 22, p. 33).

3. Kilpatrick (personal communication, August 1997).

4. Tjaden and Boyle's (1998) statement that 4,829 cases were screened out of the interview *"because there were not any adults or women in the household"* (p. 54; emphasis added) is bewildering. If there were no adults or women [*sic*] in 4,829 households, who on earth lived there? "Children" seems to be the only logical but implausible answer. If they meant to say that this enormous number of households were excluded from their sample because no adults happened to be there when the interviewer dropped by, we wonder how many times interviewers returned to these addresses.

5. Since 0.3% of their female respondents were victimized by completed and/or attempted rape in the previous 12 months (see Exhibit 2, p. 4), and since these victims averaged 2.9 rapes each (see Exhibit 3, p. 4), multiplying 0.3/100 by 2.9 provides an incidence rate of 8.7 rapes per 1,000 women. This approximates the total 876,064 victimizations obtained by Tjaden and Thoennes (1998a; see Exhibit 3, p. 4).

6. Twenty-four women were raped in the previous year and each woman experienced, on average, 2.9 rapes, making a total of 70 rapes ($24 \times 2.9 = 69.6$). To remove the effect of the rapes by the woman who reported 24 rapes, these 24 rapes were subtracted from the total of 70 rapes, leaving 46 rapes occurring to the 23 remaining victims. Dividing the 46 rapes by the 23 victims, we find that each woman, on average, experienced two rapes in the prior year.

8

◆

IS THE RAPE RATE
REALLY DECREASING?
TRENDS IN RAPE RATES OVER TIME

THE FBI'S *UCR* STATISTICS ON
CHANGES OVER TIME

The question of whether or not the rape rate in the United States is increasing or decreasing over time is an extremely controversial one. Typically, individuals wishing to inform themselves on this issue turn to the statistics on reported rapes published in the FBI's annual *Uniform Crime Reports (UCR)*. However, since most rapes are not reported to the police, and since those that are reported to the police are not representative of unreported rapes, it is virtually certain that the reported cases do not reflect the actual trends in rape rates over time (see Chapter 4).

For example, we noted in Chapter 4 that stranger rapes are much more likely to be reported to the police than date rapes and rapes by lovers and ex-lovers. The growing awareness about date rape and incestuous rape in the 1980s probably caused more such cases to be reported to the police than in the past. However, these increases cannot be assumed to reflect equally large increases in the real occurrence of these types of rapes.

Nevertheless, because so many individuals continue to rely on the *UCR* statistics, sometimes out of ignorance about the limitations but also for lack of alternatives, we decided to include the *UCR*'s data on the changes in the rates of reported rape from 1932, when these records began, until 1997—the most recent year for which these statistics were available (see Figure 8.1).

Figure 8.1 indicates that the reported incidence of rape has decreased from 84 per 100,000 females in 1992—the highest rate ever recorded—to 70 per

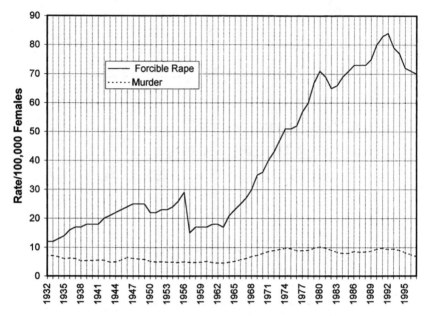

Figure 8.1. FBI Statistics on the Rates of Murder per 100,000 Inhabitants and Forcible Completed and/or Attempted Rape per 100,000 Females: 1932-1997

100,000 females in 1997 (a 16.7% decrease) (see Table A1.8.1 in Appendix 1 for the data on which Figure 8.1 is based). Many politicians have claimed that the decline in violent crime is due to their policies favoring harsher penalties against such crimes. For example, *New York Times* journalist Fox Butterfield (1997) noted that

> President Clinton and Attorney General Janet Reno immediately hailed the re-
> ported decline in rapes, but criminologists, academic experts on rape and leaders
> of women's groups divided sharply over whether the new figures were accurate
> and whether they should be seen as part of a broader trend toward an ebbing of vio-
> lent crime. (p. A1)

Rape researcher Mary Koss, for example, argues that the decline in the rape rate is not real because when the number of males in the rape-prone age groups decreases, the rape rate also decreases (Butterfield, 1997, p. A1). The implication is that the decline in rapes is due to this transitory demographic change rather than to a meaningful reduction in men's rape behavior. Koss goes on to emphasize that "the real issue is the number of women who are raped at some point in their life, and not whether the number of incidents goes up or down in any year" (Butterfield, 1997, p. A1).

When the FBI's *UCR* statistics on reported rape increase, many people speculate that the increase is due to more rapes being reported by victims rather than to a genuine increase in the incidence of rape. When rape rates decrease, however, few people suggest that perhaps fewer rape victims are reporting their experiences. However, this possibility is exactly what Koss suggests in the following statement: "It's just as legitimate for me to hypothesize that the rate of [reported] rape is going down because women are disillusioned with the criminal justice system" (Fuentes, 1997, p. 21).

Other possible reasons for the decline include the fact that certain kinds of rape are more likely to be reported than others, for example, rape by strangers, violent rapes, completed rapes, rapes by more than one perpetrator, or rapes by armed perpetrators (documented in Chapter 4). Hence, rape by strangers may have decreased because of tougher laws against rapists, while rape by intimates (e.g., dates, lovers, husbands, family members)—few of which are ever reported—may have increased. Because the vast majority of rapes are never reported (90% in Russell's study), the *UCR* cannot be assumed to reflect accurately the true trends in rape rates over time.

The considerable rise in rapists' use of "roofies" (Rohypnol)—the so-called date rape drug—in the past few years could also account for fewer reports of rape to the police. Some victims under the influence of Rohypnol or some other equivalent drug remain unaware of their victimization due to being unconscious during and after the assault. Many other victims know they have been raped or assaulted because they wake up with semen in or on their bodies, feeling sore, sweaty, etc., even though they cannot remember the attack.

These theories aside, a more long-term perspective on trends in the *UCR*'s rape rates over time—as portrayed in Figure 8.1—makes it clear that the increase in reported rape between 1932 and 1997, and the far more dramatic increase between 1963 and 1992, is much more noteworthy than the decrease between 1992 and 1997.

Finally, Koss also makes the important point that the FBI's statistics on rape have always been "suspect because the agency is 'charged with controlling crime, and so they are going to make decisions to make the numbers come out on the smaller side'" (Butterfield, 1997, p. A1). As we saw in Chapter 5, this skepticism is even more applicable to the statistics reported by the *National Crime Surveys/National Crime Victimization Surveys.*

In seeking to understand the trends in the rape rate over time, it is helpful to see them in the context of the trends in the rates of other violent crimes against persons. Figure 8.1 includes the murder and forcible rape rates from 1932 to 1997 (Table A1.8.1, on which this bar graph is based, is located in Appendix 1). Table A1.8.1 reveals that the murder rate also declined from 9.3 per 100,000 inhabitants in 1992 to 6.8 per 100,000 inhabitants in 1997 (a 26.9% decrease), as did the aggravated assault rate—from 441.8 in 1992—the highest rate ever recorded—to 382.0 in 1997 (a 13.6% decrease).

The recent short-term decline in these three violent crimes suggests that it makes little sense to look for a unique explanation that applies only to rape. Instead, it is necessary to seek explanations that apply to all three crimes of violence against persons. As previously mentioned, Koss attributed the recent decline in rape to a decrease in the number of males in the more rape-prone age groups. This presumably applies to aggravated assault and murder as well, since males are the primary perpetrators of all these crimes.

In conclusion: It seems premature to get too excited about the decreases in reported rape and other crimes of violence. The decline in these rates since 1992 may well turn out to be short-lived. Focusing instead on the long-term trend, Table A1.8.1 reveals a far more noteworthy and sizeable *increase* in the rape rate from 12 per 100,000 females in 1932 to 70 per 100,000 females in 1997 (a 483% increase) (see Figure 8.1 for the visual display of the rape and murder rates). Hence, the reported rape rate was close to six times higher in 1997 than it was in 1932.

Similarly, the aggravated assault rate rose from 45.9 per 100,000 inhabitants in 1932 to 382.0 per 100,000 inhabitants in 1997 (a 732.2% increase). The murder rate, on the other hand, is virtually flat, starting out at 7.0 per 100,000 inhabitants in 1932 and decreasing to 6.8 per 100,000 inhabitants in 1997 (a 3% decrease).

An examination of the peaks and valleys in the graphic representation of rape over time suggests a particularly sizeable increase in this crime between 1963 and 1992, when it rose from 17 per 100,000 females to 84 per 100,000 females, respectively (i.e., an increase of 394%). During those same years, aggravated assault increased even more—from 78.4 per 100,000 inhabitants to 441.8 per 100,000 inhabitants in 1992 (an increase of 463.5%).

Because the NCS/NCVS include reported *and* unreported rapes, their statistics on trends over time should provide a more accurate picture than the FBI's statistics on trends. However, as we will show, the NCS/NCVS's statistics confuse the picture even more.

THE NCS/NCVS'S STATISTICS ON CHANGES OVER TIME

Figure 8.2 is a graph of the NCS/NCVS's rape rates per 1,000 females aged 12 and older from 1973 to 1994 (the figures on which Figure 8.2 is based are located in Appendix 1, Table A1.8.2). Although the NCS/NCVS's statistics typically include males as victims, separate data were available on females.

In striking contrast to the 78.7% increase in the FBI's *UCR* rape rate from 1973 to 1994 (from 47 to 84 per 100,000 females), Table A1.8.2 in Appendix 1 shows that the NCS/NCVS's rape rate actually declined slightly from 1.8 per 1,000 females from the inception of these surveys in 1973, to 1.4 per 1,000 females in 1991. If the NCS/NCVS data could be assumed to be reasonably sound, the contrast between its findings and those of the *UCR* on the trends in the rape rate over time would highlight how poorly the *UCR*'s statistics on rapes reported to the police represent authentic data on rape rates over time. However, as we have documented in Chapter 5, there are no reasonable grounds for thinking that the NCS/NCVS's findings on rape rates over time are any more valid than the *UCR*'s. In fact, they may well be less accurate—for reasons that will shortly become apparent.

From 1992 onward, the magnitude of the rape rates was affected by the methodological changes made. The graphic display of the unadjusted rape rate in Figure 8.2 and the statistics provided in Table A1.8.2 in Appendix 1 (on which the graph is based) reveal a sharp increase in the rape rate from 1992 to 1993.

The NCVS has subsequently recalculated the rape rates reported by the NCS from 1973 to 1992 "to make data comparable to data after the redesign" (*BJS,* http://www.ojp.usdoj.gov/bjs/glance/viotrd.txt). The adjusted incidence rate for completed and attempted rape was calculated in the following way: In 1992-1993, the NCS methodology was administered to half of the sample, and the revised NCVS methodology was administered to the other half. The difference in the incidence rates obtained by both the old and the revised NCVS methodology was then determined. The difference was then applied proportionally to the incidence rates between 1973 and 1991 to estimate what the incidence rates would have been *if the revised definition of rape had been used throughout this period.* Comparisons of the adjusted rape rate with

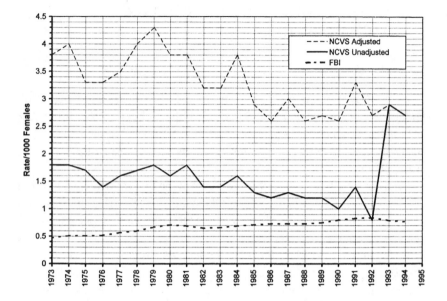

Figure 8.2. A Comparison of the Adjusted and Unadjusted Incidence Rates for Completed and/or Attempted Rape per 1,000 Females for the National Crime Surveys, the National Crime Victimization Surveys, and the Rate of Completed and/or Attempted Rape per 1,000 Females for the FBI's *Uniform Crime Reports* From 1973 to 1995

NOTE: To compare this figure with Figure 8.1, it is important to realize that the FBI data points for the years 1973 to 1994 in this figure represent the number of incidents of female rape for each *1,000* females, whereas the FBI data points for the years 1932 to 1997 in Figure 8.1 represent the number of incidents of female rape for each *100,000* females. Thus, the numbers on the left axis in Figure 8.1 are 100 times larger than the comparable numbers in Figure 8.2 (100,000/1,000 = 100), although they represent a similar percentage.

the unadjusted rape rate are graphically portrayed in Figure 8.2 (see Table A1.8.2 for the statistics on which this figure is based).

However, because the revised methodology included a greatly expanded definition of both completed and attempted rape, it is not legitimate to apply this new definition retrospectively. It is unacceptable to assume that it is possible to predict how women would have answered a different set of questions about rape over a period of almost two decades. Many rape-relevant historical changes were made during this period: for example, the recognition of rape in marriage, date rape, incestuous rape, oral and anal rape, rape with a foreign object, rape of incapacitated women, and a decrease in blaming attitudes toward rape victims. It is reasonable to believe that some of these changes may have affected rape victims' reporting behavior.

Despite fairly large fluctuations over the years (ranging from a high of 4.3 per 1,000 in 1979 to a low of 2.6 per 1,000 females in 1986, 1988, and 1990), the NCVS's adjusted incidence rate for completed and attempted rape declined from 3.8 per 1,000 females in 1973 to 2.7 per 1,000 females in 1992, after which no further adjusted rates were calculated. This represents a 29% decrease in the rape incidence rate from 1973 to 1992. This fairly gradual decline over almost two decades is inconsistent with the enormous increase reported in the FBI's statistics (published in the *UCR*) for completed and attempted rape. The only point of agreement between these two sources is that there has been a decline in the rape rate over the past few years. For the NCVS, the decline has been from 3.3 per 1,000 females in 1991 to 2.7 per 1,000 females in 1994 (i.e., a decline of 19%), while for the FBI's statistics on reported rape the decline has been from 84 per 100,000 in 1992 to 70 per 100,000 in 1997 (a decline of 16.7%).

Russell's survey offers a unique opportunity to evaluate whether or not the prevalence of rape and other types of sexual assault had actually been increasing at the time of her study in 1978.

Russell's Data on Changes in the Rape Rate Over Time

Russell's respondents ranged in age from 18 to over 80, so rape experiences that occurred before 1900 can be compared to those that occurred before 1978. One way to execute this comparison is to analyze the prevalence of rape for different cohorts of women (subgroups of women who were born around the same period of time).

COHORT RATES FOR COMPLETED AND ATTEMPTED RAPE OF SAN FRANCISCO WOMEN

Figure 8.3 shows the cumulative proportion of women who disclosed one or more experiences of completed or attempted rape at some time in their lives, for five different cohorts of women:

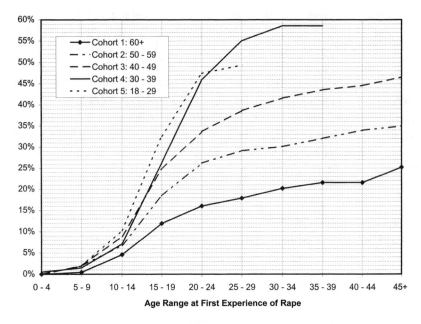

Figure 8.3. Cumulative Percentages of Five Cohorts of San Francisco Women Reporting Their First Experience of Completed and/or Attempted Rape in Russell's Survey in 1978

Cohort 1: those born in 1918 and earlier, who were 60 and older at the time of the interviews

Cohort 2: those born between 1919 and 1928, who were in their 50s

Cohort 3: those born between 1929 and 1938, who were in their 40s

Cohort 4: those born between 1939 and 1948, who were in their 30s

Cohort 5: those born between 1949 and 1960, who were from 18 to 29 years of age

When women disclosed more than one experience of completed or attempted rape, only their first experiences have been tabulated. This choice biases the data toward the younger age groups. Had we decided instead to select the most recent experience of rape, this choice would have biased the data toward the older age groups.

Figure 8.3 reveals that the percentage of women who reported a first experience of completed or attempted rape accelerated rapidly for all age groups during the teenage years (the raw data for Figure 8.3 are recorded in Table A1.8.3 in Appendix 1). Although the acceleration dropped greatly in their

early 20s, increases in the percentage of women who were ever raped continued more gradually until age 45 and over for the three cohorts that reached
that age.

Far more significant, however, is the strong linear relationship between the
current age of the cohort and the percentage of the cohort who reported being
a victim of completed or attempted rape at any age. The younger the current
age of the cohort, the higher the prevalence of completed and attempted rape
was found to be. More specifically,

♦ The oldest women (aged 60 years and more) reported a cumulative prevalence of
rape of 21.5%

♦ Women between the ages of 50 and 59 reported a cumulative prevalence of rape of
33.9%

♦ Women between the ages of 40 and 49 reported a cumulative prevalence of rape of
46.2%

♦ Women between the ages of 30 and 39 reported a cumulative prevalence of rape of
58.7%

♦ And women between the ages of 18 and 29 reported a cumulative prevalence of
rape that was already 53.2%

These data predict that the prevalence of rape for women who were in their
teens and 20s will eventually be still higher. By age 20, the percentage of respondents who reported one or more completed or attempted rapes had increased steadily from 11% of women 60 and older to almost 30% of the youngest group. These findings suggest that rape increased dramatically up until
1978 when Russell's survey was conducted. However, it could also be that the
younger women were more willing than the older women to admit their rape
experiences.

An effort to ascertain which of these explanations is correct, we examined
whether the younger women also reported more experiences of child sexual
abuse than the older women. We reasoned that if older women were less willing than younger women to disclose experiences of rape, they would also be
less likely to disclose experiences of child sexual abuse. Figure 8.4 shows that
the prevalence of child sexual abuse was significantly lower for the two older
age cohorts of respondents (50 years and older) than for the three younger age
cohorts (aged 18 to 49 years). More specifically, the prevalence rate of child
sexual abuse for respondents who were 60 years and older was only 28.5%,
whereas for respondents between the ages of 18 and 29 years, the prevalence
rate was 43.5% (chi square = 16.719, p = .005 for child sexual abuse; chi

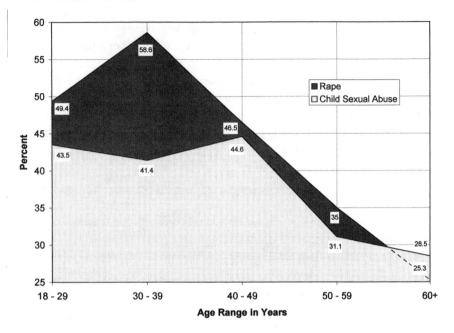

Figure 8.4. A Comparison of Child Sexual Abuse Prevalence Versus Rape Prevalence by Age of Respondent in Russell's 1978 Study

square = 55.611, $p < .001$ for rape), revealing a significantly lower rate of child sexual abuse for older women than younger women.

However, in contrast to the prevalence of rape, for which there was a marked linear relationship for the four older age cohorts (from 25.3% for respondents who were 60 and older to 58.6% for respondents who were between 30 and 39), there were only minor differences in the prevalence rates for child sexual abuse for the three younger age cohorts of respondents (see Figure 8.4). One other difference between the rape and child sexual abuse patterns is that respondents aged 30 to 39 were more likely than any other age cohort to report an experience of rape (58.6% for respondents aged 30 to 39 as compared to 49.4% for respondents aged 18 to 29, who had the next highest prevalence of rape).

This comparison confirms that the women aged 50 and over had significantly lower prevalence rates for both rape and child sexual abuse. While these comparisons do not clarify whether the older respondents were less willing to disclose experiences of child sexual abuse, they do suggest that age was not relevant to the prevalence of child sexual abuse obtained for the large majority of women aged 49 and younger. Although this finding appears to be in striking contrast to Russell's prevalence of rape for the younger three cohorts, it is important to bear in mind that Russell's 18-year-old respondents had already passed the age where they could have any additional experiences of child sexual abuse, whereas this was not the case for rape. This presumably explains why the prevalence of rape was higher for the 30- to 39-year-olds than for the respondents who were 18 to 29 years old. However, this same logic does not apply to the prevalence of rape disclosed by the respondents aged 40 and older. Either this linear decrease in the prevalence of rape by age reflects a decrease in the percentage of women being raped as they get older, or it reflects a decline in their willingness to report it.

In conclusion: Russell's finding that age is relevant to the prevalence rates for child sexual abuse reported by women aged 50 and older, but not for women who are younger than 50, contrasts with her cohort analysis of rape rates in which there was an almost perfect linear relationship between age and prevalence rates. We believe this confirms the validity of Russell's conclusion that the differences in prevalence rates for rape—at least for the three younger cohorts—are real, not the results of differential willingness to disclose such experiences. Hence, we believe that most of the increases over time revealed by Russell's cohort analysis reflect increases in the real rape rate over time (prior to 1978).

DISCUSSION

We noted above that the FBI's statistics on reported rape suffer from the fact that only a small percentage of rapes are ever reported to law enforcement agencies. We also pointed out in Chapter 5 that the National Crime [Victimization] Surveys' repeated claims that rape is an infrequent crime in the United States are totally incorrect. Findings by the methodologically superior representative studies evaluated in Part I of this book make it abundantly clear that rape is a widespread problem in the United States. The reason the NCVS consistently finds otherwise is due to its inadequate methodology. Hence, this official source of rape statistics seriously misleads the public by repeatedly describing rape as a rare occurrence.

Even if the official sources of rape statistics severely underestimate the problem of rape in the United States, the fact that the *UCR*'s and the NCS's methods for collecting statistics have remained the same through the years—until the methods of the NCS were finally revised in 1992—leads some individuals to believe that at least their statistics on trends over time are sound. Furthermore, because no other researchers (besides Russell) have chosen to analyze trends in their study's incidence or prevalence of rape over time, those needing this information have no alternative source to which they can turn.

However, since these federal government sources reveal only the tip of the iceberg as far as rape is concerned, we think it highly probable that their trend data are subject to many other influences (e.g., those mentioned by Koss earlier in this chapter). We believe Russell's cohort analysis was far more successful than the federal government's in estimating trends in the rape rate before 1978. Her cohort analysis suggests that rape increased dramatically over time until 1978 when her data were gathered. It is most unfortunate that other researchers have not analyzed changes over time. Perhaps other studies have obtained too few rape victims in their samples to conduct this kind of analysis.

The strongest evidence confirming the unreliability of the FBI's and the NCVS's rape rates over time may be the fact that they completely contradict each other prior to the past few years. While the FBI's rape rate shows a substantial increase in reported rapes until 1992, the NCS's rate of rape actually declined from 1973, when these surveys began, until 1992, when the methodological changes were made (see Figures 8.1 and 8.2).

Russell's survey, on the other hand, offers the first solid basis for determining whether or not the FBI's increase in reported rape over the years reflects a real increase in the rape rates. The tragic finding of Russell's survey is that there appears to be a far greater increase in the rape rate over several decades than the FBI's statistics indicate. When tracing the rape rates for five different cohorts of women, it is evident that the rates become significantly higher for every younger cohort. By age 20, the percentage reporting one or more completed or attempted rape had increased steadily from 11% of the women who were 60 and older to almost 30% of the youngest group.

In 1978, the cumulative prevalence of completed or attempted rape for women between the ages of 30 and 39 was 58.7%. For women between 18 and 29, it was already 53.2%. These increases are also evident when tracing the rates of completed and attempted rape between 1931 and 1976, except for a decline between 1971 and 1976 for most age groups.

Since Russell's data on trends in the prevalence of rape over time take us only to 1976 or 1978, there is no way of knowing if the rape rates continued to rise over the next two decades. It is vital that new research on changes in the rape rate over time be conducted so that scholars, policymakers, politicians, journalists, and interested members of the public are not forced by lack of alternatives to depend on the *UCR* and the NCS/NCVS, whose statistics on trends in the rape rate over time are so totally inadequate.

We also urge that research be conducted to determine whether the recent decline in the *UCR*'s rates of reported rape can be explained by addressing questions such as: Is this decline in the rate of rape related to a decline in the population of males at risk of raping females? Are fewer women reporting rape than in the past? Given that the decline in the rape rate reported by the *UCR* between 1992 and 1997 (16.7%) is associated with a similar decline in aggravated assault (13.6%) and murder (26.9%), have the rates of incarceration for these crimes increased and/or has the length of the sentences increased, thereby leaving fewer of these criminals in a position to offend? Of the rapists who are incarcerated, what percentage of them raped strangers as opposed to intimates and other females known to them? If a large percentage of incarcerated rapists were convicted for raping strangers, this might have contributed to a decline in stranger rapes because these are the rapes that are most likely to be reported to the police. However, there may not be any decrease, or there may even be an *increase,* in the much greater number of largely unreported rapes by men known to the victim.

In conclusion: Without further research, it is impossible to know whether the recent decline in reported rapes represents a real or an apparent decrease in this crime. Whatever the answer turns out to be, it would take a very long time for even a substantial and long-lasting decline in the rape rates to justify complacency about this problem. A decline does not herald the end of the epidemic of rape in the United States. The volume and rates of rape, like other violent crimes, are vastly higher in this country than in other Western nations (e.g., see Kangspunta et al., 1998, and Newman, 1999, pp. 52-53). Certainly, any declines in the real rape rate deserve to be celebrated. More important, any real decline should motivate analyses of what caused it. If the decline turns out to be policy related, the policy could be implemented more widely.

PART **II**

The Scope of
Child Sexual Abuse

9
◆

CHILD SEXUAL ABUSE, THE LAW, AND RESEARCHERS' DEFINITIONS

HISTORY OF LEGAL STATUTES

Until the late 1800s, most states prohibited "carnal knowledge," "carnal abuse," or sexual intercourse with females under the age of 10 (Kocen & Bulkley, 1985). Females of this age were considered too immature to consent knowledgeably to sexual activity with another person. Those older than 10 were protected by criminal statutes only from forcible rape (Kocen & Bulkley, 1985, p. 2). However, by the 1950s and 1960s, most states had raised the age of prohibition to as high as 17 years, regardless of whether or not consent had been given (Haugaard & Reppucci, 1988, pp. 19-20). These statutes became known as statutory rape laws.

In addition to these statutory rape laws, most states enacted legislation designed to protect children "from 'indecent liberties,' 'lewd and lascivious acts,' or 'molestation.'" These provisions covered sexual behavior other than sexual intercourse, such as the touching of the young child's private parts or genitals" (Kocen & Bulkley, 1985, p. 3). The term *sexual intercourse* was also redefined to include oral and anal intercourse as well as vaginal intercourse (Kocen & Bulkley, 1985, p. 2).

In the mid-1960s and continuing into the 1970s, substantial reforms in rape laws were initiated. The newer statutes prohibited a range of sexual acts, and the severity of the penalties depended on which of a number of factors—including the victim's age, the perpetrator's age, the relationship between them, and whether or not violence was used—characterized the crime (Kocen & Bulkley, 1985, p. 3). Currently, adult sexual activity with children is a crime in every state. However, state statutes differ in their definitions of what constitutes child sexual abuse. According to Haugaard and Reppucci (1988),

The criteria that most legal definitions depend on tend to be the ages of the child and the perpetrator and the type of act. However, wide variations exist from state to state, especially in regard to the specific acts that are defined as constituting sexual abuse. In general, children under the age of eighteen are protected [sic][1] from sexual activity with a parent or anyone who is in a parental or custodial position. Children who are thirteen or fourteen tend to be protected [sic] from sexual activity with anyone three or more years older than they are. Children under the age of thirteen are protected [sic] from all sexual activity. Children over the age of fourteen tend to be protected [sic] from sexual activity with someone other than a custodial figure only if they do not consent to the sexual activity. (pp. 23-24)

As complex as Haugaard and Reppucci's attempt is to summarize the elements included in most legal definitions in the United States, the reality is even more complicated. For many states, the term *sexual abuse* is only one of several forms of child sexual maltreatment. No wonder researchers typically do not use the law as their model for developing their definitions of this crime. As of 1991, every state except Ohio, Rhode Island, and Washington[2] also had incest statutes that prohibit sexual intercourse and marriage between close relatives (Liz Wohlken, NVC Policy Specialist, personal communication, February 22, 1995). Unlike the laws relating to child sexual abuse, most of the incest statutes ignore the ages of the parties involved.

Haugaard and Reppucci (1988) note that, "Every state with incest laws limits the criminal act of incest to sexual intercourse," regardless of whether or not force is used (p. 21). This means that sexual contact involving oral or anal intercourse, or sex acts other than vaginal intercourse, cannot be prosecuted under the incest laws in most states. However, they *can* be prosecuted under the broader child sexual abuse statutes. This very restricted prohibition was presumably due to the fact that incest laws in the United States were originally designed "primarily to protect against biological risk of dysgenic effect on the offspring of consanguineal relations" (Wulkan & Bulkley, 1985, p. 53).

In response to the proliferation of reports of incestuous abuse, starting in the late 1970s and early 1980s, many states revised their laws on incest with the intention of "preserving the sanctity of the family by adding stepparents and adoptive parents" to the list of prohibited sexual relationships (Wulkan & Bulkley, 1985, p. 60).

Statute of Limitations

Most states have statutes limiting the time during which crimes other than murder can be prosecuted. In recent years, many states have adopted extensions to their criminal and civil statutes of limitations for cases of child sexual abuse, although state statutes differ on the length of the extension (National Victim Center [NVC], 1995).

The states that have extended their statutes of limitations have done so because they came to accept the fact—elucidated by child sexual abuse researchers and clinicians—that the power imbalance between child victims and adult perpetrators, particularly when they are family members, renders child victims more easily intimidated into silence. Perpetrators' threats of terrible consequences to the child who tells, perpetrators convincing the child that she is to blame for the abuse, the child's inability to recall the sexual victimization, the child's ignorance about how to report the abuse, and/or the child's failure to understand that a crime has been committed, are some of the reasons that "many legislatures have extended the limitations period for the prosecution of child sexual offenses" (NVC, 1995, p. 1).

More recently, claims made by the False Memory Syndrome Foundation—that memories of child sexual abuse retrieved in therapy or in survivor groups or as a result of reading certain materials (e.g., Bass & Davis's *The Courage to Heal* [1988]) are usually false—have led to reductions in the statute of limitations for the prosecution of cases of child sexual abuse in some states. A growing number of other states are considering doing the same.

Reporting Child Sexual Abuse to the Police

The Child Abuse Prevention and Treatment Act of 1974 grants funding to states on condition that they have formal child abuse reporting laws. As a result, every state now has these laws. Legally, those who report are not required to have proof of their suspicions; they only have to have "reasonable" suspicion. Although all states accept calls from anyone reporting a case of suspected abuse, 30 states mandate certain types of professionals to report suspected abuse. These usually include medical professionals, law enforcement officers, teachers, and mental health professionals. The other states require anyone with a suspicion of abuse to report. The identities of those who report are supposed to be kept confidential. All states but four now have specific criminal penalties for those mandated to report who fail to do so. However, although prosecutions do occur, they are rare.

As expected, rates of reporting child sexual abuse increased dramatically after these reporting laws were enacted. It is important to note, however, that other factors could also have contributed to this increase (Pence & Wilson, 1994). Specifically, media attention to the problem of child sexual abuse intensified, much literature on the topic became available, and, as a consequence, public awareness increased. Thus, child sexual abuse reports grew from 7% of all child abuse reports in the late 1970s to 16% in 1986. Since then, rates have declined to 14% in 1993 (U.S. Department of Health and Human Services, 1995) and 11% in 1995 (Daro, 1995). This decline is probably due both to the backlash and to a child protective service (CPS) system that has become severely overburdened.

Even with the overall increase in reporting over the past two decades, a substantial percentage of suspected abuse remains unreported. In 1986, the second National Incidence Study found that 54% of all child abuse and 30% of child sexual abuse cases known to professionals were not reported to child protective services. Thus, even with the increase in reporting rates, the majority of cases known even to professionals remained unreported.

Substantiation

Even with the known underreporting, a backlash has developed by critics of the child welfare system, who "assert that too many families are being reported" (Pence & Wilson, 1994, p. 72). Concern has been voiced by Douglas Besharov (1994), among others, that with the greater numbers of reported abuse, fewer substantiated reports are occurring.

Yet, substantiation rates appear to have changed little over approximately the past 20 years. For example, the substantiation rate for all child abuse and neglect was 39% in 1993 (U.S. Department of Health and Human Services, 1995) and 37% in 1994 (U.S. Department of Health and Human Services, 1996), as compared to 40% in the 1980 NIS study (Pence & Wilson, 1994). Since 1990, substantiation rates have averaged 41% (U.S. Department of Health and Human Services, 1996).

It would be foolish to presume that every reported sexual abuse case is a valid, prosecutable offense. It is equally foolish—and much more dangerous—to deny that many valid cases are erroneously discounted because of entrenched myths about the sexual victimization of children and/or because children are manipulated or threatened into retracting their disclosures.

Removal of the Child From Her Home

Once the case has been substantiated, child protective services move to intervene with the intention (supposedly) of protecting the child. Yet in 40%

to 55% of substantiated cases of child sexual abuse, it is the child who is removed from the home (Hunter, Coulter, Runyon, & Everson, 1990; Jaudes & Morris, 1990; Pellegrin & Wagner, 1990). This removal rate is higher than that for other types of child maltreatment (Finkelhor, 1983; Pence & Wilson, 1994). Surprisingly, the most important factor related to removal is whether the child made the original disclosure (Finkelhor, 1983; Jaudes & Morris, 1990). Children who made the original disclosure were more often removed from their homes. This was also likely to be the fate of victims who lived in the same home as the perpetrator (Hunter et al., 1990).

What factors explain the high removal rate for victims of child sexual abuse? The most important factor may be the mother-blaming perspective of many CPS workers. In an early study, Christine Dietz and John Craft (1980) found that child protective workers placed equal blame on nonoffending mothers and fathers who abused their daughters. More recent studies find that the attitudes of child protective workers toward nonoffending mothers have improved, but workers still place a significant amount of blame on the mother (Kelley, 1990). Even some treatment centers that work with families of incestuous abuse victims often insist that mothers apologize to their daughters as part of the treatment program (Giarretto, 1982, 1989).

The misogyny evident in these judgments is supported by research that finds that at least 75% to 95% of mothers of victims of father-daughter incest are unaware of the ongoing abuse (Faller, 1990; Myer, 1985); that most mothers believe their children's disclosures (Sirles & Franke, 1989); and that 44% to 82% of mothers are supportive of their children upon disclosure (Everson, Hunter, Runyon, Edelsohn, & Coulter, 1990; Gomes-Schwartz, Horowitz, & Cardarelli, 1990; Lyon & Kouloumpos-Lenares, 1987; Myer, 1985). Thus, it is possible that a portion of the removals from the home may be based upon the worker's pejorative and often unfounded views of nonoffending mothers.

Perhaps even more important is the fact that the father is typically the only or primary breadwinner. Removing him from the home could jeopardize this role by alerting his employer to his crime, or by risking his refusal to continue providing for the family. The economic dependence of the family on him has been found to contribute to mothers' siding with their husbands at the expense of their victimized daughters (Myer, 1985).

The unfairness of removing the victim rather than the perpetrator from the home is compounded by the fact that most incest perpetrators abuse more than one child (Ballard et al., 1990). Hence, after the daughter's removal from the home, the perpetrator can continue the abusive behavior or may even start sexually abusing another child. The father's continued presence is a matter of great concern.

Prosecution

Finally, the majority of substantiated cases of incestuous abuse are not prosecuted, even though more of these cases have criminal charges filed (17%) than any other type of maltreatment (Pence & Wilson, 1994). In an early study by Carl Rogers (1982), only eight of 233 cases in the District of Columbia that were referred for prosecution came to trial, and only seven of these resulted in conviction. In a later study by Tausha Bradshaw and Alan Marks (1990), 30% of perpetrators in 490 cases of child sexual abuse referred for prosecution pleaded guilty prior to the trial, and less than 5% were convicted at trail. Two factors were related to conviction: the presence of medical evidence and the presence of a statement by the perpetrator. In other words, the victim's statement about the abuse was disregarded in determining whether the perpetrator was convicted.

Summary and Conclusion

Only approximately half of the cases of incestuous abuse known to professionals are reported. Of reported cases of suspected abuse, only approximately 40% are substantiated. Once substantiated, the "punishment" for the victims is often quick, as approximately 40% to 50% are removed from their homes. Further, only approximately 17% of perpetrators have criminal charges filed against them. Of these, approximately 65% are not convicted. Thus, for every 100 *substantiated* cases of incestuous abuse, only approximately 11 of the perpetrators are convicted of their crimes, and for every 100 cases of *reported* abuse, only four perpetrators are convicted. The tragedy is that these numbers represent only those child sexual abuse cases that come to the attention of officials.

Although the stated purpose of child sexual abuse legislation is to protect children, we see that the opposite is often accomplished. Many children remain in untenable situations or are placed in worse situations after they disclose the sexual abuse (Armstrong, 1994). Even in cases where they are not overtly blamed for their sexual victimization, being removed from the home constitutes a powerful message of blame and responsibility. How can it possibly be seen as just by them or anyone else? It is hard to imagine that their removal from the home does not convey the same message to their incestuous fathers.

RESEARCHERS' DEFINITIONS OF CHILD SEXUAL ABUSE

Researchers typically do not use the legal definitions of incestuous abuse or of child sexual abuse. For example, they do not limit their definition of incestuous abuse to intercourse with blood relatives. And just as states are not in agreement on the legal definitions of child sexual abuse or incestuous abuse, nor are researchers. In Timothy Wynkoop, Steven Capps, and Bobby Priest's (1995) review of data collection procedures for ascertaining the incidence and prevalence of child sexual abuse, they conclude that the gravest problem in arriving at reliable prevalence rates may well be "the variability between studies in the definitions of dependent variables" (p. 57) (also see Wyatt & Peters, 1986a). This is a serious obstacle to comparing the findings of different prevalence studies.

After reviewing 19 child sexual abuse prevalence studies, Finkelhor (1994) noted disagreements between researchers on the following definitional issues:

Whether or not to include non-contact experiences such as verbal propositions, exhibitionism, photographing of nude children, and showing children pornography.
What age to use to define the end of childhood (usually 16 or 18 years).
Whether or not to include peer sexual abuse. (p. 34)

Other definitional issues about which there is no consensus among researchers include:

Whether or not to use the perpetrator's age as a criterion of child sexual abuse (some researchers confine their definition to the euphemistic concept of "adult-child contacts").
Whether or not to use age differences between perpetrators and victims as a defining feature of child sexual abuse, and if so, whether or not to use one or more age differences depending on the age of the victim. For example, Finkelhor and Hotaling (1984) favor "5 or more years for a child 12 or under; 10 or more years for a child 13 to 16" (p. 31).

What forms of sexual abuse to include, for example, child prostitution; commercial sexual exploitation; pornography-related abuse; unwanted kisses and touches on the buttocks.

How to handle attempted child sexual abuse, such as attempted penetration, attempted fondling, and attempted touching of buttocks. Some attempts involve contact and some do not. If the researcher has decided to exclude noncontact forms of sexual abuse, does this mean including only those cases of attempted abuse that involve contact?

Whether or not to differentiate between incestuous and extrafamilial child sexual abuse. If so, whether or not to have different definitions for these two forms of abuse.

Whether or not to have a different definition of sexual abuse for children and adolescents.

Whether or not to confine child rape to forcible penetration or to include nonforcible penetration.

Other things being equal, the definition of child sexual abuse has a great impact on the prevalence rates obtained by different studies: The broader and more inclusive the definition, the higher the prevalence rate is likely to be. Hence, when comparing two studies whose definitions of child sexual abuse differ significantly with respect to breadth, the upper age limit for children, and the inclusion or exclusion of peers, it would be erroneous to assume that their different incidence and/or prevalence rates necessarily reflect anything more than their different definitions.

NOTES

1. The term *sic* has been inserted in this quotation because of the assumption it conveys that these laws *succeed* in protecting children from sexual abuse, rather than that they are designed to punish those who all too frequently transgress these statutes.

2. The fact that these states do not specifically prohibit incest does not mean that incest is legal in these regions, because there are statutes that preempt or subsume incest.

10

◆

THE INCIDENCE OF
CHILD SEXUAL ABUSE

There are three official sources on the incidence of child sexual abuse in the United States: (a) The National Incidence Studies of Child Abuse and Neglect (NIS); (b) The Fifty-State Survey of Child Abuse and Neglect (Daro, 1995); and (c) The National Child Abuse and Neglect Data System (NCANDS) (U.S. Department of Health and Human Services, National Center on Child Abuse and Neglect, 1996).

Because both the NCANDS report on the 1996 compendium of the annual statistics on child maltreatment (including child sexual abuse) and the Fifty-State Survey of Child Abuse and Neglect fail to provide information on the incidence of child sexual abuse of females, these databases are excluded from this analysis.[1]

THE THIRD NATIONAL INCIDENCE STUDY
OF CHILD ABUSE AND NEGLECT (NIS-3)
(1993/1994)

The National Incidence Study (NIS) is "a congressionally mandated, periodic effort of the National Center on Child Abuse and Neglect (NCCAN)" to collect data on reported and unreported child abuse in the United States during a one-year period (Sedlak & Broadhurst, 1996b, p. 1-2). The first National Incidence Study (NIS-1) was conducted in 1979 and 1980; NIS-2 was conducted in 1986 and 1987, and NIS-3 was conducted in 1993.

The fieldwork for NIS-3 was done during a period of three months by Westat, Inc., and its subcontractor James Bell Associates in 1993.

NIS-3 Project Director Andrea Sedlak and Senior Researcher Diane Broadhurst (1996a) describe the NIS as "the single most comprehensive source of information about the current incidence of child abuse and neglect in the United States" (p. v). Finkelhor (1994) describes NIS-3's statistics as "possibly the most reliable" (p. 35) of the three sources mentioned above. Since child sexual abuse is one of the types of child abuse included in NIS-3, these assessments presumably apply to this form of abuse as well.

The NIS-3 was based on counts of cases obtained from a nationally representative sample of counties. Estimates of national incidence rates are based on extrapolations from these counts (Finkelhor, 1994, p. 35). The statistics gathered by child protection and law enforcement agencies are also included in these counts, along with estimates of the number of cases seen by mandated reporters (such as "doctors and other health care and mental health providers, educators, and child care providers") who did not report these cases to child protection or law enforcement agencies (Finkelhor, 1994, p. 35; also see Sedlak & Broadhurst, 1996b, p. 2-5). This information was obtained from interviews with these professionals. Included also are cases that had been screened out by CPS (child protective services) without being investigated (Sedlak & Broadhurst, 1996a, p. 1). Finkelhor (1994) points out that "there may also be unreported cases of which professionals *are* aware, which they do not reveal to NIS researchers" (p. 35; emphasis added).

More specifically, the NIS-3 was based on 842 agencies serving a nationally representative sample of 42 counties; in each, the CPS agency provided information "on all the children who were reported and accepted for investigation" during the fieldwork period (Sedlak & Broadhurst, 1996a, pp. 1-2). Additional data were obtained from a representative sample of these cases (p. 2). Another representative sample of 5,612 professional staff in 800 non-CPS agencies were also queried to determine if they had identified any suspected cases of child sexual abuse.

Definitions

According to Sedlak and Broadhurst (1996b), "To a considerable extent, state legislatures have left it up to professionals in the field to interpret what constitutes 'abuse' or 'neglect'" (pp. 2-7). This translates into a lack of agreement on how to define these terms, including sexual abuse. However, the NIS researchers have their own definition, and "Only those cases that fit the [NIS] standards are considered 'countable' and used as the basis for generating incidence estimates" (Sedlak & Broadhurst, 1996b, p. 2-7). All eight of NIS-3's standards had to be met in order for a case of child sexual abuse to qualify as countable.

At the time of the sexual abuse, the child had to be: "a noninstitutionalized dependent of parent(s)/substitute(s)" and under 18 years of age. She also had to live in one of the study counties at some time during the study period. The sexual abuse had to be "nonaccidental and avoidable" and had to "occur during the study period that applied to the respondent agency." In addition, "there were requirements concerning the allowable *nature of the abusive acts or neglectful omissions* that could be included, concerning the *perpetrator* of the acts/omissions, and concerning the degree of *harm* to the child" (Sedlak & Broadhurst, 1996b, p. 2-8, emphasis in original). For example, under the "Harm Standard requirements" all maltreatment, including child sexual abuse, was limited to cases that were "perpetrated or permitted by a parent [or parent-substitute such as a foster parent or step-parent] or caretaker" (Sedlak & Broadhurst, 1996a, p. 2-8; also see 1996b, p. 2-9).

In addition, the NIS-3 (Sedlak & Broadhurst, 1996b) differentiated between the following three types of child sexual abuse:

Intrusion: "Evidence [i.e., credible information] of oral, anal, or genital penile penetration or anal or genital digital or other penetration."

Molestation with Genital Contact: "Acts where some form of actual genital contact had occurred, but where there was no specific indication of intrusion."

Other or Unknown Sexual Abuse: "This category was used for unspecified acts not known to have involved actual genital contact (e.g., fondling of breasts or buttocks, exposure) and for allegations concerning inadequate or inappropriate supervision of a child's voluntary sexual activities." (p. 2-14)

Each child was included only once in the database, and the data were annualized into estimates reflecting a full year.

Findings

Sedlak and Broadhurst (1996b) reported an estimated 300,200 sexually abused children in 1993 (p. 8-5), of whom we calculate that 198,732 were female.[2] *The estimated incidence rate for female victims of child sexual abuse was 6.8 per 1,000* compared to 2.3 per 1,000 for males (p. 4-7). Hence, girls experienced substantiated sexual abuse about three times more frequently than boys.

Evaluation

Many professional service workers in the field of child abuse and neglect, including child sexual abuse, rely on the findings of the National Incidence Studies. This makes it all the more serious that these studies suffer from numerous flaws. As noted by Finkelhor and Hotaling (1984), the vast majority of cases of child sexual abuse uncovered by NIS-1 were limited to those disclosed to child protective services (83%) or to "other investigatory agencies such as police" (9%; p. 24, i.e., adding up to 92%). Hence, these studies are glaring failures in achieving their goal of collecting data on unreported as well as reported cases.

Furthermore, "whatever fraction of the true incidence was captured by the National Incidence methodology, it is in all likelihood not a representative fraction" (Finkelhor & Hotaling, 1984, p. 25).

Because NIS's definition of child sexual abuse limits these acts to those that are perpetrated or permitted by a parent or caretaker, most experiences of child sexual abuse do not qualify as such; for example: sexual abuse by siblings, neighbors, and acquaintances who are not in a caretaking role (Sedlak & Broadhurst, 1996b, p. 3-1), as well as sexual abuse by strangers, gangs, or peers, and "even numerous seductions [sic] by adults or adolescent acquaintances of the child where the parents were not neglectful" (Finkelhor, 1994, p. 35). Furthermore, several studies have found that sexual abuse by nonrelatives is much more prevalent than sexual abuse by relatives (e.g., Finkelhor, Hotaling, Lewis, & Smith, 1990; Kilpatrick et al., 1992; Russell, 1984; Siegel, Sorenson, Golding, Burnam, & Stein, 1987).

Although NIS-3's definition of child sexual abuse is broader than some other investigators' definitions because of its inclusion of noncontact acts (exposure of genitals), it may be the narrowest ever devised by virtue of its requirement that the perpetrators be caretakers in order to qualify as sexual abusers. This is undoubtedly one of the reasons that the National Incidence Studies find such a low incidence of child sexual abuse.

Several other studies have found that only 5% to 7% of cases of child sexual abuse were perpetrated by a parent (Finkelhor et al., 1990; Russell, 1983a; Saunders, Villeponteaux, Lipovsky, Kilpatrick, & Veronen, 1992) and that approximately 70% of child sexual abuse cases were extrafamilial (Finkelhor et al., 1990; Russell, 1983a; Wyatt, 1985). In contrast, 29% of the children reported in the NIS-3 were sexually abused by a biological parent and 25% were sexually abused by a parent substitute such as a stepfather. This comparison dramatizes the fact that the National Incidence Studies set out to gather data on only a very small percentage of cases of child sexual abuse. Clearly, these studies would be far more useful if they used a much more inclusive definition of perpetrators comparable to the better prevalence studies.

With regard to the gender of the perpetrators, Finkelhor and Hotaling (1984) criticize NIS-1 for making it "difficult to distinguish in data summaries between an adult who actually commits the sexual abuse and one who allows it to happen or who may even give encouragement to another adult to do it" (p. 27). To our knowledge, the NIS is unique in defining as perpetrators those who allow the sexual abuse to happen, and we believe this definition is totally out of step with the definitions used by all other child sexual abuse researchers. As Finkelhor and Hotaling note, "there is a vast degree of difference between playing such a role [allowing sexual abuse to happen] and being the person who actually physically molests the child" (p. 27).

It is a well-documented fact that approximately 95% of child sexual abuse perpetrators are male (e.g., Finkelhor et al., 1990; Russell & Finkelhor, 1984; Wyatt, 1985) and, as already mentioned, that the vast majority of mothers are not aware of the ongoing sexual abuse by their partners (De Jong, 1988; Faller, 1990; Margolin, 1992; Myer, 1985; Sirles & Lofberg, 1990). Since it is typically males who sexually abuse children, especially those to whom they are related, and mothers who are considered the responsible negligent caretakers, the NIS's continuing failure to make a distinction between fathers who sexually abuse their children and mothers who are judged to have failed to protect their children, is also exceedingly sexist.

The NIS-3 provides very little data on gender aside from the gender of the perpetrators. Hence, there is very little information available on the sexual abuse of females in their lengthy report. This is extremely disturbing, especially since it is well established that gender is a key factor in virtually all aspects of child sexual abuse.

Incidence estimates based on reported cases of child sexual abuse are inherently biased because they are limited to suspected cases of child sexual abuse and the small minority of children who choose to disclose their abuse experience(s) to someone who then has to report it to the appropriate authorities. Even though reporting has increased over the past several years (Pence & Wilson, 1994), far fewer cases are reported than actually occur. In addition, it is up to child protective services to decide whether or not to substantiate the case. Only cases that have been substantiated or indicated (i.e., there is a very strong suspicion that they are valid, but they do not quite meet the substantiation guidelines) are included in the official incidence statistics.

In conclusion: It is evident that the National Incidence Studies' estimates of the incidence of child sexual abuse in the United States are totally inadequate, misleading, and sexist (manifested in mother-blaming), and vastly underreport the problem of child sexual abuse in this country.

Besides the problem of stigma, the NIS investigators also believed that a household survey would be too costly (Sedlak & Broadhurst, 1996b, fn. 2, pp. 2-3 & 2-4). While we are in no position to judge the financial wisdom of this claim, this does not justify spending millions of dollars on studies that fail to meet even NIS's own goals—let alone the goals that knowledgeable researchers and policymakers would find more useful.

GALLUP POLL ON DISCIPLINING CHILDREN IN AMERICA, 1995

In 1995, the Gallup Organization conducted interviews with a nationwide representative sample of 1,000 parents "which primarily concerned disciplinary practices and violence toward their children" (Finkelhor, Moore, Hamby, & Straus, 1997, p. 1). This poll "focused on how parents discipline their children and how parents were themselves raised as children" (Moore, Gallup, & Schussel, 1995, p. 1).

Moore et al. (1995) used random digit dialing to obtain and screen for households with children under the age of 18. If there was more than one eligible child, one child was randomly selected for an interview. If the child had two parents, only one of them was randomly selected for an interview. Almost two thirds (65%) of the respondents were mothers or mother substitutes, 32% were fathers or father substitutes, and 2% were other kinds of adult caretakers (Finkelhor et al., 1997, p. 2).

Once all the data were collected, they were weighted on the ages and genders of the children, as well as on race/ethnicity, region of the country, and education of the parents, to reflect the latest U.S. Census statistics (p. 22).

Definition

No specific definition for child sexual abuse was provided. Hence, the questions served as the operational definition for this crime.

Questions

Following are two of the four questions that were designed to ascertain the incidence of child sexual abuse.

30. What about the experience of your own child. As far as you know, IN THE PAST YEAR, has your child been touched in a sexual way by an adult or older child, when your child did not want to be touched that way, or has he/she been forced to touch an adult or an older child in a sexual way—including anyone who was a member of your family, or anyone outside your family? (If "Yes," ask:) Has it happened more than once? (If "No," ask:) Has it ever happened?
31. In the last year, has your child been forced to have sex by an adult or an older child—including anyone who was a member of your family, or anyone outside your family? (If "Yes," ask:) Has it happened more than once? (If "No," ask:) Has it ever happened? (Moore et al., 1995, p. 20)

The respondents' answers to these questions provided an incidence rate for this survey, and, in combination with the answers to the follow-up question: "Has it ever happened?," they provide a prevalence estimate as well.

Participation Rate

The Gallup Poll's refusal rate was 19% and the participation rate was 57% (Moore et al., 1995, p. 22).[3] The latter included telephone numbers that were busy or never answered (Finkelhor et al., 1997).

Findings

The Gallup Poll's incidence rate for the sexual abuse of girls was 17/1,000 or 1.7% in the prior 12 months of 1994-1995 (Moore et al., 1995, Table 6, p. 17). Remarkably, the Gallup Poll's incidence rate for the sexual abuse of boys was 20/1,000 or 2.0% in the prior year—slightly higher than the incidence rate for girls (Moore et al., 1995, Table 6, p. 17). This finding is, to our

knowledge, unprecedented (see Finkelhor et al., 1997, p. 6), and will be discussed in the next section.

Moore et al. (1995) note that the mothers in the sample were more likely
than fathers to report the sexual abuse of their child in the past year. More specifically, mothers reported that "23 children per thousand were sexually
abused last year, compared with 9 per thousand reported by fathers" (p. 16).
Unfortunately, no gender breakdown for the children is provided. However,
we can infer from this finding that the incidence rate of child sexual abuse is
lowered by the lesser knowledge or disclosures of the fathers.

Although mothers reported higher rates of child sexual abuse than fathers
in two-parent households (17 per 1,000 vs. 2 per 1,000, respectively), in one-
parent families, "single fathers report[ed] 46 victims per thousand in the past
year compared to 32 per thousand reported by single mothers" (Moore et al.,
1995, p. 16). This finding is consistent with a finding by Finkelhor et al.
(1990) in which children in male-only households were at a very high risk of
being sexually abused. This anomaly, however, does not negate the more general finding of higher disclosures by mothers.

Evaluation

Because the major goal of the Gallup Poll was to find out about how Americans discipline their children, the sample was limited to parents who had a
child under the age of 18 living in the home. Consequently, many adults were
excluded from participation in this survey: child-free adults, adults whose
children had left home, divorced adults who did not have custody of their children, as well as those typically omitted by surveys—the homeless and the
institutionalized. Although the term *parents* does not necessarily exclude
those who are lesbian or gay, it seems likely that the study was limited to parents who were living as heterosexuals. Were this not the case, they presumably would have mentioned that they had included same-sex couples. Adults
without telephones were also excluded.

Perhaps the most serious methodological shortcoming of the Gallup Poll
is the fact that the incidence of child sexual abuse was "based on what their
parents report about their child's experience" (Moore et al., 1995, p. 15). One
of the best established findings about child sexual abuse is that many victims
do not disclose their victimization experience(s) to anyone (Russell, 1986;
Saunders et al., 1992). If they do disclose to a parent, it is typically the mother
they tell (e.g., see Sauzier, 1989). The more problematic children's relation-

ships are with their parents, particularly their mothers, the less likely they are to disclose to them.

Several studies indicate that from 75% to 95% of mothers are unaware of the sexual abuse of their children (De Jong, 1988; Faller, 1990; Margolin, 1992; Myer, 1985; Sirles & Lofberg, 1990), and that a minority of mothers do not believe their children's disclosures of sexual abuse when they are informed about them (Faller, 1984; Herman, 1981; Russell, 1986).

Nor can we assume that parents who *do* know that their child has been sexually abused will disclose this to a Gallup Poll interviewer (Finkelhor, 1984), particularly if the perpetrator is, or was, a family member. Parents may also fail to disclose their child's sexual abuse because they feel ashamed about how they reacted to their child's disclosure; they may feel guilty for this "evidence of defective parenting" or that they will be considered bad parents; they may not know that they are supposed to report the sexual abuse to the authorities; the mother may be afraid of her husband's reaction; certain cultural values may prescribe keeping "family problems" within the family; minority parents may be reluctant to report to authorities who represent a white majority; and so on. Hence interviewing parents is a very unwise methodological choice for arriving at a sound estimate of the incidence and/or prevalence of child sexual abuse.

As noted above, the Gallup Poll's finding that the incidence of sexual abuse rates for boys was slightly higher than for girls is unprecedented. Typically, girls predominate over boys as victims of child sexual abuse at a ratio of from 2:1 to 4:1 (Finkelhor et al., 1997, p. 6). Moore et al. (1995) suggest that girls may be less willing than boys to report their experiences of child sexual abuse to their parents "for reasons of intimidation, or perhaps because they feel guilty about it" (p. 15). These authors also speculate that, because sexual abuse of boys is often perpetrated by older males,

> it may be that parents are especially sensitive to such homosexual advances. Or it may be that boys are more willing to share the trauma with their parents, especially if it is homosexual in nature, because they are more confident their parents will not hold them responsible. (p. 16)

We find all these reasons unconvincing. Given the overwhelming evidence showing much higher rates of sexual abuse of girls than boys, it is reasonable to assume that this also applies to the children of the Gallup Poll's respondents. Furthermore, studies on disclosure do not report gender differences

(Faller, 1990; Farrell, 1988; Sauzier, 1989), suggesting that the process of disclosure for boys and girls is similar.

Finkelhor et al. (1997) offer several other possible explanations for this anomalous finding. Because females are more likely than males to be incestuously abused, it may be that the girls in the Gallup Poll study were less willing to disclose these experiences to their parents—particularly when one or both of their parents were the perpetrators. Sauzier's (1989) finding that children were less likely to disclose parental sexual abuse supports this explanation. It could also be that parents were less willing to report incestuous abuse to Gallup Poll interviewers (Finkelhor et al., 1997, p. 6). Whatever the explanation, however, these problems suggest that this method is a poor one for ascertaining the incidence of child sexual abuse.

The NIS-3 incidence rate of 6.8 per 1,000 for girls compares with the Gallup Poll's incidence rate of 17 per 1,000. Hence, the Gallup Poll incidence rate for girls is two-and-a-half times higher than the NIS-3's incidence rate, despite the fact that the Gallup Poll's rate is based on the typically incomplete knowledge of parents about their daughters' experiences of child sexual abuse. This highlights the poor quality of the NIS-3's estimate of the incidence of child sexual abuse for females. No wonder Finkelhor (1994) considers it appropriate to conclude that, "Because sexual abuse is usually a hidden offense, there are no statistics on how many cases actually occur each year" (p. 32).

SUMMARY AND CONCLUSION

No satisfactory method for obtaining a sound estimate of the incidence of child sexual abuse exists at the current time. Finkelhor suggests that researchers should consider interviewing young children and asking them about what experiences of sexual abuse they may have had, or may be having. However, this possibility raises serious ethical issues. For example, the usual vitally important assurance of confidentiality would be in conflict with mandatory reporting requirements. In addition, it may be traumatizing for children to be asked to disclose experiences of sexual abuse, particularly incestuous abuse. It remains to be decided at what age it becomes unethical and unproductive to interview adolescents and children. Who will decide this, is unclear.

Perhaps a task force of the best prevalence researchers should be invited to develop a policy regarding how best to solve the ethical, methodological, and feasibility issues involved in conducting sounder child sexual abuse incidence studies.

In the interim, it is essential that professionals and others who cite the NIS or the Gallup Poll incidence statistics understand their serious limitations. Because of their methodological defects, there are no studies that provide anything close to satisfactory estimates of the incidence of child sexual abuse. All grossly underestimate the problem. Using these estimates to support policy decisions is therefore unwarranted.

NOTES

1. Although the NCANDS report (U.S. Department of Health and Human Services, 1998) provided information on the number of female victims of child sexual abuse in 1996 (21,867, pp. 2-10), there are too much missing data to be able to extrapolate the rate per 1,000 females. For example, the gender breakdown is limited to only 25% of all victims. We hope future NCANDS reports will provide estimates of the incidence of child sexual abuse based on complete information.

2. Given a ratio of 2.3 males to 6.8 females, males constituted approximately 33.8% of all 300,200 child sexual abuse cases, whereas females constituted 66.2% of these cases; $300,200 \times .662 = 198,732$ females.

3. Finkelhor et al. (1997) describe the overall participation rate as 52% without explaining why their figure differs from the 57% reported by Moore et al. (1995).

11

◆

RUSSELL'S SURVEY ON THE PREVALENCE OF CHILD SEXUAL ABUSE IN SAN FRANCISCO

Russell was the first researcher to conduct a probability survey to ascertain the prevalence of incestuous and extrafamilial child sexual abuse. This chapter is devoted to describing her child sexual abuse-related methodology and prevalence rates.

RUSSELL'S SAN FRANCISCO SURVEY CONDUCTED IN 1978

Definitions

Russell's primary definition of child sexual abuse excluded noncontact experiences (except in some cases of attempted contact) in the hope that whatever prevalence figures she obtained would be taken seriously and not trivialized.

Since incestuous abuse was expected to be generally more traumatic than extrafamilial child sexual abuse, Russell (1986) used a broader definition for incestuous abuse than for extrafamilial child sexual abuse. She defined *incestuous child abuse* as

> any kind of exploitive sexual contact or attempted sexual contact that occurred between relatives, no matter how distant the relationship, before the victim turned eighteen years old. (p. 60)

Experiences involving sexual contact with a relative that were both wanted *and* with a peer were regarded as nonexploitive (e.g., sex play between cousins or siblings of proximate ages). A peer relationship was defined as one in which the respondent was less than five years younger than the "perpetrator." The 40 cases of exploitive sexual contact between relatives where the respondent was 18 years or older when it started were excluded from this analysis.

In 1978, when the interviews for Russell's survey were conducted, California law defined child molestation as "all sex acts upon children under the age of fourteen, when the intent of sexually stimulating either party is involved" (Beserra, Jewel, & Matthews, 1973, p. 160). Hence Russell differentiated between the kinds of sex acts that qualified as extrafamilial child sexual abuse before and after the age of 14 and between the ages of 15 and 17. In general, however, the term *child* in her study included all individuals under the age of 18 years.

Another reason for Russell's decision to use a broader definition for extrafamilial sexual abuse of adolescents than of children was her desire to avoid including as sexual abuse adolescent females' very common experiences of unwanted sexual kisses and fondling in dating situations. She preferred to use a conservative definition that could not be dismissed for including insignificant experiences of child sexual abuse. Hence she limited her definition of adolescent (those aged between 14 and 17 years) extrafamilial child sexual abuse to rape and attempted rape. At least, it was her intention to do so.

However, after reanalyzing child sexual abuse on a case-by-case basis, Bolen found that some of the experiences that had been included as instances of adolescent extrafamilial child sexual abuse were in fact less serious than completed or attempted rape. However, in all cases the perpetrators were over 18 years of age and more than five years older than the victim. Hence, Russell's definition of this form of child sexual abuse had to be revised as follows:

> *Extrafamilial child sexual abuse* involves one or more unwanted sexual experiences with unrelated persons, ranging from attempted sexual fondling[1] to rape, before the victim turned 14 years, completed or attempted forcible rape experiences from the ages of 14 to 17 years (inclusive), *and attempted or completed sexual fondling from the ages of 14 to 17 years (inclusive) by adult perpetrators (over 18 years of age) who were five or more years older than the victim.*[2]

Despite this revision, Russell's definitions of these two forms of child sexual abuse are narrower than those used by many other researchers, most of whom include in their definitions exhibitionism and/or other experiences such as verbal propositions that involve no actual sexual contact or attempt at contact.

In many states, 18 is the age of consent; it is also the age specified in the Child Abuse and Neglect reporting statute. Hence, Russell's prevalence rates will be reported for respondents who were sexually abused before they turned 18.

Other Terminology

We prefer the term "perpetrator of child sexual abuse" over the terms sexual offender, sexual abuser, or sexual predator. The term *sexual offender* is typically used for sexual perpetrators who have been arrested, prosecuted, and/or incarcerated. Since only a very small percentage of perpetrators of child sexual abuse are ever apprehended, this term will be avoided. The term *sexual abuser* sounds too mild to apply to the more severe types of child sexual abuse such as child rape. And because males in the United States are typically raised to behave in a predatory fashion toward females, the term *sexual predator* is too broad and undifferentiating.

The Interview Schedule and Screening Questions

Russell surmised that respondents' abilities to recall their experiences of child sexual abuse (as well as rape) on request in an interview situation required several different questions. Hence, she included in her interview schedule five questions that asked about child sexual abuse experiences in a wide variety of ways, and nine additional questions that applied to females of all ages. The words in parentheses in these questions were read by the interviewer only if the respondent had already mentioned an experience of child sexual abuse. The percentages of the 930 women who answered in the affirmative to these questions appear at the end of each question.

1. Before you turned 14, were you ever upset by anyone exposing their genitals?— 27%
2. Did anyone ever try or succeed in having any kind of sexual intercourse with you against your wishes before you turned 14?—9%
3. In those years, did anyone ever try or succeed in getting you to touch their genitals against your wishes (besides anyone you've already mentioned)?—4.5%

4. Did anyone ever try or succeed in touching your breasts or genitals against your wishes before you turned 14 (besides anyone you've already mentioned)?—19%
5. Before you turned 14, did anyone ever feel you, grab you, or kiss you in a way you felt was sexually threatening (besides anyone you've already mentioned)?—14%
6. Before you turned 14, did you have any (other) upsetting sexual experiences that you haven't mentioned yet?—9%

The following questions do not stipulate an age limit. However, because information on age was obtained for those respondents who answered these questions in the affirmative, some of these questions yielded additional experiences of sexual abuse before the age of 14— especially of teenagers from 14 to 17 years of age. However, the frequencies indicated at the end of each question apply to adults as well as children.

7. At *any* time in your life, have you ever had an unwanted sexual experience with a girl or a woman?—8%
8. At any time in your life, have you ever been the victim of a rape or attempted rape?—22%
9. Some people have experienced unwanted sexual advances by someone who had authority over them, such as a doctor, teacher, employer, minister, therapist, policeman, or much older person.[3] Did *you ever* have *any* kind of unwanted sexual experience with someone who had authority over you, at *any* time in your life?—31%
10. People often don't think about their relatives when thinking about sexual experiences, so the next two questions are about relatives. At *any* time in your life, has an uncle, brother, father, grandfather, or female relative ever had *any kind* of sexual contact with you?—15%
11. At any time in your life, has anyone less closely related to you such as a stepparent, stepbrother, or stepsister, in-law or first cousin had *any* kind of sexual contact with you?—10%
12. In general, have you *narrowly missed* being sexually assaulted by someone at any time in your life (*other* than what you've already mentioned?)—12%
13. And have you *ever* been in any situation where there was violence or threat of violence where you were also afraid of being *sexually* assaulted—again *other* than what you've already mentioned?—8%
14. Can you think of any (other) unwanted sexual experiences (that you haven't mentioned yet)?—18%

Separate mini-interview schedules were completed only for those experiences that met Russell's definitions of incestuous or extrafamilial child sexual abuse. For those cases that qualified as sexual abuse, interviewers were instructed to obtain sufficiently detailed descriptions of the experience to ensure that the level of intimacy violated could be precisely coded. The numbers of mini-interview schedules relevant to different forms and degrees of child sexual abuse constituted the basis for calculating prevalence rates rather than the percentages of respondents who answered "yes" to any of the questions. This is because a respondent could answer two or three questions in the affirmative on the basis of only one experience; for example, a woman who had been incestuously raped as a child might have answered "yes" to questions 1, 7, and 9 above. In addition, if a respondent's description of her sexual abuse experience revealed that it did not meet the study's definitions, the incident was disqualified.

Findings

Table 11.1 shows that *16% of the sample of 930 women reported at least one experience of incestuous abuse before the age of 18 years.*[4] *Applying the narrower definition of extrafamilial child sexual abuse, almost a third (31%) of the sample of 930 women reported at least one experience of sexual abuse by a nonrelative before the age of 18 years.*

As might be expected, there is some overlap between the respondents who had experienced incestuous child abuse and those who had experienced extrafamilial child sexual abuse. When these two categories of sexual abuse are combined, *38% of the 930 women reported at least one experience of incestuous and/or extrafamilial sexual abuse before the age of 18 years* (see Table 11.1).

Russell's survey uncovered unexpectedly high prevalence rates for child sexual abuse. Nevertheless, these figures would have been much higher had Russell defined child sexual abuse to include noncontact experiences such as exhibitionism, being viewed by a Peeping Tom, being the recipient of verbal sexual propositions, and requests to pose for pornographic pictures. Some respondents answered the two questions on incest—which specifically asked about incidents involving sexual contact—by describing experiences that did not involve actual or attempted physical contact. It is probable that many other respondents would also have revealed such experiences had they been asked about them.

Despite the incompleteness of these inadvertently obtained data, they made it possible to derive an incomplete prevalence figure based on a broader

TABLE 11.1 The Number and Prevalence of Incestuous and Extrafamilial Child Sexual Abuse Obtained by Russell: Different Measures

Type of Sexual Abuse[1]	Prevalence	Number of Victims	Number of Incidents With Different Perpetrators[2]
		Contact Sexual Abuse	
Incestuous abuse[3]	16%	152	186
Extrafamilial sexual abuse[3]	31%	290	461
Incestuous and/or extrafamilial sexual abuse	38%	357	647
		Contact and Noncontact Sexual Abuse[4]	
Incestuous and/or extrafamilial sexual abuse	54%	504	

NOTES: 1. Prevalence rates for children under the age of 14 years were listed in Tables 10.2 and 10.3 in Russell (1984), pp. 184-185, for the four types of child sexual abuse listed here.

2. When perpetrators sexually abused victims more than once, it was counted as only one incident. When victims were sexually abused by more than one perpetrator, it was also counted as only one incident.

3. For the definitions of incestuous and extrafamilial child sexual abuse, see "Definitions" at the beginning of this chapter.

definition of child sexual abuse than the one that guided Russell's research. Quantitative data were also obtained about respondents who had been upset by witnessing someone exposing their genitals before they were 14 (27% replied in the affirmative) and extrafamilial child sexual abuse involving unwanted sexual kisses, sexual hugs, and other nongenital touching.

When Russell added these incomplete data on noncontact experiences of incestuous and extrafamilial child sexual abuse to her study's completed and attempted contact experiences of these crimes, she found that *54% of the 930 women in her sample reported at least one experience of incestuous and/or extrafamilial child sexual abuse before 18 years of age.* This prevalence rate would undoubtedly be substantially higher had more than one question (the one on genital exposure) been asked on a systematic basis. Furthermore, that question excluded all the respondents' genital exposure experiences between the ages of 15 and 17 years.

EVALUATION

The methodology of Russell's study was thoroughly evaluated in Chapter 3. Only methodological factors that are specific to child sexual abuse will be mentioned here.

Russell included 14 screen questions about child sexual abuse or sexual assaults at any age, including two questions that were specifically related to sexual abuse by relatives. Presumably, Russell's 14 questions contributed greatly to the high prevalence rate she obtained. After reviewing 19 surveys, Peters, Wyatt, and Finkelhor (1986) concluded that

> the most dramatic variations were not primarily explained by the definitions used, the sampling techniques, the response rates, the socioeconomic status of respondents, or whether subjects were interviewed by phone, in person, or with self-administered questionnaires. *Most important was the number of specific questions that were asked to ascertain a possible history of abuse.* (cited in Finkelhor, 1994, p. 37; emphasis added)

It is safe to assume that at least some of Russell's 930 respondents were unwilling to disclose experiences of child sexual abuse to the interviewers, particularly incestuous abuse. It is also highly probable that a significant number of respondents failed to remember their experiences (see Williams, 1994). These factors are likely to be more pronounced with Russell's study than the studies that followed, since in 1978, when she conducted her study, incestuous abuse was still a far more taboo topic than it has subsequently become. More recent studies have probably benefited from more women being able to remember their childhood sexual abuse experiences as well as more of them being willing to disclose these experiences to survey interviewers—assuming sound methodology.

In Chapter 3 we suggested that Russell's low 64% participation rate is probably the weakest factor in her study. There are two contradictory hypotheses regarding the impact of low participation rates on the prevalence of child sexual abuse. "The more common hypothesis," Peters et al. (1986) maintain,

> is that sexual abuse victims will, if given the opportunity, decline to participate in surveys because they are traumatized in a way that makes them distrustful. The implication is that low response rates mean artificially low prevalence rates as

victims screen themselves out. . . . . The second opposing hypothesis is that these same low response rates mean inflated prevalence rates. This would be because sexual abuse victims select themselves preferentially into surveys because they are looking for an opportunity to confide their history to someone who appears to be interested and concerned about this subject. However, the response rate remains low because nonvictims with nothing to discuss select themselves out. (p. 35)

On comparing the relationship between low participation rates and the prevalence of child sexual abuse obtained in 10 different studies, Peters et al. (1986) conclude that "low response rates are [not] consistently associated with either low or high prevalence" (p. 36). In a meta-analysis, Bolen and Scannapieco (1999) also found that the participation rate was not significantly related to the prevalence rate.

Although further research is needed on this issue, the conclusion of both of these research teams suggests that Russell's relataively low participation rate probably had no significant impact on her prevalence rate for child sexual abuse.

CONCLUSION

Despite the fact that the definitions used by Russell's study were narrower than those used in the other studies to be evaluated in the next two chapters, astonishingly high rates of child sexual abuse were disclosed. More specifically, Russell found that *well over one third (38%) of the women in her San Francisco sample had been sexually abused before the age of 18.* In addition, 16% (one in approximately six women) of Russell's 930 respondents had been victimized by incest before the age of 18. However, we have also explained why these rates constitute an underestimate of the true prevalence of these crimes.

According to Finkelhor (1994), "The most commonly cited specific figures for [the sexual abuse of] females are 27% from the *Los Angeles Times* study because of its national scope and 34% [this should be 38%] . . . from the Russell study because of its careful methodology" (p. 37). Elsewhere, Finkelhor refers to Russell's "often-cited" study as being "among the most meticulous in its methodology" (p. 37).

NOTES

---

1. The term *sexual fondling* has replaced *petting* because of the imprecision of the latter term as well as its connotation of relative harmlessness.

2. The revision is indicated in italics. Having to revise this definition is most unfortunate because Russell's previous definition has been cited frequently in the literature.

3. Authority figures such as physicians, employers, and professors are often much older than the children they molest, as well as having authority by virtue of their profession. The criterion for qualifying someone as a "much older adult" was not strictly based on the age of the perpetrator, nor on the age difference between the perpetrator and the victim. Instead, an attempt was made to ascertain from what respondents said, what had determined the perpetrators' status as an authority figure in their eyes. While this method is somewhat subjective on both the coders' and the respondents' parts, it seemed preferable to applying "objective" age criteria that are arbitrary and of dubious meaning.

4. Eight cases of incestuous abuse were excluded from the prevalence rates because the respondents' ages at the time of the abuse were missing, and two other cases were excluded because the interviewers failed to determine whether actual sexual contact had occurred or been attempted by the woman's relative.

12

◆

THE PREVALENCE OF
CHILD SEXUAL ABUSE:
OTHER REPRESENTATIVE SAMPLES,
PART 1

In this chapter we will describe and evaluate the prevalence findings and prevalence-related methodology of the following four surveys:

1. Glen Kercher and Marilyn McShane, Texas Survey, 1980
2. Gail Wyatt, Los Angeles County Survey, 1981-1984
3. Dean Kilpatrick, Connie Best, Lois Veronen, Angelynne Amick, Lorenz Villeponteaux, and Gary Ruff, Charleston County, South Carolina Survey, 1983
4. Judith Siegel, Susan Sorenson, Jacqueline Golding, Audrey Burnam, and Judith Stein, The Los Angeles Epidemiologic Catchment Area Project, 1983/1984

All of these representative surveys and those presented in Chapter 13 obtained their prevalence rates from retrospective studies of adults. According to Finkelhor (1994), these studies "provide the best window on undisclosed abuse" (p. 49). This is a vital achievement since, as emphasized earlier, underdisclosure is perhaps the most challenging problem for prevalence researchers to overcome. A comparison of the methodology and prevalence findings for all nine of the surveys described in this chapter and Chapter 13 can be found in Table A2.12.1 in Appendix 2.

The methodology of the surveys conducted by Wyatt and by Kilpatrick et al. were described in Chapter 6 on the incidence and prevalence of rape. Only their methodology that relates specifically to child sexual abuse will be described and evaluated in this chapter. These studies will be presented in chronological order according to when their fieldwork was conducted.

GLEN KERCHER AND MARILYN MCSHANE, RANDOM SAMPLE SURVEY IN TEXAS, 1980

In 1980, Kercher and McShane (1984) replicated the sampling procedure, the sample size, and the method of data collection of two earlier Texas research teams whose research was never published.[1] They sent self-administered questionnaires about child sexual abuse to a random sample of 2,000 adult Texas residents who held valid Texas driver's licenses. "Every nth name was taken to provide the size sample [*sic*] required" (p. 497).

Definition. Kercher and McShane (1984) defined child sexual abuse in the introduction to the questionnaire as

> contacts or interactions between a child and an adult when the child is being used for the sexual stimulation of the perpetrator or another person. Sexual abuse may be committed by a person under 18 when that person is significantly older than the victim or when the perpetrator is in the position of power or control over another child. (p. 487)

In addition, child sexual abuse included

> the obscene or pornographic photographing, filming or depiction of children for commercial or personal purposes, or the rape, molestation (fondling), incest, prostitution or other such forms of sexual exploitation of children under circumstances which indicate that the child's health or welfare is harmed or threatened thereby. (p. 497)

No age ceiling was provided in this definition; however, people could obtain driver's licenses in Texas at that time when they were 16 years old.

Screen Question. Kercher and McShane formulated only one screen question about the prevalence of child sexual abuse: "As a child, were you ever sexually abused?" (p. 497).

Participation Rate. Questionnaires were mailed to 2,000 addresses, and 1,056 questionnaires were returned, 56% (593) of which were by females (Kercher & McShane, 1984, p. 497).[2]

Findings

Kercher and McShane (1984) failed to report a prevalence rate for child sexual abuse. Extrapolating from the data they provided, we calculated *a prevalence rate of 11%;* that is, 11% of the female residents in their survey disclosed having been victims of sexual abuse in childhood (Table 1, p. 498).[3]

However, Kercher and McShane (1984) noted that 7% of the respondents failed to answer the question about child sexual abuse (p. 498). Although these 72[4] refusals should not have been included in the total number of participants when we calculated the prevalence rate for this study, the lack of information about the gender of these respondents made it impossible to exclude them from the prevalence rate for females.

No information was provided on the prevalence of incestuous abuse.

Evaluation

Kercher and McShane's study suffers from many glaring methodological weaknesses, much missing information, and several inaccurate calculations. For example, their survey suffered from a low and inaccurately calculated participation rate. Kercher and McShane noted that 7% of their male and female respondents skipped the screen question on child sexual abuse. This 7% should have been incorporated into their 56% participation rate. However, since Kercher and McShane did not indicate the gender breakdown for these refusals, all we can say is that their participation rate would almost certainly have been lowered had it included the female respondents among the 7% of question-skippers.

While there is no evidence at this time that the size of participation rates has an impact on prevalence rates (see Chapter 11 for documentation of this finding), the lower the participation rate obtained, the less reasonable it is to assume that the findings would be the same for the nonparticipants.

Kercher and McShane's exclusion of individuals without driver's licenses is another shortcoming of their study. People who could not afford cars, preferred other means of transportation, did not drive, or were ineligible for driver's licenses were therefore excluded from the study. This may have resulted in the overrepresentation of individuals who were better off financially. Given the large minority population in Texas, this could have seriously biased the results. However, Kercher and McShane (1984) maintain that "the racial/ethnic distribution of victims paralleled that of the Texas census with 77% white, 5% black, and 16% Hispanic" (p. 495).

Despite Kercher and McShane's (1984) finding that 16% of their study's victims of child sexual abuse were Hispanic, "a Spanish-language version of the questionnaire was not prepared" (p. 497). In providing a rationale for this decision, these researchers point to another study in which only 1.4% of the respondents had completed the Spanish-language questionnaire.

Finally, we find Kercher and McShane's inclusion of sexual exploitation (pornography-related abuse) in their definition of child sexual abuse commendable. Unfortunately, very few researchers have followed their example in this respect. Hence, in order for Kercher and McShane's prevalence findings to be compared with those obtained in other studies, it would have been desirable for these researchers to have separated their questions on child sexual abuse and child sexual exploitation.

Factors Reducing the
Prevalence of Child Sexual Abuse

The fact that there was only one screen question in this survey is the most serious shortcoming of the methodology and probably the key factor in the low 11% prevalence rate obtained. We have already provided ample evidence that the number of screen questions is highly related to the number of disclosures of child sexual abuse obtained.

Kercher and McShane's definition of child sexual abuse is rather long and complicated. The technical and academic style in which it is written is inappropriate for a random sample of individuals at all educational levels. This problem is compounded by the ambiguities in the definition. For example, according to the definition, "Sexual abuse may be committed by a person under the age of 18 when that person is significantly older than the victim," but it does not specify what a significant age difference is (Kercher & McShane, 1984, p. 497). Almost certainly, respondents chose different ages—a choice that it was impossible for Kercher and McShane to know.

Similarly, the screen question and definition left it up to respondents to decide what the upper age limit is for "a child" and at what age someone becomes an adult. In addition, Kercher and McShane's (1984) phrase "contacts or interactions between a child and an adult" (p. 487) is very vague. The term *interactions* should have been clarified by citing examples.

It was also left for respondents to decide whether or not a long list of different forms of sexual exploitation, including molestation and incest, had "harmed or threatened" their "health and welfare." In recognition of the fact that some victims are in denial about the effects, whereas others have no way of knowing whether or not symptoms like depression and anxiety are related to their childhood victimization, researchers should not rely only on subjective measures to define or evaluate the effects of child sexual abuse.

Furthermore, stigmatizing words, like *rape, molestation,* and *incest,* were included in the definition printed on the questionnaire. We have repeatedly pointed out that the inclusion of such words results in lowering respondents' disclosure rates.

The fact that the questionnaires were self-administered means that no interviewers were available for questions or clarifications about the meaning of words like *depiction, interactions, exploitation,* or *incest.*

In conclusion: Kercher and McShane's low 11% prevalence rate for child sexual abuse is almost certainly due to their study's weak methodology.

GAIL WYATT, LOS ANGELES COUNTY SURVEY, 1981-1984

Wyatt's methodology was described at length in Chapter 6; only those methodological features of her study that are specific to child sexual abuse will be described here. First and foremost is the fact that Wyatt's sample included roughly equal numbers of African American and white respondents 18 to 36 years old.

Definition. Wyatt (1985) defined child sexual abuse as

> contact of a sexual nature, ranging from those [*sic*] involving non-body contact such as solicitation to engage in sexual behavior and exhibitionism, to those involving body contact such as fondling, intercourse and oral sex. (p. 510)

The abuse also had to have occurred before the victim turned 18 years old, and the perpetrator had to be at least five years older than the victim. In cases where the age difference was less than five years, "only situations which were not wanted by the subject and which involved some degree of coercion were included" (p. 511).

In addition, Wyatt and Peters's (1986a) definition of child sexual abuse differentiated between childhood and adolescent victims in terms of consent:

> For incidents occurring when the victim was 12 or younger and involving an older partner, experiences were considered abusive even if the subject consented to participate. For incidents occurring between the ages of 13 and 17, however, voluntary experiences with older partners were not defined as sexual abuse. (p. 235)

Questions. The following introductory statement was read to each respondent prior to asking Wyatt's eight screen questions:

> It is now generally realized that many women, while they were children or adolescents, have had a sexual experience with an adult or someone older than themselves. By sexual, I mean behaviors ranging from someone exposing themselves (their genitals) to you, to someone having intercourse with you. These experiences may have involved a relative, a friend of the family, or a stranger. Some experiences are very upsetting and painful while others are not, and some may have occurred without your consent.
>
> Now I'd like you to think back to your childhood and adolescence and remember if you had any sexual experiences with a relative, a family friend, or stranger. Describe each experience completely and separately.

1. During childhood and adolescence, did anyone ever expose themselves (their sexual organs) to you?
2. During childhood and adolescence, did anyone masturbate in front of you?
3. Did a relative, family friend or stranger ever touch or fondle your body, including your breasts or genitals, or attempt to arouse you sexually?
4. During childhood and adolescence, did anyone try to have you arouse them, or touch their body in a sexual way?
5. Did anyone rub their genitals against your body in a sexual way?
6. During childhood and adolescence, did anyone attempt to have intercourse with you?
7. Did anyone have intercourse with you?
8. Did you have any other sexual experiences involving a relative, family friend, or stranger? (Wyatt, 1985, p. 512)

The interviewer then asked a series of additional questions of respondents who had answered any of the above questions in the affirmative.

Findings

Wyatt found no statistically significant differences in the prevalence rates for sexual abuse in childhood between African American and white women. Hence, her prevalence findings for these ethnic groups are combined. Wyatt (1985) states that *62% (154) of her sample of 248 women "reported at least one incident of sexual abuse prior to age 18"* (p. 513). This is the highest prevalence rate found to date for contact and noncontact forms of child sexual abuse.

When Wyatt distinguished between sexual abuse experiences that involved body contact (from fondling to vaginal or oral intercourse) and those in which there was no body contact (e.g., verbal propositions, penis exposure, and witnessing a man masturbating), she obtained the following prevalence rates: 21% of the respondents reported at least one experience of incestuous abuse; 32% reported at least one experience of extrafamilial child sexual abuse; and 45% reported at least one experience of incestuous *or* extrafamilial child sexual abuse (Wyatt & Peters, 1986a, Table 5, p. 237).

Evaluation[5]

Wyatt's definition of child sexual abuse is contradictory since it starts out by defining child sexual abuse as "contact of a sexual nature," then states that it includes noncontact experiences, "ranging from those involving *non-body contact* such as solicitation to engage in sexual behavior and exhibitionism" (Wyatt, 1985, p. 510; emphasis added).

As broad as Wyatt's definition of child sexual abuse generally is, this does not apply to experiences between peers (i.e., age differences that do not exceed five years and where the victim is younger than the perpetrator). In cases where the age difference was less than five years, "only situations which were not wanted by the subject and which involved some degree of coercion were included" (p. 511). More significantly, although child sexual abuse researchers often require an age difference of five years between the perpetrator and the victim, this condition denies the often great power differences between siblings even one year apart in age.

Factors Elevating the Prevalence of Child Sexual Abuse

The Number of Interviewers and Their Intensive Training. The four "highly trained and experienced women" interviewers in Wyatt's study (1987) underwent "an intensive three-month training program" (p. 510). This amount of training is far longer than the training provided in any other prevalence study. Also, it is presumably much easier to select four highly skilled interviewers than it is to select a large number.

The Length of the Interview. The 3- to 8-hour interviews are much longer than the interviews conducted in other prevalence studies.

The High Number of Screen Questions. Eight screen questions is higher than in any other study except Russell's. As stated earlier, a high number of such questions has been found to be related to higher prevalence rates (Bolen & Scannapieco, 1999).

The Relative Youthfulness of Wyatt's Respondents. Research has established that younger women typically report more child sexual abuse than older women. Russell's and Wyatt's prevalence rates for child sexual abuse will be compared shortly after adjusting for the different age range of their respondents and their definitions of child sexual abuse.

The Matching of the Ethnicity and Gender of Interviewers and Respondents.

The Broadness of Wyatt's (1985) Definition of Child Sexual Abuse. Wyatt's prevalence rate was 45% when confined to contact experiences; the inclusion of noncontact experiences added 17% to this rate. Noncontact sexual abuse included experiences like exhibitionism and "solicitation to engage in sexual behavior" (p. 510).

Whether or not the study's location in California played a role in Wyatt's high prevalence rate (as well as Russell's) will be discussed at the end of Chapter 14.

Wyatt's study shows that a high rate of child sexual abuse can be obtained when the methodology used encourages high disclosure. Of course, the purpose of prevalence studies is not to strive to obtain the highest rate possible. In fact, we believe that broad definitions of child sexual abuse that include noncontact experiences are more likely than narrower definitions to be seen as trivializing the issue of child sexual abuse. We think it preferable to confine the definition of child sexual abuse to contact or attempted contact experiences of sexual abuse. While Wyatt is to be commended for also providing a prevalence rate that was limited to contact experiences, it is her 62% preva-

TABLE 12.1ᵃ The Prevalence of Incestuous and Extrafamilial Child Sexual Abuse by Age: A Comparison of Russell's and Wyatt's Surveys

Type and Definition of Child Sexual Abuse	Russell Survey: 18 Years Plus		Russell Survey:[a] 18- to 36-Year-Olds		Wyatt Survey:[b] 18- to 36-Year-Olds	
	%	N = 930	%	N = 470	%	N = 248
Incestuous abuse of females involving sexual contact	16	(152)	19	(91)	21	(51)
Extrafamilial sexual abuse of females involving sexual contact	31	(290)	35	(164)	32	(80)
Incestuous and/or extra-familial sexual abuse of females involving sexual contact	38	(357)	43	(200)	45	(112)
Incestuous and/or extra-familial sexual abuse of females, broad definition[1]	54	(504)	59	(276)	62	(154)

SOURCES: a. Russell, 1986, p. 70.
b. Wyatt and Peters, 1986a.

NOTE: 1. The broad definition includes noncontact experiences such as exhibitionism, verbal propositions, posing for porn..

lence rate that includes noncontact experiences that appears to be the primary prevalence rate associated with her study.

Comparisons Between Russell's and Wyatt's Studies

When Russell excluded Wyatt's noncontact experiences from her (Wyatt's) prevalence rate for child sexual abuse and recalculated her own sample's prevalence rate for the 18- to 36-year-old age group to match the age range of Wyatt's respondents, the prevalence rates for these two studies became astonishingly similar, never exceeding a 3% difference (see Table 12.1). This similarity was evident despite the fact that Russell's definition of extrafamilial child sexual abuse from the ages of 14 to 17 was much narrower than Wyatt's definition for this age group.[6]

This comparison shows that Wyatt's younger sample of 18- to 36-year-old women is a significant factor in the magnitude of her prevalence rates. Indeed, a desire to obtain a greater proportion of child sexual abuse victims from whom to obtain data may have been the reason she confined her sample to this age group.

Despite Wyatt's report that the 18- to 26-year-old women in her sample disclosed a slightly *lower* prevalence of child sexual abuse than the older cohort of 27- to 36-year-olds (60% and 64%, respectively), this minute difference is probably not statistically significant (Peters et al., 1986, p. 28). In addition, the difference between these two young cohorts of women is not an adequate test of the relationship between age and prevalence of child sexual abuse. Furthermore, it is based on her broad definition of child sexual abuse, and may not apply to her narrower definition.

Because of the limited 19-year range of Wyatt's survey, her prevalence rates are not strictly comparable to samples of all adult women without adjustments being made (and few studies *can* be adjusted by anyone besides their author[s]). There are no other surveys in the United States that have calculated their prevalence rates for 18- to 36-year olds. There is also no reason to anticipate that there will be other such studies, because there is no sociological meaning to this particular cohort of women.

While the exceptionally lengthy duration of the interviews in Wyatt's study likely contributed to her high prevalence of child sexual abuse, it is presumably a major reason for Wyatt's relatively small sample size of 248 respondents. Had the interviews been much shorter—say, less than two hours—it would have been possible to increase the sample size while keeping within the same budget.

In addition, Wyatt's small sample size may have been responsible for there being no significant differences between the child sexual abuse prevalence rates for African American and white women for both noncontact (57% and 67%, respectively) and contact (40% and 51%, respectively) abuse. Furthermore, the small sample size limited the kinds of analyses Wyatt was able to conduct.

Another important problem with Wyatt's small sample size is that it precludes generalizations to the larger population of women in Los Angeles within reasonable limits of accuracy.[7]

In conclusion: Wyatt succeeded in doing an excellent study of the prevalence of child sexual abuse. It seems reasonable to conclude that she may have obtained sound prevalence rates for the age group that she studied. However, because of her small sample size, the margin for error is unacceptably high. In addition, her limited age range makes it misleading to compare her study with other studies unless there is a way to compensate for the higher rates of sexual abuse disclosed by younger women. This fact invariably seems to be forgotten by researchers who cite her prevalence rates.

DEAN KILPATRICK, CONNIE BEST, LOIS VERONEN, ANGELYNNE AMICK, LORENZ VILLEPONTEAUX, AND GARY RUFF'S CHARLESTON COUNTY SURVEY, SOUTH CAROLINA, 1983

The methodology of Kilpatrick et al.'s 1983 survey (1985) was described in Chapter 6, so only those aspects that apply to child sexual abuse will be described here.

Definitions. Kilpatrick et al.'s (1985) definition of completed "sexual molestation" required that victims had to be "forced to engage in a sexual act other than sexual intercourse, oral sex, or anal sex." Attempted molestation required that "serious unwanted sexual advances had been made but . . . no sexual activity of any kind had occurred" (p. 868).

Screen Question. The following question was the only screen question on child sexual abuse. Hence, it is the operational definition of child sexual abuse for this survey.

> Have you ever had any *other* experience in which someone tried to molest you sexually—that is, made serious, unwanted sexual advances but did not attempt full sexual relations? (Kilpatrick & Amick, 1984, p. 6; emphasis added)[8]

Findings

The prevalence rates for completed and attempted sexual molestation of children had to be extrapolated from Kilpatrick et al.'s (1985) data. The 55 victims of completed child molestation yielded a prevalence rate of 2.7%. The 37 victims of attempted child molestation yielded a prevalence rate of

1.8%. And the 92 victims of completed and attempted child molestation yielded a prevalence rate of 4.6%.[9]

Although Kilpatrick et al. (1985) did not provide any information on incestuous abuse, data on the number of perpetrators of incestuous abuse were provided in an earlier unpublished paper by Kilpatrick and Amick (1984) based on this same survey. Based on the 26 perpetrators, we inferred that there were also 26 incest victims. Our inference was based on the fact that although the numbers of victims and perpetrators can differ, the difference, if any, is usually very small. Hence we estimated Kilpatrick et al.'s approximate prevalence rate for incestuous abuse to be 1.3% (26 × 100/2,004 [the sample size]; see Kilpatrick & Amick, 1984, Table 2, p. 20). On the basis of this extrapolation, we inferred that there were 66 victims of extrafamilial child sexual abuse (92 [total victims of completed and attempted child molestation] − 26 = 66). Thus, the approximate prevalence rate for extrafamilial child sexual abuse would have been 3.3% (66 × 100/2,004)—assuming no victims reported multiple incidents.

When calculating these two forms of child sexual abuse as percentages of the number of victims of such abuse, 28% were incest victims and 72% were victims of extrafamilial child sexual abuse.

Evaluation

Kilpatrick et al.'s 4.6% prevalence rate for child sexual abuse is exceedingly low. This was also the case for their prevalence of rape (see Chapter 6). The following factors probably contribute to the failure of these researchers' methodology to yield a more realistic assessment of the prevalence of child sexual abuse.

Factors Reducing the Prevalence of Child Sexual Abuse

1. Only one screen question on child sexual abuse.
2. Poor quality of the screen question.

The screen question on child sexual abuse (quoted on p. 179) followed two screen questions on rape, both of which could have yielded respondents' experiences of rape in childhood as well as rape as adults. However, inclusion of the word *other* in the screen question on child sexual abuse reveals that respondents' experiences of completed and attempted rape in childhood were omitted from the prevalence rates for child molestation. The fact that the screen question specifically precludes "attempt[ing] full sexual relations" (Kilpatrick & Amick, 1984, p. 6) from the definition of child molestation confirms this, as also does the fact that the different categories of abuse are described as "mutually exclusive." No rationale is provided for this method-ological decision.

In addition, the child sexual abuse screen question asked respondents if "someone *tried* to molest" (Kilpatrick & Amick, 1984, p. 6) them sexually rather than asking them if someone had tried *or succeeded* in sexually abus-ing them when they were children (emphasis added). This oversight might have resulted in an underreporting of completed child sexual abuse experi-ences.

Just as using the term *rape* is inadvisable unless there are several screen questions, it is probably inadvisable to use the term *molest,* especially if it is used in the only screen question. Some victims of child sexual abuse probably do not identify with this stigmatizing label.

Requiring that respondents confine themselves to reporting "unwanted" sexual advances is problematic, particularly for young children and for inces-tuous abuse. Many survivors of incestuous abuse are ambivalent about their victimization experiences, and some recognize that they enjoyed or were aroused by certain acts involved in the sexual abuse, or by rewards given to them by the perpetrator. These experiences should still qualify as abuse un-less the respondent and her "perpetrator" were peers or the respondent was in a position of power vis-à-vis the "perpetrator." Otherwise enjoyment is irrel-evant when the power relationship between perpetrator and victim makes consent impossible.

The term *sexual advances* suggests a seductive approach to a child rather than a sexual attack. This may have discouraged respondents from disclosing sexually abusive experiences in which they were taken by surprise and/or sex-ually attacked.

The screen question lacks behaviorally specific terminology to help re-spondents understand what Kilpatrick et al. meant by the terms *molestation, serious sexual advances,* and *full sexual relations* (Kilpatrick & Amick, 1984, p. 6). Leaving it to respondents to decide the meaning of these terms in-troduces inconsistencies because of peoples' different interpretations of them. Moreover, Kilpatrick et al. had no way of knowing how their respon-dents interpreted these terms. The same experience could yield a "no" from one respondent and a "yes" from another. The word *serious* is particularly open to a wide range of interpretations.

In conclusion: The very low prevalence of child sexual abuse reported by Kilpatrick and his colleagues appears to result from the many serious methodological flaws that we have pointed out rather than revealing that South Carolina enjoys a low prevalence rate for these crimes.

JUDITH SIEGEL, SUSAN SORENSON, JACQUELINE GOLDING, AUDREY BURNAM, AND JUDITH STEIN, THE LOS ANGELES EPIDEMIOLOGIC CATCHMENT AREA PROJECT, 1983/1984

Siegel et al.'s (1987) data on child sexual abuse[10] were obtained from a supplement to the Los Angeles Epidemiologic Catchment Area Project as part of a five-site collaborative effort to estimate the incidence and prevalence of mental disorders in the United States. This survey also attempted to ascertain the lifetime prevalence of sexual assault for both adults and children. This research was supported by the Epidemiologic Catchment Area Program and by supplemental funds from the National Center for the Prevention and Control of Rape (fn. 3, p. 1141). The data on child sexual abuse were gathered during the first of three waves. Hence, the description of the methodology will be limited to this period.

Siegel et al. (1987) selected a household sample, stratified by catchment area, "using a two-stage probability technique, with census blocks as primary sampling units and households as secondary sampling units" (pp. 1143, 1145). The sample was drawn in two areas of Los Angeles, one largely Hispanic and the other largely non-Hispanic white, providing each household with an equal chance of being selected. One adult aged 18 or over was then drawn at random from each household (p. 1145). A total of 3,125 adults were interviewed in person, 1,645 of whom were women (Table 2, p. 1146).

Forty-seven percent ($n = 766$) of the women in the sample were Hispanic, 41% ($n = 678$) were non-Hispanic white, and 12% ($n = 114$) belonged to some other ethnicity. A total of 85% of the Hispanic American women were described as being of Mexican cultural or ethnic origin (percentages calculated from data in Siegel et al., 1987, Table 2, p. 1146).

Siegel and her colleagues (1987) maintain that their study is "the largest existing community-based study of childhood sexual assault," and that "it is the only study that systematically samples from a community with a high proportion of Hispanic residents" (p. 1143).

Definition and Screen Question. Siegel et al. (1987) defined child sexual abuse as "incidents before age 16 years which involved pressure or force for sexual contact" (p. 1141). Following is their only screen question on child sexual abuse:

> In your lifetime, has anyone ever tried to pressure or force you to have sexual contact? By sexual contact I mean their touching your sexual parts, your touching their sexual parts, or sexual intercourse. (Siegel et al., 1987, p. 1146)

Respondents who answered affirmatively to this question were next asked "if they had ever been forced or pressured for sexual contact before age 16 years" (p. 1146). Only abuse that occurred before the age of 16 qualified as child sexual abuse.

Interviews and Interviewers. Respondents were interviewed in person. They and the 113 interviewers (56% female and 39% Hispanic) were not matched for gender. No information was provided regarding whether or not respondents and interviewers were matched for ethnicity. However, the fact that Siegel et al. employed 44 Hispanic interviewers and that the Hispanic respondents could choose the language in which they preferred to be interviewed, suggests that they probably did match Hispanic respondents and interviewers.

Participation Rate. Siegel and her colleagues (1987) described "the overall completion rate" as 68% for their household sample (p. 1145). They did not provide another rate for the *individuals* in the households. Hence, their participation rate may be lower than the 68% they report it to be.

Findings

Siegel et al. (1987) reported that *6.8% of the 1,645 women in their Los Angeles sample had been sexually abused before the age of 16* (Table 3, p. 1147).

The *prevalence of child sexual abuse disclosed by non-Hispanic white women was 12%* (Siegel et al., 1987, p. 1151)[11]—significantly higher than the 6.8% prevalence for both ethnic groups combined (see Table 3, p. 1147). Siegel et al. did not report a comparable prevalence rate for Hispanic women separate from men. However, it is possible to extrapolate from their data in Tables 2 and 4 that only *3.9% of the Hispanic women disclosed having been sexually abused in childhood.*[12] Hence, the prevalence rate for Hispanic women is only approximately one third of the prevalence rate for non-Hispanic white women. It was not possible to extrapolate a prevalence rate for those who were categorized as belonging to "other" ethnic groups.

No information was provided on the prevalence of incestuous abuse.

Evaluation

Since most of the methodological features of Siegel et al.'s survey in Los Angeles were developed for all five of the collaborating epidemiological research studies, the strengths and weaknesses of their methodology have implications for all these studies.

Siegel et al.'s (1987) inclusion of a large sample of Hispanic women (*n* = 766) could have been an important contribution to the field. However, it is undercut by the fact that very little of these researchers' analyses provide separate data on females. This shocking oversight is becoming increasingly common as more studies of sexual assault include males in their samples (e.g., Tjaden & Thoennes, 1998a; the revised National Crime Victimization Surveys).

It has repeatedly been shown that women and girls are victimized by rape and child sexual abuse far more frequently than men and boys, and that only a small percentage of the perpetrators of these crimes are females. This is one of the reasons that most of the early research in this field focused exclusively on females. It is very distressing that the new trend to include males in these surveys has resulted in a significant loss of data on female victims.

It is important to remember that prevalence rates that underestimate the problem of child sexual abuse yield distorted findings on the other topics being studied. For example, the investigators in the five-site collaborative effort, of which Siegel et al.'s survey is a part, are engaged in studying mental health. Those of the five surveys that obtained unrealistically low prevalence rates for child sexual abuse will likely have compromised the validity of their mental health assessments. If these assessments are based on a mere fraction of the real prevalence of child sexual abuse, this fraction cannot be assumed to represent the universe of child sexual abuse experiences in the population.

Factors Reducing the Prevalence of Child Sexual Abuse

Siegel et al.'s prevalence rate of 6.8% for women respondents who were sexually victimized in childhood is exceedingly low. Several methodological factors undoubtedly contribute to this low prevalence rate.

The Inclusion of Hispanic Women in the Survey. While a 12% prevalence rate of child sexual abuse for non-Hispanic white women is also low, the much lower 3.9% prevalence rate for Hispanic women reduced the study's overall prevalence rate to only 6.8%. This makes it clear that the inclusion of a large number of Hispanic women in the sample (46%) is a major factor in lowering this study's prevalence rate of child sexual abuse.

In contrast to Siegel et al.'s (1987) very low prevalence for child sexual abuse among Hispanic women, Russell's (1984) comparable child sexual abuse prevalence rate for Hispanic women in her San Francisco sample was 45.5%. Moreover, Russell's prevalence rate for the child sexual abuse of Hispanic women was very slightly higher than her prevalence rate for non-Hispanic white women (which was 42%). Similarly, Kercher and McShane (1984) obtained a prevalence rate of 22% for Hispanic women's experiences of child sexual abuse compared with only 10% for non-Hispanic white women (p. 498).

However, it is also quite possible that all these different prevalence rates for Hispanic women may be due to differences in class status, level of acculturation, and/or region of the country. For example, Hispanic women living in Texas with driver's licenses may be very different from Hispanic women living in a barrio in Los Angeles who may be poorer, undocumented, and so on. Supporting the acculturation explanation is the finding that "Hispanic respondents [males and females] who completed the interview all or partially in Spanish reported much lower rates of childhood abuse (1 percent) than Hispanics who completed the interview in English (5 percent)" (Siegel et al., 1987, p. 1151). Siegel et al. (1987) note that,

Since language of choice is often used as a proxy for acculturation, these data suggest that assimilation is associated with higher rates of childhood sexual abuse. [However,] alternative explanations, including less acculturated individuals being more hesitant to discuss assault . . . cannot be ruled out. (p. 1151)

Koss also found that the Hispanic women in her current study seemed more reluctant to disclose their experiences of child sexual abuse than white women (public lecture at APA Conference, 1998).

Siegel et al. (1987) also suggest the possibility that Hispanics might feel more uncomfortable than non-Hispanic whites about discussing child sexual abuse, or that

> cultural factors (such as the protectiveness of Hispanic families toward women, or spending childhood in a country where assault is believed to be less prevalent) may have had some influence on the actual occurrence of assault. (p. 1151)

These cultural factors may include feelings of guilt and shame associated with Catholicism, as well as fears of bringing shame to the family.

Yet another possibility, particularly for those who were interviewed in Spanish, is that illegal immigrants and those who share this history or who have relatives, friends, or neighbors who do, may be afraid of being interviewed by community outsiders.

Whatever the best explanation(s) for the particularly low 3.9% prevalence rate of child sexual abuse disclosed by Hispanic women in Siegel et al.'s Los Angeles sample, methodological factors undoubtedly contributed to it.

Only One Screen Question. Siegel et al. (1987) themselves note that studies with much higher prevalence rates, like Wyatt's and Russell's, engaged in the "prompting of respondents," whereas their respondents "were asked only once if they had ever experienced pressure or force for sexual contact" (p. 1151).

Poor Quality Screen Question. Although Siegel et al. (1987) list the types of pressure or force used by perpetrators that were reported by their respondents (Table 6, p. 1150), the screen question *"Has anyone ever tried to pressure or force you to have sexual contact?"* (Siegel et al., 1987, p. 1146) excludes many common types of child sexual abuse. For example, it is common for girls who are fondled by their fathers when they are in bed at night to pretend to be asleep. In addition, child molesters often touch very young children without exerting any pressure or force. Sexual contact may be in the context of a game (e.g., a doctor-patient game), or when a caretaker takes advantage of an opportunity to bathe a child, or he may simply take her by surprise, and so on. Even if the researcher might consider that some of these examples qualify as pressure, it is the respondents' perceptions that the screen question asks about—not the researchers'.

Evidence That Many Women Were Unwilling to Disclose Their Experiences. For those respondents who answered "yes" to the screen question, Siegel et al. (1987) found that they disclosed a high mean number of childhood sexual abuse incidents (i.e., 3.9, p. 1148). The fact that the vast majority of respondents reported no childhood experiences while a small minority reported a high mean number of such experiences raises a red flag.[13] It seems highly unlikely that women either experienced no abuse or a lot of abuse, but nothing in between. It seems to us to suggest an unwillingness to disclose among the majority of respondents.

Lack of Privacy for Interviews. Siegel et al.'s (1987) failure to ensure that their respondents had complete privacy during the interview is the most shocking of their methodological shortcomings. They admit that "other persons were within hearing range [of the interview] about half of the time," but claim that tests showed that this lack of privacy "did not change these [prevalence] rates" (p. 1151). The notion that women would as readily disclose such taboo experiences in the presence of others, some for the very first time, flies in the face of our knowledge about the secretiveness of many women about their experiences of child sexual abuse.

Given Hispanic women's more deprived economic status as compared with white non-Hispanic women, they probably live in more crowded conditions, which may have resulted in their having less privacy when they were interviewed than non-Hispanic white women. This in turn may be a factor in the very low prevalence rate for child sexual abuse obtained for Hispanic women.

Failure to Match for Gender. As previously mentioned, Siegel et al. (1987) claim that their failure to match the gender of their interviewers with the gender of their respondents was determined by tests to have had no impact on the prevalence rate (p. 1151). This is difficult to comprehend because of the ample evidence that women who have been sexually abused in childhood are significantly more distrustful of men (e.g., Russell, 1986).

Exclusion of Noncontact Child Sexual Abuse. While Siegel et al.'s exclusion of noncontact abuse in no way qualifies as a methodological shortcoming, other things being equal, it inevitably lowers prevalence rates. This also applies to these researchers' selection of 16 years of age rather than 18 years as their criterion for adulthood. This decision excludes the experiences of sexual abuse for 16- and 17-year-old adolescent females, thereby contributing to the low prevalence rate for child sexual abuse.

Siegel et al. claim that the inclusion of many older women in their study lowered their prevalence rate. However, their mean age for women respondents was 41 years, which is about the same as the National Women's Study's (Kilpatrick et al., 1992) mean of 40 years, Kilpatrick et al.'s (1985) mean of 42 years, and Russell's mean of 43 years.

Siegel et al. noted that the methodology of their study was the same as the methodology used in the other four epidemiological sites in different regions of the United States. The many methodological shortcomings that have contributed to their obtaining an unrealistically low prevalence rate for child sexual abuse suggests that the studies at the other sites may be equally defective. Consequently, their prevalence rates can also be expected to be unrealistically low.

In conclusion: We believe that Siegel et al.'s poor methodology resulted in their obtaining unsound prevalence rates for child sexual abuse.

Four more studies of the prevalence of child sexual abuse will be described and evaluated in the next chapter.

NOTES

1. In addition to not publishing their studies, these two research teams in Texas—Sapp and Carter (1978) and Riede, Capron, Ivey, Lawrence, and Somolo (1979)—failed to differentiate between males and females when they reported the very low prevalence rates they obtained.

2. There are several minor arithmetic errors here: 593 + 461 add to 1,054; 56% of 1,056 = 591, not 593; and 44% of 1,056 = 465, not 461; furthermore, the number of female survey participants adds to 592 in Table 1, page 498. We will arbitrarily assume that the number 592 is the correct one.

3. 65 female victims/592 female respondents × 100 = 10.97%.

4. The correct number of refusals is 74 (7 × 1,056/100 = 73.92).

5. The methodology of Wyatt's study was described and evaluated in Chapter 6. Only new aspects of her study will be evaluated here.

6. Wyatt and Peters (1986a) used a different method to compare Wyatt's and Russell's prevalence findings: They recalculated her prevalence rate for child sexual abuse involving contact and adjusted her definition of extrafamilial child sexual abuse so as to be consistent with Russell's—that is, they limited it to completed and attempted rape from the ages of 14 to 17 years. (Since Russell did not have access to Wyatt's data, she did not make this adjustment.) Wyatt and Peters (1986a) did not, however, recalculate Russell's prevalence rate to apply to women aged 18 to 36 years. Nevertheless, they also concluded that "once adjustments have been made for differ-

ences in definition, the prevalence rates derived from these two studies are very similar" (p. 237).

7. The rule of thumb requires a 95% confidence level and a ±5% confidence interval. For example, the researcher wants to be able to say, with a 95% level of confidence, that the prevalence is within ±5% of the obtained statistic.

8. Kilpatrick et al. (1985) did not include this screen question in their published article on this study. This is troublesome, particularly as it suffers from many serious problems (to be discussed shortly). Most researchers are probably unaware of the earlier unpublished paper by Kilpatrick and Amick (1984) that includes the screen question, particularly as it is not referred to in Kilpatrick et al.'s 1985 article, nor does it even appear in their references.

9. Given the interest in prevalence rates for sexual assault by 1984 (when Kilpatrick et al. conducted their study) and the need for studies on this subject, it is surprising and remiss of Kilpatrick et al. not to calculate and report the prevalence rates for rape and child sexual abuse in their 1985 article. Interested researchers have to do several extrapolations in order to ascertain the prevalence of child sexual abuse. It is not surprising, then, that some researchers have failed to include Kilpatrick et al.'s survey when comparing the prevalence rates obtained by different studies (e.g., Finkelhor, 1994; Gorey & Leslie, 1997).

10. Siegel et al. consistently use the term *child sexual assault* instead of *child sexual abuse*. However, the screen questions do not ask about more severe cases of child sexual abuse than the other studies of the prevalence of child sexual abuse.

11. Siegel et al. did not explain how they calculated this prevalence rate. However, it can be extrapolated from their Tables 2 and 4: 15.2% of 353 = n of 54; 8% of 325 = n of 26; hence 80/678 × 100 = 11.8.

12. Table 2 provides data on the numbers of Mexican Americans and Other Hispanics in the sample for two different age groups. Following is our method of extrapolating the prevalence of child sexual abuse disclosed by Hispanic women: 382 + 72 = 454 Hispanic women 18-39 years old; 270 + 42 = 312 Hispanic women 40+ years old. Table 4 reveals that 4.6% of Hispanic women 18-39 were sexually abused as children, and 2.8% of Hispanic women 40+ were sexually abused as children; 4.6 × 454/ 100 = 21%; 2.8 × 312/100 = 9%; finally, 30/766 × 100 = 3.9% (when 21% + 9% = 30% and 454 + 312 = 766).

13. Despite the high 3.9 mean number of childhood sexual abuse experiences disclosed, Siegel et al. (1987) excluded 13 reports of very high numbers of incidents. For example, one respondent claimed to have been sexually abused more than 95 times before she was 16 years of age, and 12 respondents said they had been abused lots of times or too many times to count (p. 1148).

13

◆

THE PREVALENCE OF
CHILD SEXUAL ABUSE:
OTHER REPRESENTATIVE SAMPLES,
PART 2

This chapter will be devoted to describing and evaluating the prevalence findings and the prevalence-related methodology of the following four surveys:

5. I. A. Lewis, Los Angeles Times Poll, National Survey, 1985
6. John Murphy, Minnesota survey, circa 1989-1990[1]
7. Ronald Kessler, Amanda Sonnega, Evelyn Bromet, and Michael Hughes, National Comorbidity Survey, 1990-1992
8. David Moore, George Gallup, and Robert Schussel, Gallup Poll, National Survey, 1995

These studies are presented in chronological order according to when the fieldwork was conducted.

I. A. LEWIS, LOS ANGELES TIMES POLL,
NATIONAL SURVEY, 1985

In 1985, I. A. Lewis, the Director of the Los Angeles Times Poll, conducted the first national survey of adult Americans on the prevalence of child sexual abuse. Five years later, Finkelhor, Hotaling, Lewis, and Smith (1990) wrote it up for publication.

Lewis drew a sample of 2,625 adults 18 years and older from residential telephone numbers, including unlisted numbers, within the 50 United States. His sample included 1,481 women, who constituted 56% of the respondents. The respondents were interviewed for approximately 30 minutes over the telephone on topics related to child sexual abuse. Despite a refusal rate of 24% (or a participation rate of 76%), Finkelhor et al. (1990) noted that the final sample remained representative of the demographics for the United States as a whole. The results were weighted to take into consideration household size and "times at home" (whatever that means) (p. 20).

Screen Questions. Following are the four screen questions on child sexual abuse devised by Lewis:

1. When you were a child . . ., can you remember having any experience you would now consider sexual abuse—like someone trying or succeeding in having any kind of sexual intercourse with you, or anything like that?
2. When you were a child, can you remember any kind of experience that you would now consider sexual abuse involving someone touching you, or grabbing you, or kissing you, or rubbing up against your body either in a public place or private— anything like that?
3. When you were a child, can you remember any kind of experience that you would now consider sexual abuse involving someone taking nude photographs of you, or someone exhibiting parts of their body to you, or someone performing some sex act in your presence—or anything like that?
4. When you were a child, can you remember any kind of experience that you would now consider sexual abuse involving oral sex or sodomy—or anything like that? (Finkelhor et al., 1990, p. 20)

If the respondent answered "yes" to the first question, the interviewer skipped the others and started asking questions about the incident disclosed.[2] No information was obtained about more than one incident.

Findings

According to Finkelhor and his colleagues, 27% of the Los Angeles Times Poll's women respondents disclosed at least one experience of child sexual abuse. (In fact, 416 women out of 1,481 women respondents who reported being victims of child sexual abuse comes to 28%, not 27%.)

Finkelhor et al. (1990) did not report a separate prevalence rate for incestuous abuse. Extrapolating from the data provided, we calculated that 8% of the women respondents had reported experiencing incestuous abuse,[3] and 14%[4] of the women respondents reported having been victimized by rape or attempted rape in childhood.

Lewis's data also revealed "a markedly higher [prevalence] rate of abuse for Pacific states than the seven other regions examined (California, Oregon, Washington, Alaska, and Hawaii)" (Finkelhor et al., 1990, p. 25): a 40% prevalence rate in the Pacific states compared with a 28%[5] prevalence rate for the country as a whole (Table 8, p. 25). At 42%, "The rate in California for women was particularly high" (p. 25).

Evaluation

The Los Angeles Times Poll was the first national survey of adults' experiences of child sexual abuse ever conducted. This is a very significant achievement. Of the nine representative surveys (including Russell's) on child sexual abuse that qualified for inclusion in our sample, this poll's 28% prevalence rate for child sexual abuse was the fourth highest (after Wyatt, Russell, and the Gallup Poll's prevalence rate for mothers). Nevertheless, this 28% prevalence rate is less than half of Wyatt's 62% prevalence rate despite the fact that they both included noncontact experiences. And it is substantially less than Russell's 38% prevalence rate that *excluded* noncontact experiences.

Thus we need to address what methodological features may account for the Los Angeles Times Poll's obtaining a higher prevalence rate than several other studies, and a lower rate than others. As with the other studies we have evaluated, we will also point out methodological flaws—regardless of their impact on the prevalence rate.

Factors Elevating the
Prevalence of Child Sexual Abuse

Very Broad "Definition" of Child Sexual Abuse. Although Lewis did not provide a definition of child sexual abuse, the definition implied in the screen questions is very broad. First, it includes noncontact abuse—exhibitionism and someone taking nude photographs of the respondent. Second, it includes "someone performing some sex act in your presence." This would include a respondent having seen her parents engaged in sex play or sexual intercourse. Since the "performers" of such sex acts may not even be aware of being seen, or may experience no sexual arousal from being seen and/or may have no interest in sexually arousing the child who sees them, such acts do not qualify as child sexual abuse by most definitions.

Third, each screen question ends with the phrase, "or anything like that?" There is no knowing how respondents might interpret this invitation to include additional experiences that they perceive as similar in some way to those mentioned in the screen questions. As Finkelhor et al. (1990) point out, "experiences of a minor nature that many researchers would exclude could have been counted because of a respondent's broad interpretation of the phrase, 'anything like that'" (p. 20). For example, men and women quite often perceive experiences that they regard as having been sexually traumatic (such as enemas, insensitive comments about their bodies, hearing their parents engaged in sex) as instances of sexual abuse. However, it is important to distinguish between sexually abusive behavior and behavior that may cause sexual trauma.

The broader and more inclusive the definition of child sexual abuse is, other things being equal, the higher the prevalence rate is likely to be. However, it does not follow that very broad definitions are the best—as we noted in our evaluation of Wyatt's study in Chapter 12.

Lewis's inclusion of four screen questions in the Los Angeles Times Poll exceeds the number provided in several other studies. As we noted previously, there is a positive relationship between the number of screen questions and the prevalence rate obtained.

The Age of Victims of Child Sexual Abuse. The Los Angeles Times Poll included sexual abuse reported by 18-year-olds—probably in error since 18-year-olds are legally adults (Finkelhor et al., 1990, Table 2, p. 21). Since all the screening questions started with the phrase "When you were a child," it is surprising that any respondents disclosed experiences they had when they were 18 years old and, in fact, only six experiences of sexual abuse of 16- to 18-year-old female respondents were disclosed.

The Los Angeles Times Poll also included sexual abuse by peers (no minimum age difference between the perpetrator and the victim was required).

Factors Reducing the
Prevalence of Child Sexual Abuse

Too Few Screen Questions. The disclosure rate would presumably have been higher had more than four questions been asked.

Short Interviews. The brevity of the interviews (only 30 minutes) provided little time to build rapport before asking about taboo experiences like child sexual abuse. Other things being equal, it seems likely that the shorter the interview, the lower the disclosure of child sexual abuse is likely to be.

Telephone Interviews. We noted before that privacy for telephone interviews can be difficult to accomplish. Lewis said nothing about how his poll handled the privacy issue despite its importance to the disclosure rates obtained.

Training of Interviewers. Lewis also provided no information about the training, if any, that his poll interviewers received about child sexual abuse.

Other Methodological Problems

Respondents' Definitions of Child Sexual Abuse. Finkelhor et al. (1990) point out that relying on respondents to define what constitutes child sexual abuse means that, "Experiences some researchers might define as abuse could be left out because the respondent did not consider them as abuse" (p. 20). In addition, the prevalence rate obtained may reflect differences in respondents' ideologies. For example, a respondent with a nudist or sexually libertarian philosophy might consider having been photographed nude, or someone exhibiting parts of his body to her, or someone performing a sex act in her presence, as nonabusive, whereas another respondent might consider all these experiences abusive. However, it is impossible to know the effect of this methodological problem on the prevalence rate found.

Finally, it would have been helpful if Lewis had made it possible to differentiate contact from noncontact forms of child sexual abuse so as to enable more precise comparisons to be made with the findings of other studies.

In conclusion: Although there were some methodological factors that undoubtedly decreased the prevalence rate obtained by the Los Angeles Times

Poll, including the likelihood that no child sexual abuse-appropriate method-ology was utilized, this is nevertheless one of the sounder of the child sexual abuse prevalence studies.

JOHN MURPHY, MINNESOTA SURVEY, CIRCA 1989-1990[6]

John Murphy used random digit dialing to obtain a random sample of Minnesota adults 18 years and older at the time of the interview. Although he failed to mention the size of his sample, extrapolation from other informa-tion he provided yields the figure of 1,195 eligible respondents. In order to ensure a random selection of respondents within each household, Murphy used a selection process that alternated randomly between men and women and older and younger respondents.

Overall, 777 female and male respondents were asked 65 questions that took them only 10 to 15 minutes to complete (no breakdown by gender was provided). The interviews were carried out over a five-day period. Murphy re-ported a 65% participation rate for his study. Since 3% of the respondents failed to answer the questions on child sexual abuse, we calculated a 63% par-ticipation rate for the relevant questions on child sexual abuse.[7] These figures are for males and females.

Definition and Screen Questions. Murphy (1991) defined child sexual abuse as an

experience with one, or all, of the following behaviors before the age of 18:

1. an adult exposing himself to the child;
2. an adult touching or fondling breasts or sexual parts of the child's body when he/she was not willing;
3. having to touch an adult's body in a sexual way when the child did not want to;
4. an adult sexually attacking the child or forcing the child to have sexual inter-course;
5. an adult taking nude photographs of the child or performing a sexual act in the child's presence;
6. experiencing oral or anal sex with an adult. (p. 83)

Findings

Eighteen percent of the female respondents in Murphy's study were sexually abused before the age of 18. No breakdown was provided for the prevalence of contact versus noncontact sexual abuse, or for the prevalence of incestuous abuse and extrafamilial sexual abuse.

Evaluation

Given the remarkably brief 10- to 15-minute interview, it is surprising that Murphy was able to obtain a prevalence rate for child sexual abuse as high as 18%. Had Murphy undertaken this study 10 years earlier, it seems doubtful that it would have been this successful. American women appear to be increasingly willing to talk about this formerly much more taboo topic.

Factors Elevating the Prevalence of Child Sexual Abuse

Broad Definition. Screen questions 1 and 5 asked about noncontact experiences, such as male exhibitionism, taking nude photographs of the respondent when she was a child, or performing a sex act in her presence. The term *sex act* could theoretically include a sexual kiss, a sexual caress on the buttocks, or the squeeze of a breast. However, no information is provided on how respondents interpreted these questions.

Number of Screen Questions. Six screen questions is more than most other studies ask their respondents.

Factors Reducing the Prevalence of Child Sexual Abuse

Screen Questions Limited to Unwilling Victims. Murphy's second and third screen questions asked about women's unwanted experiences with adult perpetrators, despite the fact that most researchers consider the child's feelings to be irrelevant in cases of child sexual abuse by older perpetrators, particularly adults. The exclusion of all incidents of child sexual abuse by older perpetrators that are wanted and/or about which the child feels ambivalent can be assumed to have lowered the prevalence of child sexual abuse obtained by Murphy's study.

Telephone Interviews. We have already noted that it is more difficult to ensure privacy for interviews by telephone.

Brevity of the Interview. The fact that the interviews lasted only 10 to 15 minutes makes it hard to believe that good rapport and trust could have been developed between the interviewer and respondent in that brief time.

Other Methodological Problems

Little information is provided about the study's methodology, making it difficult to evaluate. For example, who interviewed the respondents, what was their gender and what was their training? What were the demographic characteristics of the respondents? How was privacy ensured, if at all?

Murphy noted that 777 interviews were completed and 418 persons refused. However, he provided no information about all the homes where no one answered the telephone, or where an ineligible person like a child or a visitor answered the telephone but no one called back. Is it reasonable to exclude such outcomes from the participation rate? If so, a double standard is operating regarding how participation rates for samples obtained by random digit dialing are calculated as compared to samples obtained by knocking on the doors of all households drawn in the sample.

Murphy often failed to provide separate information on gender. For example, he reported that 8% of the male and female respondents reported experiencing a male exposing himself. Presumably this percentage would have been significantly higher had it excluded male respondents. We commented earlier on the unfortunate tendency for researchers to combine their findings for both genders.

In conclusion: Given all the missing information we have noted, Murphy's description of his study is clearly woefully inadequate. This makes it impossible to do a thorough evaluation of his methodology. That Murphy succeeded in obtaining an 18% disclosure rate for child sexual abuse is probably due to the number of screen questions and the broadness of his definition of this crime.

RONALD KESSLER, AMANDA SONNEGA, EVELYN BROMET, AND MICHAEL HUGHES'S NATIONAL COMORBIDITY SURVEY, 1990-1992

The methodology of Kessler and his colleagues' study as it relates to rape was described and evaluated in Chapter 6, so only those features that apply specifically to child sexual abuse will be described here. There was only one screen question on child sexual abuse asking respondents if they had ever been "sexually molested." The study's definition of this concept immediately followed in parentheses: "someone touched or felt your genitals when you did not want them to" (Kessler et al., 1995, p. 1051). No ceiling age for children was provided in this definition.

Findings

Of the female respondents in Kessler et al.'s study, 12.3% were sexually abused in childhood. No information was provided on the prevalence of incestuous abuse.

Evaluation

We identified three major factors that probably contributed to Kessler et al.'s low 12.3% prevalence rate for child molestation.

Factors Reducing the Prevalence of Child Sexual Abuse

Narrow Definition of Child Molestation. Kessler et al.'s (1995) question on child sexual abuse omits any kind of penetration experience, as well as milder sexually abusive experiences that involve sexual contact without genital contact, such as sexual kissing, sexual touching of the rectum, thighs or buttocks. Furthermore, it is likely that a number of women do not know precisely what "genitals" refers to, specifically whether breasts (or chests, in the case of prepubescent girls) qualify or not. Hence, Kessler et al.'s definition of child molestation is unclear as well as very narrow.

Number of Screen Questions. The fact that Kessler et al. (1995) used only one screen question on child sexual abuse is certain to have contributed to their low prevalence rate.

Quality of Screen Question. We pointed out earlier that the use of the term *sexual molestation* in a screen question is inadvisable in prevalence studies, unless there are several other questions that do not use this word. We argued that Kilpatrick and Amick's (1984) use of this term probably contributed to their very low 4.6% prevalence rate for child sexual abuse (see Chapter 12).

In conclusion: Because of budget problems, Kessler et al.'s (1995) methodology for the subsample used to assess the prevalence of child sexual abuse was so compromised that it is impossible to evaluate whether or not its representativeness was jeopardized (see Chapter 6 for more details on this problem). This problem, combined with the use of but one poorly phrased screen question and a very narrow definition of child sexual abuse, makes this a very weak study for estimating the prevalence of child sexual abuse.

In short, we suggest that Kessler et al.'s low 12.3% prevalence rate for child sexual abuse is due to severe underdisclosure by their respondents.

DAVID MOORE, GEORGE GALLUP, AND ROBERT SCHUSSEL, GALLUP POLL NATIONAL SURVEY, 1995

Most of the methodology of the 1995 Gallup Poll on parents' disciplinary practices and violence toward their children was described in Chapter 10 on incidence studies. This Gallup Poll had two measures of the prevalence of child sexual abuse: Parents in the sample were asked about the sexual abuse experiences of their children as well as about their own experiences of sexual victimization before the age of 18.

Almost two thirds (65%) of the parental respondents were mothers and mother substitutes, almost a third (32%) were fathers and father substitutes, and 2% were "adults in other caretaking relationships to the child" (Finkelhor et al., 1997, p. 2). The gender of the latter 2% was not reported, so these cases are excluded from the analysis. The preamble preceding the screen questions was as follows:

> Now I would like to ask you something about your own experiences as a child that may be very sensitive. As you know, sometimes, in spite of efforts to protect them, children get sexually abused, molested, or touched in sexual ways that are wrong. To find out more about how often they occur, we would like to ask you about your own experiences when you were a child. (Moore et al., 1995, p. 20)

Following are the two screen questions designed by Gallup to ascertain the prevalence of child sexual abuse[8] disclosed by mothers and mother substitutes to the interviewers:

28. Before the age of 18, were you personally ever touched in a sexual way by an adult or older child, when you did not want to be touched that way, or were you ever forced to touch an adult or older child in a sexual way—including anyone who was a member of your family, or anyone outside your family?

29. Before the age of 18, were you ever forced to have sex by an adult or older child—including anyone who was a member of your family, or anyone outside your family? (Finkelhor et al., 1997, p. 3)

Findings

Thirty percent of the mothers in the Gallup Poll's national sample reported at least one experience of childhood sexual abuse before the age of 18 (Moore et al., 1995, p. 18; see also Finkelhor et al., 1997, p. 3). No separate prevalence rate was reported for the incestuous abuse of the mothers when they were children.

Evaluation

While prevalence rates based on national studies are obviously greatly preferred over limited regional studies, there are several problems with relying on a sample of mothers with at least one child living in the home to ascertain a prevalence rate for child sexual abuse. This sample excludes all child-free women and mothers who no longer have a child living in the home. Although the percentage of these excluded women in the population in 1995 is unknown, it is presumably quite substantial. Furthermore, the relationship between being child-free and the prevalence of child sexual abuse is also not known. In addition, mothers and mother substitutes with a child under 18 in the home are presumably young in comparison to older mothers whose children have left home. Although this factor does not necessarily have an impact on the prevalence rate, it nevertheless highlights the selectiveness of the women on which the Gallup Poll's prevalence rate for mothers was based. Hence, it is not strictly comparable to the other surveys included in this chapter and Chapters 11 and 12.

Factors Reducing Prevalence

Number of Screen Questions. The fact that the Gallup Poll used only two screen questions to measure the prevalence of mothers' experiences of child sexual abuse can be assumed to have reduced its prevalence.

Quality of Screen Questions. While a sensitive preamble introduces the screen questions, Finkelhor et al. (1997) note that "no additional definition was given of any of the specific terms such as 'touched in a sexual way' or 'forced to have sex'" (p. 3). Clearly these phrases do not qualify as behaviorally specific—a quality now known to be more successful at eliciting abuse experiences. Examples should have been given to explicate the meaning of "touched in a sexual way." And if "forced to have sex" was supposed to convey sexual intercourse, it would have been preferable to explain whether this meant penile-vaginal intercourse only, or anal and oral penetration as well. In general, because of women's reluctance to disclose experiences of child sexual abuse, ambiguous and vague questions are likely to result in lower disclosure.

Regardless of the pros and cons of interviewing parents for research that is unrelated to prevalence, we believe that using samples of mothers to ascertain prevalence rates for child sexual abuse is definitely not to be recommended. We have noted how selective such samples necessarily are. Hence, the prevalence rates that would emerge from such studies would have no relevance to the prevalence of child sexual abuse in the general population. Nor do we see why knowledge of the prevalence of child sexual abuse disclosed by mothers would be intrinsically more important or interesting than having this same knowledge about divorced or single women.

CONCLUSION

After comparing the prevalence rates obtained by some of the studies of child sexual abuse in the next chapter, we will attempt to arrive at the prevalence estimate we consider to be the most sound.

NOTES

1. Murphy neglected to report when he conducted this study. Hence, 1989-1990 is a guess based on the fact that his findings were published in 1991.

2. This information was obtained from the Los Angeles Times Poll's unpublished questionnaire, available by writing to the Los Angeles Times Poll, Times Mirror Square, Los Angeles, CA 90053, or by calling 213-972-7676.

3. The prevalence of incestuous abuse was extrapolated from the Los Angeles Times Poll's data as follows: Table 3 reveals that 29% of the 416 female respondents were sexually abused by a relative (Finkelhor et al., 1990, p. 22); $29/100 \times 416 = 121$; $121/1,481 \times 100 = 8\%$.

4. This figure was obtained as follows: 49% of 416 women were the victims of completed or attempted rape, that is, 204 women; $204 \times 100/1,481$ [the number of respondents] = 13.7.

5. The discrepancy between the 28% national prevalence of child sexual abuse for women reported in Table 8 in Finkelhor et al. (1990, p. 25) and the 27% national prevalence rate for women reported in Table 7 (p. 25) and on page 19, is neither acknowledged nor explained.

6. See note 1.

7. Seven hundred seventy-seven respondents $\times$ 65% (Murphy's participation rate) = 505 completed questionnaires. Since 3% of the sample failed to answer the questions on child sexual abuse (Murphy, 1991, p. 83), this reduced the number of usable questionnaires to 482 ($3 \times 777/100 = 23$; $505 - 23 = 482$). Hence, the corrected participation rate is $482 \times 100/777 = 62\%$.

8. The screen questions designed to estimate the incidence of child sexual abuse based on the parents' disclosures to the interviewers about their children's experiences of this crime can be found in Chapter 10.

14

◆

COMPARISONS OF CHILD SEXUAL ABUSE PREVALENCE RATES

The nine representative studies analyzed in Part II of this book obtained immense differences in their prevalence rates for the sexual abuse of girls, ranging from a low of 4.6% for Kilpatrick et al.'s (1985) Charleston County survey in South Carolina (which excluded completed or attempted rape) to a high of 45% for Wyatt's Los Angeles survey when noncontact sexual abuse is excluded, and 62% when noncontact abuse is included (see Figure 14.1 and Table A2.12.1 in Appendix 2). However, it is important to remember that Wyatt's prevalence rates are elevated by their being based on relatively young respondents aged 18 to 36. The other high prevalence rates were obtained by Russell (38%, excluding noncontact abuse) in San Francisco, by the Gallup Poll for mothers and mother substitutes (30%, excluding noncontact abuse) throughout the nation, and by the Los Angeles Times Poll (28%, including noncontact abuse), also throughout the nation.

Only four of the studies reported separate prevalence rates for incestuous child sexual abuse ranging from a low of 1% in Kilpatrick and Amick's study (excluding noncontact abuse) to a high of 21% in Wyatt's survey (excluding noncontact abuse, and 23% including noncontact abuse). Only three of the studies reported separate prevalence rates for extrafamilial child sexual abuse, ranging from a low of 5% in Kilpatrick and Amick's study to a high of 32% in Wyatt's survey (excluding noncontact abuse).

We have shown in Chapters 12 and 13 that a number of methodological factors affected the size of the prevalence rates obtained by different studies. However, one potentially important factor that we have not adequately

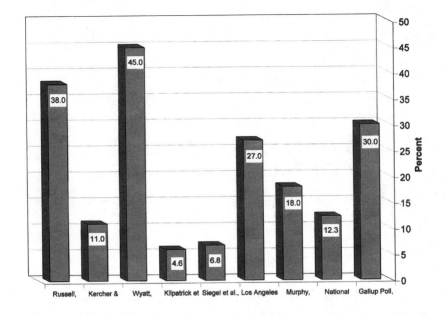

Figure 14.1. A Comparison of Prevalence Rates for Child Sexual Abuse Obtained by Nine Surveys

addressed is the impact on these prevalence rates of the geographical location in which these studies were conducted.

COMPARISONS OF PREVALENCE RATES IN CALIFORNIA STUDIES

Some individuals dismissed the high prevalence rates of child sexual abuse first found by Russell by attributing them to the uniqueness and "weirdness" of San Francisco.[1] After Wyatt's study found even higher rates, some individuals dismissed the high prevalence rates of both studies as being due to their location in California. For example, Peters et al. (1986) noted that,

Because of a popular perception that California harbors a greater degree of sexual license, the question has been raised whether or not the high rates in California studies might reflect a true regional difference in sexual abuse. (p. 30)

After reviewing 19 prevalence studies of child sexual abuse, Peters et al. (1986) concluded that no strong regional trends were apparent "with the exception of the high prevalence rates reported by two of the three studies conducted in California"—these being the studies by Russell and by Wyatt (p. 30). In addition, the Los Angeles Times Poll's prevalence rate for women respondents who disclosed being victimized by sexual abuse as children was 42% in California compared to only 28% for respondents in the country as a whole. This poll also found almost as high rates for Oregon, Washington, Alaska, and Hawaii.

However, Siegel et al.'s study, which was conducted in Los Angeles and which obtained the second lowest prevalence rate for child sexual abuse (6.8%) of the nine studies we compared, is an outstanding exception to these findings. Furthermore, Wyatt and Peters (1986b) noted that "a more detailed examination of the prevalence rates in Wyatt's sample using the nine regional designations developed by the U.S. Census Bureau failed to show evidence of regional variations" (p. 245). In addition, the meta-analysis conducted by Bolen and Scannapieco (1999) found no regional differences in the prevalence of child sexual abuse after accounting for the number of screen questions, the year in which the study was conducted, and the size of the sample. Peters et al. (1986) also point out that "regional differences in respondent candor" is another factor to be taken into account when interpreting regional differences in prevalence findings (p. 31).

Clearly, more research is needed to settle the regional question as it applies to California and other locations. Peters et al. (1986) recommend that future prevalence studies find out "(1) where victims are currently residing, (2) where they actually grew up, and (3) where they were when they were sexually abused" (p. 31).

COMPARISON OF INCESTUOUS AND EXTRAFAMILIAL CHILD SEXUAL ABUSE VICTIMIZATIONS

Many individuals believe that incestuous abuse, and especially father-daughter incest, are the most prevalent types of child sexual abuse.

TABLE 14.1 Comparison of Incestuous and Extrafamilial Child Sexual
Abuse Victimizations as a Percentage of All Sexual Abuse
Victimizations

	Russell		Wyatt		LA Times Poll	
Type of Abuse	%	(N)	%	(N)	%	(N)
Incestuous	29	(187)	24	(72)	32	(121)[1]
Extrafamilial	71	(461)	76	(233)	68	(258)[1]
Total	100	(648)	100	(305)	100	(379)[2]

SOURCES: Russell, 1984, Tables 10.4 and 10.5, pp. 186, 187; Wyatt, 1985, Table 5, p. 517; Finkelhor et al., 1990,
Table 22, p. 22.

NOTES: 1. These numbers were extrapolated from Finkelhor et al., 1990, Table 22, p. 22.

2. 9% (n = 37) of the perpetrators were classified as "other." Because there was no way of
determining who they were, they are omitted from this table.

This belief appears to be confirmed by the NIS-3 (Sedlak & Broadhurst, 1996b), in which the vast majority of reported and investigated child sexual abuse cases are incestuous. However, this finding is not supported by Russell's prevalence survey (of all nine studies, Russell's is the only one to provide an assessment of the prevalence of child sexual abuse by the type of perpetrator). She found that 7% of her respondents had been sexually abused as a child by a stranger, 16% by a relative (4.5% by biological, step-, and adoptive fathers), and 28% by someone known to the victim.

When the focus is on *victimizations,* not victims, Table 14.1 reveals that the percentage of all child sexual abuse cases that are incestuous versus extrafamilial in Russell's study is quite similar to the percentages found in Wyatt's and Lewis's studies. Based on the mean percentages of these three surveys, 28% of all cases of child sexual abuse were incestuous while 72% were extrafamilial. These studies therefore contradict the view that most child sexual abuse is incestuous.

CHILD SEXUAL ABUSE BY TYPE OF PERPETRATOR AS A PERCENTAGE OF ALL SEXUAL ABUSE INCIDENTS

Table 14.2 compares the percentages of child sexual abuse incidents that were perpetrated by strangers, relatives, and others known to the

TABLE 14.2 Type of Perpetrator as a Percentage of Child Sexual Abuse Incidents: A Comparison of Three Studies

Perpetrator/Victim Relationship	Russell (%)	Siegel et al. (%)	LA Times Poll (%)
Strangers	11	22	23[1]
Relatives	29	23	32[1]
Others known to victim	60	56	45[1]
Total	100	101	100[2]

SOURCES: Russell, 1984, p. 187; Siegel et al., 1987, p. 1152; Finkelhor et al., 1990, Table 3, p. 22.
NOTES: 1. These numbers were extrapolated from Finkelhor et al., 1990, Table 3, p. 22.
2. 9% (*n* = 37) of the perpetrators were classified as "other." Because there was no way of determining who they were, they are omitted from this table.

victim. The fact that Russell's percentage of child sexual abuse perpetrated by strangers is only half of those reported by Siegel et al. and Finkelhor et al. raises the question as to whether these researchers used different definitions of *stranger.* Russell reserved the word *stranger* for complete strangers, reserving the word *acquaintance* for perpetrators with whom the victim had some familiarity. However, neither Siegel et al. nor Finkelhor et al. provided a definition for stranger.

What else might explain the fact that the percentages of child sexual abuse incidents that were perpetrated by strangers in Lewis's Los Angeles Times Poll and Siegel et al.'s study are double the percentage obtained in Russell's study, we do not know.

CONCLUSION: THE SOUNDEST ESTIMATE OF PREVALENCE

After comparing 19 retrospective surveys in the United States and Canada that obtained data on the prevalence of child sexual abuse, Finkelhor (1994) maintains that,

> These prevalence studies have led most reviewers to conclude that at least one in five adult women in North America experienced sexual abuse (either contact or noncontact) during childhood. (p. 37; Finkelhor cites Peters et al., 1986, and Leventhal, 1990)

We do not agree with Finkelhor that the best estimate of child sexual abuse is only 20%—a figure that is identical to the prevalence estimate that Alfred Kinsey and his colleagues (Kinsey, Pomeroy, Martin, & Hebhard, 1953) reported more than 40 years earlier. Although Finkelhor (1994) states that he based this figure on the "more methodologically sophisticated studies" (p. 37), he does not identify these studies, nor does he mention what definition of child sexual abuse he has in mind. He merely states that "enough credible figures cluster around or exceed 20% to suggest that the number [percentage] of female victims has been at least this high" (p. 37). Moreover, Finkelhor maintains that this 20% prevalence rate applies to contact or noncontact sexual abuse, despite the fact that the inclusion or exclusion of noncontact abuse typically has a great impact on the size of the prevalence rate obtained. Hence, we feel bound to conclude that the basis for Finkelhor's "best estimate" is very unsound.

Although we do not know which figures Finkelhor regards as "credible," let us assume he is referring to the studies that achieved the highest disclosures. The mean of the nine studies that obtained prevalence rates for child sexual abuse that were 20% and higher is 31%—a far cry from 20%.[2]

Despite having calculated this mean, we do not in fact endorse this way of arriving at the best estimate of the prevalence rate for child sexual abuse. We consider it preferable to select the studies with the soundest methodologies for estimating the prevalence of child sexual abuse, and disqualifying the other studies.

The results of Bolen and Scannapieco's (1999) meta-analysis based on 22 random sample studies conducted in North America are helpful in arriving at the best estimate of the prevalence of child sexual abuse. They set out to find out which of several variables would be most highly related to the prevalence of child sexual abuse. The number of screen questions turned out to be the most significant variable—the more screen questions, the higher the prevalence rate. However, the rate of the increase in prevalence slowed as the number of screen questions increased (p. 293). The number of respondents in the study was the second most predictive variable, with "a greater number of respondents being related to smaller prevalence estimates" (p. 293). The third most predictive variable was the year in which the study was first reported, "with studies done in more recent years having higher prevalence estimates" (p. 294). Together, these variables explained 58% of the differences in prevalence rates across 22 studies (p. 291).

As Bolen and Scannapieco (1999) point out, "one would expect that sampling *more* individuals would give a better estimate of the prevalence of child sexual abuse" (p. 294; emphasis added). As a reason for this unexpected finding, they suggest that "greater attention can be paid to respondents in smaller samples" (p. 294). It is also probable that the smaller surveys are not farmed out for survey research firms to conduct.

Bolen and Scannapieco (1999) used the results from the meta-analysis to create a predictive model based on all the significant variables they found. It predicted that a study done in 1997 with 14 screen questions and 1,000 respondents would yield a prevalence rate for child sexual abuse of 40% (see their Table 8). Despite the approximately 20-year difference between the year in which Russell's study was conducted (1978) and the year to which Bolen and Scannapieco's 40% prevalence prediction applied (1997), these researchers' predicted prevalence rate is remarkably close to Russell's 38% prevalence rate for San Francisco.[3]

Of the three national surveys evaluated in Chapters 12 and 13, the methodology of the Gallup Poll and the National Comorbidity Study are so poor as a basis for estimating the prevalence of child sexual abuse, that they have to be rejected out of hand. Consequently, the Los Angeles Times Poll with its 27% prevalence estimate for child sexual abuse, is the only national study that qualifies as worthy of consideration. However, we noted in Chapter 13 that this study suffers from several serious methodological problems. For this reason Finkelhor et al. (1990) "caution against relying on findings from this study alone in [the] absence of supporting evidence from other research" (p. 27).

Given that the six remaining studies that we evaluated are all confined to a very limited region of the United States, none of their estimates can be generalized beyond these locations. Furthermore, the generalizability of all of the studies, including the national ones, are limited to the dates when their field work was conducted. While bearing these limitations in mind, we decided to base our evaluation of the soundest estimate of the prevalence of child sexual abuse on the study (or studies) with the soundest methodology.

Our conclusion is that Russell's prevalence rates for child sexual abuse are based on the most sound methodology. Were it possible to adjust Wyatt's prevalence rate to correct for the youthful age range of her respondents, we would conclude that Wyatt's and Russell's surveys together provide the soundest methodological basis for estimating the prevalence of child sexual abuse.

A brief reminder of Russell's findings on the prevalence of child sexual abuse are in order here: she obtained a 16% prevalence rate for incestuous abuse of females under the age of 18; a 31% prevalence rate for extrafamilial child sexual abuse; and a 38% prevalence rate for incestuous and extra-familial child sexual abuse combined. We consider all these prevalence rates to be underestimates. First, Russell's sample excluded women in institutions and those who were not living in households, that is, the groups considered to be at very high risk for child sexual abuse. This problem is common to the other eight studies as well. Second, it is clear that some women were unwilling to disclose their experiences of child sexual abuse to the interviewers. Russell had a few self-administered questions at the end of the interview that asked the respondents if they had been unable to be frank about some topics. Several admitted that this was the case for child sexual abuse.

Third, some women do not remember their experiences of child sexual abuse. This is particularly likely to have applied in 1978 when Russell's research was conducted, since this was before the era when child sexual abuse became part of the cultural discourse.

In conclusion, while spokespeople for the backlash continue to claim that researchers are seriously exaggerating the prevalence of child sexual abuse, exactly the opposite is true for the superior surveys described in this volume. Nevertheless, there is an urgent need for a prevalence study that is national in scope and that—like Russell's survey—employs rigorous and child sexual abuse-relevant methodology.

NOTES

1. David Finkelhor, personal communication, 1984; Kilpatrick, public statement at the second National Family Violence Research Conference, Durham, New Hampshire, August 1984.

2. However, Bolen and Scannapieco note that half of the research reviews they examined also estimated the prevalence of child sexual abuse to be approximately 20% (Gorey & Leslie, 1997; Leventhal, 1990; Salter, 1992) (see Bolen & Scannapieco, 1999, pp. 283-284).

3. The effect of predicting a study done in 1984 with 1,000 respondents and 14 screen questions would be to lower the prevalence rate. For an explanation of this statement, see Bolen & Scannapieco, 1999.

15

◆

THE EPIDEMIC OF CHILD RAPE: REALITY AND NEW MYTH

Rape in America is a tragedy of youth.

Kilpatrick, Edmunds, & Seymour, 1992, p. 3

Child rape has been seriously neglected by researchers on rape and child sexual abuse. This is because these two forms of sexual violation have typically been treated as separate areas of study, each with their own researchers, literature, helping and treatment services, as well as activist organizations. Child sexual abuse researchers have documented that most prepubertal child sexual abuse involves genital fondling and other kinds of sexual touching that are less serious than sexual intercourse. Although many child sexual abuse researchers report the frequency of these different degrees of severity, the prevalence of child rape is rarely singled out, and the concept of child rape is rarely used.

With children, statutory rape laws make it irrelevant whether or not force and/or threat of force are used by nonpeer perpetrators of sexual intercourse. All children are assumed to be unable to consent to those who are older than they are (the actual number of years older varies by state). Hence, this legally based definitional difference distinguishes the rape of children from the rape of adult women. This is another reason why analyses of child rape and rape of adults have typically been separated.

Rape researchers who have conducted retrospective studies of the lifetime rape experiences of adult women have necessarily obtained data on child rapes (e.g., Kilpatrick et al., 1992; Russell, 1983b, 1984). Because the researchers have not applied separate definitions to the rape of children and adult women in these studies, the rapes of children are typically limited to acts of forcible rape. While this practice has the disadvantage of omitting nonforceful cases of child rape, it makes possible a direct comparison between the prevalence of child rape and adult rape.

Kilpatrick, Edmunds, and Seymour's *Rape in America: A Report to the Nation* (1992) shocked the country with its national survey finding that *61% of the completed forcible rapes disclosed by women in their sample occurred when they were children or adolescents.* Twenty-nine percent of these rape incidents occurred when the respondents were younger than 11 years old, while close to a third (32%) occurred when they were between the ages of 11 and 17 (p. 3). Hence Kilpatrick et al. concluded that, "Rape in America is a tragedy of youth" (p. 3). Since 1992, these findings of the National Women's Study (NWS) have become widely accepted in and outside the profession.

We noted, however, that a concomitant finding reported by Kilpatrick et al. was that only 6.1% of the completed forcible rapes disclosed by women in their sample occurred when they were over the age of 29. How was such a low percentage possible? And why had no survey found this before?

Just as we thought we had figured out what aspects of the NWS's methodology appeared to be responsible for the dramatic findings about the young age at which most rapes occurred, Tjaden and Thoennes (1998a) published the results of their National Violence Against Women (NVAW) survey. They reported that more than half of the female rape victims in their study had been raped when they were children and adolescents, and, like the NWS researchers, they also concluded that, "Rape should be viewed as a crime committed primarily against youth" (p. 11). A major goal of this chapter is to evaluate the validity of this conclusion.

In short, this chapter is our attempt to answer two questions: Has the prevalence of child rape reached epidemic proportions in the United States? If so, has it become a more widespread problem than the rape of adult women, or is this a new myth that needs to be demolished?

The data on child rape reported by six of the representative surveys evaluated in this book will be presented below in the following order: Russell's survey, conducted in 1978; Lewis's Los Angeles Times Poll, 1985; the National Women's Study, 1992; the National Survey of Family Growth, 1995; the Gallup Poll National Survey, 1995; and the National Violence Against

Women Survey, 1996. The other studies did not provide information on child rape. The methodology for these surveys was described and evaluated in Chapters 3 through 7 and 11 through 13.

RUSSELL'S SURVEY
IN SAN FRANCISCO, 1978

The Prevalence of Child Rape

Russell's narrowest definition for child rape is based on the same definition that she used for the rape of adult women: forced penile-vaginal penetration, penile-vaginal penetration because of threat of force, and penile-vaginal penetration when the victim was unable to consent because she was physically incapacitated in some way, such as being unconscious, drugged, asleep, or in some other way totally physically helpless.

The "under 18" column in the upper half of Table 15.1 shows the prevalence rates for completed child rape, attempted child rape, and completed and attempted child rape combined for forcible child rape (18.8%), whereas the lower half shows these prevalence rates for the broader and more appropriate definition of child rape that includes nonforceful acts of penetration (20.6%).

The Prevalence of Child Rape
Versus Adult Rape

Forcible Rape

In order to compare the prevalence of child and adult forcible rape, we need to base our calculation of the prevalence of child rape on the total number of respondents who were raped *as children* (this was calculated above), and we need to base our calculation of the prevalence of adult rape on the total number of respondents who were raped *as adults* (as opposed to basing the calculation on the total number of victims who were *ever* raped).

Table 15.2 compares the prevalence of completed forcible rape and completed and attempted forcible rape combined for adult women and for female children and adolescents. This table shows that *the prevalence of completed forcible rape in adulthood (19.4%) in Russell's survey is nearly three times*

TABLE 15.1   Russell's Cumulative Prevalence Rates for Different Types of Completed and/or Attempted Rapes for Female Children and Adolescents by Victims' Age Group

	UNDER 11		UNDER 14		UNDER 18	
Type of Rape	*Preva-lence*	*Number of Victims*	*Preva-lence*	*Number of Victims*	*Preva-lence*	*Number of Victims*
Forcible Only						
Penile penetration	1.0%	(9)	2.2%	(20)	6.6%	(61)
Attempted penile penetration	1.0%	(10)	4.9%	(46)	13.9%	(129)
Completed & attempted penetration	2.0%	(19)[1]	5.5%	(51)[1]	18.0%	(167)[1]
Penile penetration & other forms of penetration and attempts	2.5%	(23)	6.0%	(56)	18.8%	(175)
Forcible and Nonforcible						
Penile penetration only	1.0%	(9)	2.5%	(23)	18.3%	(170)
Attempted penile penetration	2.5%	(23)	6.5%	(60)	18.4%	(171)
Penile penetration & other forms of penetration and attempts	3.5%	(33)[1]	7.7%	(72)[1]	20.6%	(192)[1]

NOTE: 1. The percentages in rows 1 and 2 cannot be totaled to arrive at the percentage in row 3, since some respondents were victimized by both completed and attempted rapes.

higher than the prevalence of the completed forcible rape of children (6.6%), and that the prevalence of completed and attempted forcible rapes combined for adult women (32.5%) is nearly double the prevalence of completed and attempted forcible child rape (18%).[1]

Forcible and Nonforcible Child Rape

When we compare the prevalence of forcible rape of adult women with the broader and more appropriate definition of rape for female children and adolescents that includes nonforceful acts of oral, anal, and penile-vaginal penetration, Table 15.2 reveals that the same 32.5% prevalence for adult rape compares with 20.6% for child rape. *Even with this more appropriate definition of child rape, the rape of adult women is just over one-and-a-half times higher than child rape.*

These comparisons make it abundantly clear that Russell's data are not in agreement with Kilpatrick et al.'s and Tjaden and Thoennes's notion that

TABLE 15.2   Comparison of Russell's Prevalence of Completed and/or
Attempted Rapes of Adult Women and Female Children
and Adolescents

	Adult Women		Children and Adolescents			
			Forcible		Forcible & Nonforcible	
Type of Rape	%	*(N)*	%	*(N)*	%	*(N)*
Penile penetration	19.4	(180)	6.6	(61)	18.3	(170)
Completed and attempted penetration	32.5	(303)	18.0	(166)		
Penile penetration and other forms of penetration and attempts	n/a		n/a		20.6	(192)

NOTE: n/a = not applicable

child rapes are a more widespread problem than the rapes of adult women.
This does not, of course, mean that child rape is not a very serious problem for
female children and adolescents.

Ages of Rape Victims When Forcibly Raped

Another way to determine if Russell's data support or contradict Kilpatrick
et al.'s statement that rape is primarily a tragedy of youth is to examine the
ages of victims when they were first forcibly raped (see Figure 15.1; women
have been grouped into age categories in this figure for the sake of clarity). On
doing this, we found that 41.3% (4.5% + 36.8%) of the victims in Russell's
study were under the age of 18 years at the time of their first experience of
completed or attempted forcible rape (penile-vaginal penetration). However,
only 4.5% of the victims were forcibly raped before they were 11 years old
(see Figure 15.1).

We surmised that this 41% rate may have been this high because these
rapes were all *first* rapes, thus biasing the findings toward younger victims.
The extent of this bias can be demonstrated by comparing Russell's rape victims' ages at the time of their first and *last* (or most recent) rape experiences.
Figure 15.1 provides a graphic portrayal of the impact of selecting the first
versus the most recent rape experience.

Whereas 41.3% of the victims in Russell's study were under the age of 18
years at the time of their *first* completed or attempted rape, approximately

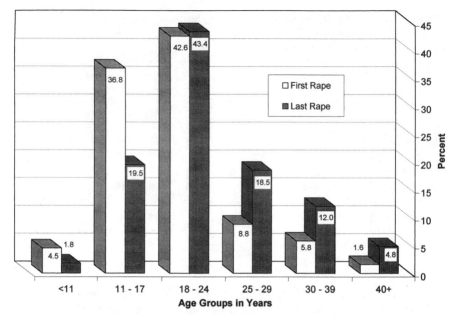

Figure 15.1. A Comparison of the Percentages of Victims' First and Last Completed and/or Attempted Rapes by Age Group in Russell's Study

half of this percentage (21.3%) were under the age of 18 at the time of their *last* completed or attempted rape. Similarly, whereas only 7.4% of the victims in Russell's study were over the age of 30 at the time of their *first* completed or attempted rape, more than twice this percentage (16.8%) were over the age of 30 at the time of their *last* completed or attempted rape (see Figure 15.1). These comparisons demonstrate the consequences of selecting the last experience of rape rather than the first experience. While it is important to demonstrate the bias introduced by selecting the first rape, selecting the last rape is equally biased in the other direction.

If we compare the risk of women who were raped at each age (see Table A2.15.1 in Appendix 2), we see that women's risk of experiencing their first rape at age 15 was .0299, indicating that 2.99% (29.9/1,000) of women not previously raped were raped for the first time at this age. This table indicates that yearly, 2% or more of all women at risk to be raped were raped for the first time between the ages of 13 and 25.[2] Yearly, 1% or more of women were raped for the first time between the ages of 12 and 34. However, the ages of greatest risk were different for women experiencing their last rape. Yearly, 2% or more of women at risk to be raped were raped for the last time between the ages of 16 and 34, and 1% or more were raped between the ages of 14 and 34.

If we were to use only the first rape experience, we would say that women are at high risk (a 2% or greater risk of rape) of being raped between the ages of 13 and 25, and at moderate risk (a 1% or greater risk) between ages 12 and 34. However, using information from both first and last rape, we conclude that women are at high risk to be raped between ages 13 and 34 and at moderate risk at age 12.

Hence, when respondents experience more than one rape, reporting their risk of being raped the first time only biases the risk of rape to women in the younger years. Based on this analysis we conclude that rape is not only a significant problem for adolescents, but also for women until their mid-thirties.

LEWIS'S NATIONAL LOS ANGELES TIMES POLL, 1985

Finkelhor, Hotaling, Lewis, and Smith (1990), who reanalyzed the Los Angeles Times Poll data, reported that "49% of the female victims (13% of all women) said they had experienced actual or completed intercourse" (p. 21), that is, child rape. According to these researchers, this 49% translates into a prevalence rate of 13% for the women respondents. This 13% prevalence for child rape differs from the 14.6% Finkelhor et al. (1990) report in their Table 1 (both on p. 21). Our extrapolation of their prevalence rate for child rape is 13.8%.[3]

Finkelhor et al. described the 49% of female victims of child rape as constituting "an unusually large amount of actual or attempted intercourse . . . compared to only 20% in Russell's survey" (p. 22). Finkelhor et al. (1990) also observed that Lewis's Los Angeles Times Poll found "an unusually small amount of coercion (only 19% of the incidents to girls in this survey compared to 41% in Russell)" (p. 22). On the basis of these two comparisons, Finkelhor et al. (1990) suggested that the differences between these two studies is "probably due to quirks of particular survey questions" asked in the Los Angeles Times Poll (p. 23). Consequently, they concluded their analysis of this Poll by saying,

Some problems with methodology however, particularly the imprecision of the screening questions, do caution against relying on findings from this study alone in absence of supporting evidence from other research. (p. 27)

The manner in which screen questions were asked in the Los Angeles Times Poll study exacerbates the criticism made by Finkelhor et al. regarding the uncharacteristically high ratio of child rapes to less serious forms of child sexual abuse. When respondents answered "yes" to the first question (see p. 192 for screen questions), the interviewer skipped the others and started asking questions about the incident disclosed. Since the fourth question asked about experiences "involving oral sex or sodomy" (Finkelhor et al., 1990, p. 20), and since this was the most likely question to be skipped (since it was the last one), it seems highly probable that this opportunity to find out about additional cases of child rape was missed in some cases. For example, if the respondent answered "no" to question 1 and "yes" to questions 2 or 3 (questions which could not elicit rape experiences), and if she would have also answered "yes" to question 4 (had she been asked), she would have been falsely classified as a non-rape victim. Hence, but for the methodology, there would almost certainly have been an even higher frequency and prevalence of child rape experiences reported by this study.

KILPATRICK, EDMUNDS, AND SEYMOUR, AND SAUNDERS ET AL.'S NATIONAL WOMEN'S STUDY, 1989-1991

The Prevalence of Child Rape

Based on the NWS database, Saunders, Kilpatrick, Hanson, Resnick, and Walker (1999) report an *8.5% (n = 339)* prevalence rate for completed forcible child rape. These rape victims disclosed 438 incidents of child rape, that is, an average of 1.29 rapes each.

The Percentage of Rape Incidents That Were Child Rapes

As noted earlier, *61% of the completed forcible rapes disclosed by women respondents in NWS's national sample of 4,008 occurred when they were children or adolescents.* Twenty-nine percent of these rape incidents occurred

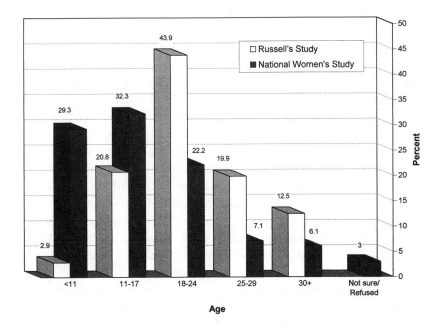

Figure 15.2. The Percentage of Completed Forcible Rape Incidents by Age Group: A Comparison of Russell's and Kilpatrick et al.'s Studies

when the respondents were younger than 11 years old, while close to a third (32%) occurred when they were between the ages of 11 and 17 (Kilpatrick et al., 1992, p. 3).

The Percentage of Rape Incidents That Were Child Rapes: A Comparison of Russell's and Kilpatrick et al.'s NWS Data

Since it was Kilpatrick et al.'s (1992) 61% finding that inspired this chapter, it is of interest to see how it compares with Russell's findings on child rape. In order to make this comparison, we separated Russell's data on completed and attempted forcible rape. In addition, we recalculated her data according to the age categories used by Kilpatrick et al. (see Figure 15.2). This comparison reveals that only 23.7% of the completed rape incidents in Russell's study involved children and adolescents under 18 years compared to Kilpatrick et al.'s 61%. *Hence, Kilpatrick et al.'s percentage of child rape incidents is more than 2.5 times higher than Russell's.*

In addition, *the percentage of rapes occurring to girls younger than 11 years old was 10 times higher in the NWS (29.3%) than in Russell's survey (2.9%).* As the age of female victims increases, this trend begins to reverse itself. The difference between the percentages of completed forcible child rapes found by these two studies is much smaller for females aged 11 to 17. Concomitantly, the percentage of completed forcible rapes of females over the age of 17 is substantially higher in Russell's survey (76.3%) than in the NWS (38.4%).

Figure 15.2 reveals that only 6% of the completed forcible rapes reported by the NWS occurred to women older than 29 years. Although Russell's comparable percentage was double the NWS's percentage (12.5% and 6.1%, respectively), her figure is also unrealistically low. One of the reasons these percentages are so low is that many of the women in the sample have not yet experienced all the rapes they may eventually experience. For example, all the women studied had already passed through their childhood and teenage years, but many of them had not yet experienced being in their thirties, forties, or older. We will demonstrate later in this chapter that another important factor is that both studies biased their findings toward the younger age groups by selecting women's experiences of first rapes.

The next section will discuss possible explanations for the large differences between the percentages of completed forcible rapes involving children and adolescents that the studies of Russell and the NWS obtained.

The Differences in the Findings of the Studies of the NWS and Russell: In Search of an Explanation

One possible explanation for why Kilpatrick et al. (1992) found much higher percentages of child rape incidents than Russell may be that women in 1989-1991 reported more incidents of child rape because they had better memories of their experiences of sexual abuse in childhood than women in 1978. Better memories would be in keeping with the greatly increased awareness about child sexual abuse in 1990 as compared with 1978. An alternative explanation is that Kilpatrick et al.'s respondents, who were generally born more recently than Russell's, may have had greater numbers of rape experiences. Still another possibility is that more child rapes were being fabricated because of the expectations and pressures of therapists, law enforcement personnel, survivor groups, anxious parents, and the like (the so-called false memory syndrome). When there is such a plethora of possible explanations, it is advisable to start by looking closely at methodology.

Rules for Counting Incidents of Child Rapes. In Chapter 1, we mentioned several different ways in which the incidents of rape can be counted. We described Russell's method of counting incidents as the most conservative because she counted only the number of incidents in which rapes were perpetrated by different men. Hence, multiple rapes by the same perpetrator were counted as one rape. In addition, a single rape incident involving multiple rapists was also counted as only one rape.

Kilpatrick et al. (1992) counted a "series" of several rapes by the same perpetrator over "a restricted time period" as one incident of rape. These researchers usually defined "restricted time period" as a year and/or allowed the respondent to determine the amount of time involved (Saunders, personal communication, January 6, 1999). According to Saunders, had a respondent been raped by her father repeatedly over a two-year period, this would have been identified as a single series of assaults. However, if she had been raped by her father over a period of a few months when she was seven years old, then raped again over a period of another few months at the age of 12, this would have counted as two series of assaults (Saunders, personal communication, January 6, 1999). Presumably this means the total count would have been two rapes. Russell, on the other hand, would have counted this as only one incident, since the child was raped by only one perpetrator. However, it is doubtful that these different methods of counting accounted for much of the discrepancy between these researchers' findings on child rape because most child sexual abuse that occurs more than one time is ongoing rather than sporadic.

Selection of Rape Incidents. Respondents in the NWS survey were instructed to follow a set of rules regarding which rape (for those disclosing more than one experience) they should select from whatever rape experiences they may have had. Information about up to three rapes per person was gathered: the first rape experienced by the respondent, the most recent rape, and the "worst" rape—*if* other than the first or the most recent rape. This means that only two rapes would be counted for respondents for whom the "worst" rape was either the first or the most recent rape.

If women tend to find their childhood experiences of rape to be the most distressing, the NWS's instructions increased the likelihood that respondents would pick a second childhood rape as the "worst" experience, thereby increasing the percentage of child rapes and lowering the percentage of adult rapes. The highly significant relationship between incestuous sexual abuse and revictimization (Russell, 1986) likely increased the contribution this factor made to the very high percentage of child rape incidents reported in this survey.

Although Kilpatrick et al. (1992) report that 44%[4] of the rape victims in their national sample were raped more than once, they do not provide information on how many of the respondents were raped more than twice or more than three times—and how many would have had to omit one or more of their rape experiences from the rape count and the data analysis. Had these researchers chosen instead to get information on every rape experience that their respondents remembered, the age at which rapes occurred may have been quite different. While it is not necessary to get information on all the rapes experienced by respondents in order to obtain valid prevalence figures, it *is* necessary to do so if one wishes to analyze the characteristics of rapes experienced by the respondents. This includes the age at which rapes occurred.

In other words, while Kilpatrick et al. (1992) reported that 61% of all the completed forcible rapes disclosed by the respondents in their sample had occurred when they were children or adolescents, these researchers presumably do not know how many completed forcible rapes had occurred to these women because they limited the number of rape experiences their respondents could disclose. Therefore, it is only legitimate for them to say that 61% of the first, last, and worst rapes occurred to children in their study.

NWS's Oversampling of Young Women. We already noted that 2,000 women in NWS's sample of 4,008 were "an oversample of younger women between the ages of 18 and 34" (Kilpatrick et al., 1992, p. 1). Kilpatrick et al. reported that they corrected for this oversampling by weighting their data "to U.S. Census projections of the 1990 (Wave One) . . . adult female population by age and race" (p. 15). Weighting procedures take into consideration discrepancies between the individuals sampled and the population from which they are sampled. The weighting procedures described by Kilpatrick et al. were applied to correct for the large number of women in the sample who were between the ages of 18 and 34. Thus, when Saunders et al. (1999) stated that 13% of women had experienced at least one completed rape, this percentage had been weighted so that it applied to women of all ages.

However, these weighting procedures were not applied to NWS's data on *incidents* (Saunders, personal communication, April 1, 1999). Therefore, when Kilpatrick et al. (1992) reported that 61% of all rapes were committed on children, they were not correcting for the rapes that were committed on the 2,000 women aged 18 to 34 who were oversampled. Because they did not weight their incidence-level data, we conclude that the high percentage of child rapes reported by these researchers is in large part a result of the youth of the sample.

Because of the oversampling of an unweighted younger sample, the youngest respondents could only report childhood rapes because they had just reached adulthood. Yet, of the women in Russell's sample who were raped as children, 47% were also raped as adults, and almost half of these women were raped more than once. Thus, oversampling an unweighted younger group likely excluded a large number of adult rapes. Biasing the selection of rape incidents to favor child rape resulted in the concomitant biasing of these incidents to overrepresent rapes committed by relatives.

Saunders et al. (1999) report that 16.4% of the completed child rapes disclosed to NWS interviewers were perpetrated by fathers and stepfathers and an additional 24.2% were perpetrated by other relatives (excluding husbands and ex-husbands), totaling to 40.6% of all the completed child rapes. This is an extraordinarily high percentage for completed incestuous child rapes. In contrast, only 6.8% of all completed child rapes were perpetrated by biological fathers and stepfathers in Russell's study, and another 8.1% were perpetrated by other relatives. NWS's implausibly high percentage of completed incestuous child rapes most likely occurred because they did not weight their incident-level data. Because (a) their sample included a disproportionate number of young women (who were too young to have experienced the years of greatest rape risk), and (b) more incestuous rapes occur during childhood, the incidents reported would have disproportionately represented childhood rapes.

Regardless of which of our three explanations, or which combination of them, accounts for the NWS's very high 61% for completed forcible rape incidents that occurred when their respondents were children or adolescents, we will point out in the next section why this 61% for child rapes cannot be generalized to the national population.

Incidents as a Basis for Generalizing

While Kilpatrick et al. (1992) did not specifically state that their 61% figure *could* be generalized to the population at large, the title of their report, *Rape in America,* implies that it is legitimate to do so. However, prevalence and incidence rates, not the percentage of incidents, are the appropriate measures for generalizing a phenomenon such as rape to the population from which the sample was drawn. NWS's breakdown of rape incidents by age is not a tenable basis for generalization, because the percentages of completed rapes reported by Kilpatrick et al. for different age groups (under 11, 11 to 17, etc.) are mutually interdependent, i.e., any over- or underreporting at any age influences the apparent rates at every other age (Howell, personal communi-cation, January 1999). To simplify: NWS's percentages of completed rapes are relative, not absolute, percentages, and relative percentages are sensitive to over- or underreporting at other ages. Prevalence rates, on the other hand, are mutually *in*dependent—not relative.

To explain this another way: It is not valid for Kilpatrick et al. to generalize to the population of all women because the "units" being percentaged are not women; they are rapes. When one does not know how many rapes there are in the general universe, one cannot say anything about the proportion of women in various age groups who get raped (Howell, personal communication, March 31, 1999).

Had Kilpatrick et al. used prevalence rates instead of incidents, each vic-tim would be counted only once, whereas their incident-based statistics made it possible for two rapes of the same victim to be counted twice in the same age group. Kilpatrick et al. made a grave mistake by using rape incidents as the basis for assessing the scope of child rape rather than calculating a victim-based prevalence rate for rape as well as ascertaining the relationship be-tween victims' ages and prevalence. For unknown reasons, these researchers chose not to report the prevalence of child rape in their first publication about the NWS (Kilpatrick et al., 1992) despite the fact that the prevalence of rape is the appropriate measure for evaluating the scope of this problem.

Although Saunders et al. (1999) later reported an 8.5% prevalence rate for child rape in their article on child rape, this information became available only after a lapse of seven years. Meanwhile, Kilpatrick et al. (1992) errone-ously implied in their *Rape in America* that their study had demonstrated that 61% of completed forcible rapes in the United States are perpetrated on chil-dren, and this has become a widely publicized and accepted conclusion.

Comparison of Child Versus Adult Prevalence Rates

Although Saunders et al. (1999) reported that the NWS obtained an 8.5% prevalence rate for completed forcible child rape, these researchers did not provide a comparable figure for NWS's completed forcible rape of adult women based on the total number of respondents who were raped *as adults*. This is the appropriate way to assess the prevalence of rape for adult women. In contrast, it is incorrect to assess the prevalence of adult rape on the basis of the women who were raped in adulthood but not in childhood. Many women are raped in childhood *and* adulthood, so it is necessary to include these rapes in adulthood when calculating the prevalence of adult rape.

Because Saunders et al. (1999) failed to calculate their prevalence rate for adult women in the correct way, their prevalence findings cannot be used to compare the percentages of respondents who were raped in childhood versus in their adult years. However, we assume that the NWS researchers have the data to ascertain the prevalence of adult rape calculated independently of the prevalence of child rape, and therefore can choose to publish this information in the future.

In conclusion: Many compelling arguments undermine the validity and interpretation of Kilpatrick et al.'s (1992) finding that 61% of the rapes in the NWS occurred to children and adolescents. For a start, Kilpatrick et al. should have based their analysis on the *prevalence* of child rape (i.e., the percentage of their respondents who were raped in childhood)—not the incidents.

Furthermore, the NWS did not succeed in doing a valid analysis of the incidents of rape because the researchers did not collect information about all these incidents, nor did they weight these incidents to account for the oversampling of younger women. The tremendous overrepresentation of incestuous rape, particularly by fathers, is a dramatic indicator that there is a very serious problem with their data on child rape incidents.

THE NATIONAL SURVEY OF FAMILY GROWTH, 1995

The National Survey of Family Growth (NSFG) obtained *a prevalence rate for completed forcible child rape of 11.8%* (Abma et al., 1997, Table 22, p. 33). Approximately 6% (5.8%) of the 10,847 women respondents "reported that they were forced to have intercourse before they were 15 and another 6% before they were 18" (p. 5).

The NSFG's data on rape were based on the first experience of this crime, thus biasing the statistics on age-related rapes to the younger years. And, like the NWS, the NSFG did not provide a figure for completed and attempted rapes of adult women based on the total number of respondents who were raped *as adults*—not just the additional women who were raped in adulthood but not in childhood. Therefore there is no valid prevalence rate for adult women to compare to their 11.8% prevalence rate for child rape.

DAVID MOORE, GEORGE GALLUP, AND ROBERT SCHUSSEL, GALLUP POLL NATIONAL SURVEY, 1995

As previously noted, close to a third (30%) of Moore, Gallup, and Schussel's (1995) national sample of mothers disclosed being sexually abused during childhood, and *12% of them disclosed having been victims of completed child rape* (i.e., they answered "yes" to the question, "Were you ever forced to have sex by an adult or older child—including anyone who was a member of your family, or anyone outside your family?" [Finkelhor et al., 1997, p. 3]).

The selectivity of the Gallup Poll's sample of mothers (discussed at length in Chapter 13) makes comparisons with studies of women in the general population problematic. And because this study was about sexual abuse in childhood, it provided no data on the rape of adult women.

TJADEN AND THOENNES'S NATIONAL VIOLENCE AGAINST WOMEN (NVAW) SURVEY, 1995-1996

Prevalence Rates for Child Rape

The prevalence rate for completed and attempted forcible rape reported by Tjaden and Thoennes (1998a) for the NVAW survey's 8,000 female respondents is 17.6% ($n = 1,408$).[5] Although these researchers do not report a prevalence rate for child rape, we were able to extrapolate this information from the data they provided in their report.[6]

Table 15.3 compares Tjaden and Thoennes's NVAW survey findings with Russell's on the ages of victims at the time of their first completed and/or attempted forcible rape experiences (combined), as well as their prevalence rates for different age groups. As indicated in Table 15.3, *the NVAW survey obtained a 9.5% (3.8% + 5.7%) prevalence rate for completed and/or attempted forcible rape of their respondents when they were children* (i.e., before the age of 18). When distinguishing between two age groups of children, 3.8% of the respondents were victimized by completed or attempted forcible

TABLE 15.3 Prevalence Rates for First Completed and/or Attempted Forcible Rape by Victims' Age Group: A Comparison of Russell's and NVAW's Findings

	Russell's Survey				NVAW Survey		
Age in Years	Number of Victims	Percentage of Victims	Previous Percentage	Age in Years	Number of Victims	Percentage of Victims	Previous Percentage
< 11	(19)	4.5	2.0	< 12	(304)	21.6	3.8
11-17	(147)	36.8	15.8	12-17	(456)	32.4	5.7
18-24	(170)	42.6	18.3	18-24	(414)	29.4	5.2
25+	(64)	16.0	6.9	25+	(234)	16.6	2.9
Total	(399)[1]	99.9[2]	42.9[3]		(1,408)[4]	100.0	17.6
Mean Age	19.5			No Information			

NOTES: 1. This total does not add up to 407 because of 8 missing observations.
2. This total does not add up to 100% due to rounding.
3. This total does not add up to 44% because of 8 missing observations as well as rounding.
4. See Note 4.

rape when they were less than 12 years old, compared to 5.7% of the respondents when they were 12 to 17 years old.

Comparison of the Prevalence of Child Versus Adult Rape

The NVAW survey's 9.5% prevalence for respondents who were victimized by completed and/or attempted forcible rape before the age of 18 compares with their 8.1% prevalence (5.2% + 2.9%) for respondents who were similarly victimized as adult women (see Table 15.3).

The Percentage of Rape Victims Who Were Children

In contrast to the NWS, Tjaden and Thoennes (1998a) based their comparison of child and adult rape on the percentage of *victims,* not the percentage of *incidents.* More specifically, they examined the age of the rape victims at the time of their first or only completed or attempted forcible rape. As indicated in Table 15.3, these researchers found that 21.6% of these women reported their first rape occurring when they were less than 12 years of age; 32.4% when they were 12 to 17 years old; 29.4% when they were 18 to 24 years old; and 16.6%

when they were 25 years and older. Hence, Tjaden and Thoennes (1998a) concluded that, "*More than half (21.6% + 32.4% = 54 percent) of the female rape victims identified by the survey were under 18 years old when they experienced their first rape*" (p. 6).

This finding is the basis for Tjaden and Thoennes's (1998a) conclusion that their survey "confirms previous reports that most rape victims are children or adolescents" (p. 11). While these researchers fail to cite any "previous reports," they presumably have the NWS in mind. However, as we pointed out, the NWS data were based on rape *incidents,* whereas Tjaden and Thoennes's data are based on rape *victims.* Be this as it may, they, like the NWS researchers, conclude on the basis of their finding that, "Rape should be viewed as a crime committed primarily against youth" (1998a, p. 11).

Comparison of Prevalence Rates of Child Rape: Russell and the NVAW Survey

As indicated in Table 15.3, Tjaden and Thoennes's *9.5% (3.8% + 5.7%) prevalence rate for completed and attempted forcible rape of their respondents when they were children* compares with Russell's prevalence rate of 17.8% (2.0% + 15.8%).[7] Hence, Russell's prevalence rate is close to double the prevalence rate obtained by Tjaden and Thoennes.

Ages of Victims at Time of First Completed Forcible Rape: A Comparison of Russell's and the NVAW Survey Data

Table 15.3 reveals that 41.3% (4.5% + 36.8%) of the victims in Russell's study were under the age of 18 years at the time of their first experience of completed or attempted forcible childhood rape compared with 54% (21.6% + 32.4%) of the victims in Tjaden and Thoennes's study. Hence, the difference between these two prevalence rates is not that large.

Table 15.3 also shows that *victims under the age of 12 in the NVAW survey accounted for 21.6% of all rape victims, whereas victims under the age of 11 in Russell's survey accounted for only 4.5% of all rape victims. Thus, the proportion of the youngest rape victims to all victims of rape in the NVAW survey was almost five times higher than in Russell's study.*

The large disparity in the prevalence rates applicable to the young children is probably due at least in part to these studies' different definitions of child rape. While Russell's narrow definition is confined to penile-vaginal penetration, Tjaden and Thoennes also include oral, anal, digital, and foreign object penetration. Had Tjaden and Thoennes provided a breakdown of the types of child rape they found (i.e., oral, anal, vaginal), it would have been possible to test this hypothesis.

Like Russell's, Tjaden and Thoennes's data on rape are based on the first or only rape, hence biasing their findings toward younger victims. Hence, the NVAW survey finding that 54% of the rape victims were children or adolescents would likely be significantly lower had the age at which the last rape occurred been selected (see Figure 15.1 for how the selection of first rapes instead of last rapes biases the data toward younger rape victims).

Nevertheless, even were this bias corrected in Tjaden and Thoennes's study, the NVAW survey's percentage of victims who are under 18 years old would probably still be high, and higher than Russell's. What factors might account for this aside from their broader definition of rape? Does this survey, like the NWS, have a much higher rate of incestuous rape than Russell's survey? Unfortunately, Tjaden and Thoennes do not provide any information on the number or percentage of women who were raped by relatives in childhood, so it is not possible to examine this question.

Rape: Primarily a Problem of Youth?

The biasing effect of selecting for the first rape in the cases of multiple assault—a biasing effect shared by all survey research-based prevalence studies—probably wipes out the small 8%-greater percentage of child victims as compared to adult victims reported by the NVAW researchers (54% vs. 46%). More important, the 8.1% prevalence rate for adult rape victims that this survey obtained (as compared with the 9.5% prevalence rate for the rape of female children and adolescents) was not calculated in the correct way. As we pointed out in the case of the NWS, Tjaden and Thoennes's prevalence rate for adult women should have been confined to adult women respondents who were raped after they were 18 years old, regardless of whether they were also raped as children. Hence, their prevalence data cannot be used to compare the percentages of respondents who were raped in childhood versus in their adult years.

However, as with the NWS, we assume that Tjaden and Thoennes have the data to ascertain the prevalence of adult rape calculated independently of the prevalence of child rape, and that they can therefore choose to publish this information in the future. Meanwhile, it is not legitimate for Tjaden and Thoennes to conclude that rape is primarily a crime against youth.

Given the small difference between the NVAW study's 9.5% prevalence rate for children as compared with the erroneously underestimated prevalence of 8.1% for adult women, it is virtually certain that a correct calculation of the prevalence rate for the rape of adult women will exceed child rape, possibly by a considerable amount.

In conclusion: This analysis suggests that the NVAW survey is not justified in concluding that rape is a more frequent tragedy for children than for adult women.

Comparison of the Prevalence of Child Rape in Six Studies

Figure 15.3 shows the prevalence rates for child rape obtained by the six studies analyzed in this chapter. As is evident from the figure, comparisons between the prevalence rates of the studies reviewed in this chapter are marred by the fact that Russell is the only researcher who has provided prevalence data for completed rape only *and* completed and attempted rape combined. Comparisons would be greatly facilitated if prevalence researchers would report both these prevalence rates in future.

The large disparity between Russell's prevalence of child rape for completed rape and completed and attempted rape combined shows how important it is not to compare one study's estimate of completed rape with another study's estimate of attempted rape.

A method needs to be devised to overcome the problem of bias introduced by selecting first rapes in cases of multiple victimization. Perhaps this could be achieved by using the mean age at which the rapes occurred instead of the first rape. In addition, instead of using the age of onset in cases of extended durations for multiple incidents of sexual abuse interspersed with one or more rapes, perhaps the mid-point of the duration of the abusive incidents should be chosen.

Whether or not these are the best solutions, it is imperative that researchers try to figure out ways to prevent biasing their findings toward the young age groups. One obvious corollary of this bias is that it results in the underestimation of the substantial risk of rape to adult women.

As already emphasized, in addition to calculating a prevalence rate for child rape based on the total number of respondents who were raped as children, researchers should calculate the prevalence of adult rape on the basis of the total number of victims who were raped *as adults* (*not* the total number

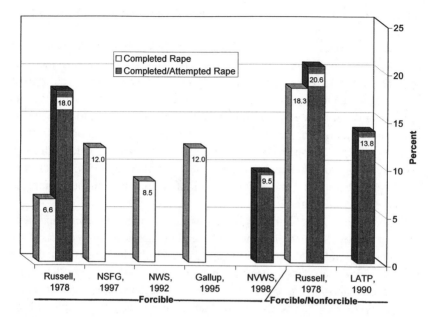

Figure 15.3. A Comparison of the Prevalence of Forcible and Forcible/Nonforcible Child Rape in Six Representative Surveys

of victims who were *ever* raped). Then it is reasonable to compare these two prevalence rates, as we have done for Russell's data at the beginning of this chapter.

CONCLUSION

It is important that rape and child sexual abuse researchers start routinely to report information on the heretofore neglected problem of child rape. Ideally, researchers should gather data on forcible child rape to enable comparisons to be made with adult rape, as well as with nonforcible child rape, which is the legal and appropriate conception of rape for children.

Of the six studies that we have compared in this chapter, three (the Los Angeles Times Poll, the National Survey of Family Growth, and the Gallup Poll) focused on child sexual abuse. Obviously, therefore, they did not have a prevalence rate for the rape of adult women with which they could compare their childhood rape rates.

Because the other three studies (Russell, the NWS, and the NVAW survey) obtained data on the prevalence of rape throughout the life span of their respondents, they have the data to compare the prevalence of rape in childhood and adulthood. However, as already noted, the NWS researchers did not calculate a prevalence rate for adult women that was comparable to their prevalence rate for children, and the NVAW researchers did not calculate a prevalence rate for adult women correctly. But more to the point, the definitions of rape that apply to adults and that were therefore also applied to children in these studies required that it be forced. This is, of course, an inappropriate requirement for child rape.

As we pointed out at the beginning of this chapter, statutory rape laws make it irrelevant whether or not force and/or threat of force are used by nonpeer perpetrators of sexual abuse and rape. All children are assumed to be unable to give their consent to those who are older than they are (the actual number of years older varies by state). However, because of our desire to evaluate the NWS researchers' conclusion that "rape is a tragedy of youth," which subsequently appeared to be confirmed by the NVAW survey, we have necessarily had to focus on forcible child rape in this chapter. And because our analysis has not supported the conclusion of these two teams of researchers that rape is a greater problem for female children and adolescents than for adult females, it could convey the impression that we are continually downplaying the prevalence of child rape. We want to dispel this impression because it is seriously inaccurate.

Figure 15.3 shows that the prevalence rates for forcible completed and attempted child rape obtained by three studies ranges from a low of 9.5% for the NVAW survey to a high of 18% for Russell's survey (the mean prevalence rate is 14%). It is alarming indeed that there are such high prevalence rates for the forcible rape of children. Furthermore, Russell's prevalence of rape for forcible *and* nonforcible completed and attempted rape of children and adolescent females, including oral and anal penetration as well as penile-vaginal penetration, is 20.6% (see Table 15.1). Hence, according to Russell's study, just over one fifth of her respondents were raped when they were children and adolescents.

Since research has consistently shown that most child sexual abuse involves fondling and other less severe forms of abuse, the 20.6% figure for completed and attempted rape becomes even more striking.

The Soundest Prevalence Rate for Child Rape

Of the six studies that had data on child rape, three are limited to forcible rape—which, as we have pointed out, is not an appropriate conception of rape for children. Because one of the two studies using a child-appropriate definition (i.e., including nonforcible penetration) did not pass the methodological rigor test (Lewis's Los Angeles Times Poll), that leaves Russell's 20.6% prevalence for child rape as the most sound estimate available at this time.

No researchers, to our knowledge, have yet tried to establish the precise size the prevalence rates for the rape of adults and/or children would have to be in order to qualify as having reached epidemic proportions. However, we think that Russell's 20.6% prevalence for child rape definitely qualifies as an epidemic.[8] However, the claim that the forcible rape of children is much greater than it is for adults—as the NWS researchers maintain—is in danger of having become a new myth.

NOTES

1. When calculating the prevalence of rape of adult women, researchers must be careful to avoid merely subtracting the prevalence of child rape from the prevalence of rape of adults and children combined. For Russell's data this erroneous calculation would have yielded a prevalence of adult rape only 8 percentage points higher than the prevalence of child rape (44% − 18% = 26%).

2. More accurately, we are reporting the hazard rate for first and last rapes. The hazard rate for first rape is computed by dividing the number of women who experienced their first rape at a given age by all women at risk to be raped. Women are classified as being at risk to be raped for the first time only if they have never been raped previously (and for the last time, if they have not yet experienced their last rape), and of course, they cannot be counted in an older group than their age places them in. For example, 18-year-olds who have never been raped can only be considered to be at risk for rape at the age of 18. These women cannot be included in calculations for ages beyond the age of 18 because they have not yet experienced that age.

3. This extrapolation was calculated as follows: 49% of the female victims × 416 (the total number of respondents who were victims of child sexual abuse)/100 = 204; 204/1,481 (the total number of women respondents) × 100 = 13.8% (see Finkelhor et al., 1990, pp. 22-23).

4. Kilpatrick et al. (1992) report that 39% of the victims were raped more than once and 5% were unsure how many times they had been raped (see Figure 1, p. 2). Since the latter group of respondents obviously had disclosed more than one experience of rape, these two categories have been combined, thus adding to 44%.

5. Although a prevalence rate of 17.6% was reported for the NVAW survey, the 1,323 total number of NVAW victims recorded in Exhibit 6 (Tjaden & Thoennes, 1998a, p. 6) constitutes a prevalence rate of only 16.7% (1,323 × 100/8,000). Extrapolating from the NVAW survey data, it appears that the correct total is 1,408, which translates to the 17.6% prevalence rate reported by this survey (17.6 × 8,000 (sample size) /100 = 1,408).

6. Because the total number of women victims recorded in Tjaden and Thoennes's (1998a) Exhibit 6 appeared to be incorrect (as noted in endnote 5), we based our extrapolations on the corrected numbers.

7. In Table 15.3, the prevalence of completed and attempted child rape adds up to 17.8% (2% + 15.8%), while in Figure 15.3 it is reported to be 18%. This discrepancy is due to the different methods of handling the eight cases in which the age of the victim of child rape was missing.

8. The other prevalence rates are no longer relevant to this discussion because they did not include nonforcible rapes.

PART **III**

Conclusion

16

THE BACKLASH: FEMINISTS BLAMED FOR CREATING A PHANTOM EPIDEMIC OF RAPE AND CHILD SEXUAL ABUSE

Diana E. H. Russell

BACKGROUND

Feminist theory and research on rape and child sexual abuse began to be taken seriously in the 1970s and early 1980s. By the mid- and late-1980s, it had radically transformed many people's thinking about these crimes. This manifested in research, law reforms, improved treatment of survivors by police, the development of rape crisis centers, and local and national anti-rape and anti-child sexual abuse organizations.

My startlingly high prevalence rates for rape (24% for completed rape and 44% for completed and attempted rape combined) were first published in 1982, and my prevalence rate for child sexual abuse (38%) was first published in 1983 (Russell, 1983a). Interestingly, my findings on rape were largely ignored, whereas my prevalence findings on child sexual abuse received a great deal of attention. (For example, the article that published my findings on child sexual abuse (Russell, 1983a) was the fifth most frequently cited of the 30 highest ranking papers on child abuse in the Science Citation Index and in the Social Science Citation Index from 1984 to 1993 [Oates & Donnelly, 1997]).

In contrast, Koss's national survey of rape and other coercive forms of sexual victimization that she conducted with Christine Gidycz and Nadine Wisniewski (1987) in 1984-1985 garnered a great deal of positive attention from their colleagues in the field as well as by the media and the public at large. Theirs was the first study ever to obtain a prevalence rate for rape based on a national representative sample of college students. Koss et al.'s 27.5% prevalence rate for rape was considered shockingly high, even though prior research of nonrandom student populations by Eugene Kanin (1957, 1970, 1971; Kirkpatrick & Kanin, 1957) had found similarly high rates.

Over the years, several other researchers used Koss's self-administered questionnaire to replicate her study—although not its national scope. These studies typically obtained prevalence rates for rape that were comparable to Koss's. However, the honeymoon period for public receptivity to feminist research on rape and child sexual abuse came to an end at the beginning of 1990.

The 1990s heralded the start of an often venomous backlash against feminism in general, as well as against feminist theory, research, and activism about rape and child sexual abuse. Many men in particular appeared to feel threatened by the obvious implication that high prevalence rates for rape and child sexual abuse might mean that a substantial minority of males must be rapists and child molesters. Feminist analyses typically stressed the normative character of rape for males and the causal link between patriarchy and the sexual victimization of women and children, particularly girls. Clearly, if these analyses were to be taken seriously, it meant that patriarchy would have to be dismantled to ameliorate the problems of rape and child sexual abuse on a very significant scale.

After Koss and I had demonstrated that many randomly selected women were willing to disclose their experiences of sexual assault to researchers, despite the taboo subject matter and despite the fact that many of these women had never disclosed these experiences to anyone before, other researchers followed in our footsteps by undertaking random sample surveys about sexual assault. As our review of some of the nonstudent studies in this book has shown, several other studies have also obtained high prevalence rates for rape and child sexual abuse. However, Koss and I—two of the pioneers in prevalence research on female victimization—are the only self-identified feminists among the researchers whose studies have been described in this book. This is an important point, as will shortly become clear.

THE BACKLASHERS

Bolen and I opened our introduction to this book with statements made by backlashers Neil Gilbert (1991c), Camille Paglia (1992), Katie Roiphe (1993), Christina Hoff Sommers (1994), and *Blade* journalists Schoenberg and Roe (1993) criticizing the high prevalence rates found by researchers and/or attacking feminists for believing these statistics and for being overly preoccupied about rape. With the exception of Paglia, whose appalling statements about rape predated Gilbert's, several of the other backlashers (e.g., Roiphe, Sommers, and the *Blade* journalists) merely restate some of Gilbert's arguments. Muehlenhard, Highby, Phelps, and Sympson (1997) have documented the fact that many of Roiphe's criticisms of feminists and researchers are mere repetitions of Gilbert's arguments.

Martin Schwartz and Mary Koss (1998) note "the enormous influence" of these backlashers (p. 6). Roiphe, who claims to be a feminist, "became the darling of the *New York Times* and much of the Eastern press" after the publication of her book, *The Morning After,* in 1993 (Schwartz, 1997, p. xii). Following is Schwartz's (1997) analysis of the important role Roiphe's book has played in the backlash against feminist research that has documented the epidemic proportions of rape in the United States:

> The arguments in her book were based completely on Gilbert's, but they were put into a wrapping of a feminist attacking feminists. What was most interesting was not that this book was published at all but that Roiphe was featured everywhere, from the cover of the *New York Times Sunday Magazine* to many of the top conservative television talk shows. After all, this particular expert was a young graduate student in literature who had never held a job, had never done research, and had made no claim to have interviewed any women except her own personal friends at Harvard and Princeton. The book itself is based on misrepresentation, mistakes, and misunderstandings. . . . Why did America's media reach out to embrace someone who obviously knew little about the subject and ignore those who had long labored in the field? The "feminists against feminists" theme was again picked up by the media when Christine Hoff-Sommers (1994) continued that attack. (p. xii)

Who Stole Feminism? (1994) is the revealing title of Sommers's well-received contribution to the backlash. As a professor of philosophy unfamiliar with rape research and social scientific method, Sommers, also a self-described feminist, could appeal to a more sophisticated audience than Roiphe. These two players, along with Paglia, owe their popularity and influence to the male-dominated media, many members of which appear to be elated to find women who share their antagonism to feminists who have raised public awareness about the widespread prevalence of sexual victimization of women by men.

Martin Schwartz (1997) notes that

> those people who represent the backlash—who argue that there are not large numbers of victimized women—are for the most part people without data, without experience in survey research, and generally without any background whatsoever in the field. (p. xi)

This is an accurate characterization of Gilbert, Roiphe, Sommers, the *Blade* reporters, and many others. Schwartz and DeKeseredy (1994) describe Gilbert, a professor at the School of Social Welfare at the University of California, Berkeley, as "the most prominent among these 'people with no data.'" They maintain that he has "turned a distinguished-but-little-known career in social work policy to achieving his most fame ever in a new calling: attacking Mary Koss and other researchers of women's victimization" (p. 5).

This chapter will focus on the arguments made by Gilbert because he stands out as by far the most prominent of the backlashers who have focused their attacks on what he refers to as a "phantom epidemic of sexual assault" (Gilbert, 1991c). This was the title of Gilbert's article that "triggered the debate" in 1991 (Schwartz & Koss, 1998, p. 7). Gilbert is also one of the few backlashers who has read some of the scholarly literature that he attacks, and who presents himself as understanding rape and child sexual abuse as well as the intricacies of prevalence survey methodology.

When criticizing the studies by Koss and myself, as well as by Kilpatrick et al.'s National Women's Study (Gilbert, 1993) and studies conducted or described by Finkelhor (Gilbert, 1994a, 1994b, 1995), Gilbert presents himself as an unbiased positivist scholar concerned about sound and objective methodological practices. His academic credentials and appearance of methodological know-how have increased his credibility. According to Schwartz and Koss (1998), Gilbert "has become a strong and acceptable mainstream criminology figure" (p. 7), despite the fact that none of his many articles on rape and child sexual abuse has ever been published in a scholarly, peer-reviewed journal (Kamen, 1993, p. 11).[1]

Gilbert's Charges

Gilbert (1991c) charges feminist researchers—that is, Koss and myself, whom he identifies as "radical feminists who promote advocacy numbers" and whom he describes as women "with an ax to grind"—with the responsibility of creating the "phantom epidemic" by manufacturing our high prevalence rates on rape and child sexual abuse in order to promote our agenda and get more funding for our cause (cited in Russell, 1992, p. 6). The following passage in Gilbert's (1991c) first published critique of sexual assault research and researchers expresses his basic thesis very clearly:

> The estimates of sexual assault calculated by feminist researchers are advocacy numbers, figures that embody less an effort at scientific understanding than an attempt to persuade the public that a problem is vastly larger than commonly recognized. . . . Under the veil of social science, rigorous research methods are employed to measure a problem defined so broadly that it forms a vessel into which almost any human difficulty can be poured. (p. 63)

Gilbert has singled out Koss as his major target among rape researchers, presumably because her national survey is the best known and most influential of all the studies. My research on rape has been Gilbert's number two target, but his prime target in the area of child sexual abuse research.

Despite the fact that Wyatt obtained a relatively high prevalence of rape (25% of her sample) and the highest prevalence rate for child sexual abuse of any study (62% for a broad definition of this form of victimization), Gilbert does not even mention her research. It is unclear why Gilbert chose to focus on Koss and myself, but not on Wyatt, unless it is that she is not identified as a feminist.

Gilbert's Agenda

Gilbert is engaged in an extended campaign to discredit the high rates of rape and child sexual abuse obtained by some survey researchers (consider, for example, his numerous publications from 1991 to 1998 in which he frequently repeats the same charges year after year). Although Koss and I are only two of the prevalence researchers who have found high rates of rape— and in my case, child sexual abuse as well—Gilbert's focus on us (in particular) *as feminists* suggests that he is engaged in a strategy to exploit the anti-feminist sentiment that became fashionable in American culture in the early 1990s (and still continues today) by associating high rates of rape with this political philosophy. This strategy is presumably designed to discredit the veracity of high prevalence rates.

Gilbert has made several revealing statements that may shed light on his motivation to discredit research that substantiates the notion that the scope of rape and child sexual abuse in the United States has reached epidemic proportions. For example, he maintains that, "The feminist prescription redefines conventional morality so as to give women complete control of physical intimacy between the sexes" (1991c, p. 61). This statement makes it appear that Gilbert is fearful of any move toward greater equality in sexual or gender relations. In another publication, Gilbert (1994b) contends that,

> [T]he sexual politics of advocacy research [Gilbert's characterization of feminist research] on violence against women demonizes men and defines the common experience in heterosexual relations as inherently violent and menacing. (p. 75)

Far more research by nonfeminists than feminists has substantiated that large numbers and percentages of women and girls have been violently and nonviolently, sexually and nonsexually, victimized by men, particularly by men they know or with whom they are, or have been, sexually engaged. (We will present some of the findings of one genre of this research in the next chapter.) It would be more appropriate to blame the perpetrators or the social and cultural institutions in the United States that foster and support violent and predatory sexual behavior by males toward females than to blame the messengers—feminists and other so-called advocacy researchers whose research has revealed the epidemic dimensions of rape and child sexual abuse in American society.

In the following statement, Gilbert (1994b) appears to cite my prevalence rates for rape and child sexual abuse (although he does not identify me as the source):

> If it is true that one-third of female children are sexually abused [presumably, Russell's 38%] and almost half of all women [Russell's 46% probability rate] will suffer an average of two incidents of rape or attempted rape at some time in their lives, one is ineluctably driven to conclude that most men are pedophiles or rapists. (p. 75)

Not only are most men not pedophiles, but most child sexual abuse is not perpetrated by pedophiles (Finkelhor, 1984; Russell, 1986). However, it does not seem unreasonable to infer from my statistics, as well as those of several other researchers, that quite a large percentage of males *are* perpetrators of rape and/or child sexual abuse. A different genre of research based on questioning male students about their likelihood of raping a woman or sexually abusing a child, if they could get away with it, is consistent with this inference (this research is described in the next chapter).

Since readers are presumably quite familiar with my study by now, from this point on the focus will be on describing and responding to Gilbert's charges against my research on rape and child sexual abuse. Another reason for this decision is that Bolen and I decided not to include our chapter on national student surveys on the prevalence of rape that included Koss's study, due to lack of space. (This chapter was selected for this fate, along with others, because student studies are not, strictly speaking, comparable with general population studies.) In addition, Koss herself, as well as many other researchers and activists, has responded to Gilbert's criticisms of her research. I (Russell, 1992), in contrast, have responded to Gilbert's charges against me only in a brief, two-page article.

Gilbert's Critique of Feminist Researchers' Methodology

As already noted, Gilbert charges feminist researchers with deliberately exaggerating the prevalence of rape and child sexual abuse by selecting methods that will achieve this goal while providing a veneer of scientific validity. Following is a list of Gilbert's objections to feminist researchers' prevalence methodology, as well as an evaluation of each of them.

Feminist Researchers Have Manufactured High Prevalence Rates

Gilbert (1994b) charges that the *prevalence* rates obtained by feminist researchers "are considerably higher than what one would infer from the official figures on child sexual abuse and rape" (p. 68). Citing the *incidence* rate for rape obtained by the greatly flawed government-funded National Crime Survey (NCS) in 1987 (see Chapter 5), Gilbert (1991c) maintains that *only about 1 in every 1,000 women is victimized by rape or attempted rape*. Gilbert concludes that "[t]he size of the discrepancies [between this rate and those of feminists] should make us skeptical" of the high rates reported by feminist researchers (1994b, p. 68).

Gilbert fails to consider whether the much higher prevalence rates obtained in several independent surveys (not just feminist surveys) should rather make *him* skeptical of the findings of the NCS, especially since detailed criticisms of the NCS had been well argued and documented by scholars in this field by the time Gilbert wrote his article in 1994 (e.g., Eigenberg, 1990; Koss, 1992, 1996; Koss & Harvey, 1991; Russell, 1984). (Gilbert's inappropriate comparison of prevalence and incidence rates will be discussed shortly.)

Feminists Formulate Overly Broad Definitions of Rape

Gilbert (1991c) singles out feminists' choice of definitions for rape and child sexual abuse as the most important methodological feature we use to exaggerate our findings on the prevalence of rape and child sexual abuse. More specifically, he accuses us of using very broad definitions of rape—so broad that "almost any human difficulty qualifies as rape" (p. 63).

Gilbert's charge against me totally misrepresents the fact that my definition of rape is, on the contrary, identical with the conservative legal definition used in California in 1978—the year my fieldwork was undertaken. This very *narrow* definition excluded oral and anal rape, as well as rape by a foreign object. Despite this narrow definition, I obtained the highest rape rate of any study. Gilbert (1995) obfuscates the truth about my narrow definition of rape by suggesting in the following quote that my theoretical argument about there being a continuum of sexual assault confirms his charge that I use a broad definition of rape. Hence he warns his readers that they

> might bear in mind Russell's perceptions about what constitutes rape. She says, "If one were to see sexual behavior as a continuum with rape at one end and sex liberated from sex-role stereotyping at the other, much of what passes for normal heterosexual intercourse would be seen as close to rape." (p. 6)

In reality, my notion of a continuum in no way contradicts the fact that I chose to use a very narrow, conservative definition of rape in my survey.

Gilbert also ignores the fact that many researchers who define rape much more broadly than I do obtained significantly *lower* prevalence rates. For example:

- Linda George, Idee Winfield, and Dan Blazer (1992), who obtained a representative sample of women aged 18 and over in North Carolina, defined sexual assault extremely broadly ("being pressured or forced to have unwilling sexual contact" [p. 110]), yet obtained a prevalence rate of only 5.9%.

♦ Margaret Gordon and Stephanie Riger (1989) obtained randomly selected telephone samples in Philadelphia, San Francisco, and Chicago, and asked their respondents "if they had ever been raped *or* sexually assaulted *at some time during their lives*" (emphasis in the original; p. 36). They obtained a minute 2% rape prevalence rate in this study (p. 36; also see Riger & Gordon, 1981, p. 76), noting that their prevalence rate may be that "high" [*sic*] "because the question asked about sexual assault as well as rape" (1981, p. 76).

♦ Even the revised National Crime Victimization Surveys use a definition of rape that is substantially broader than the legal definition of rape (e.g., it includes psychological coercion and verbal threats of rape). Nevertheless, these surveys continue to obtain very low incidence rates for rape (see Chapter 5 for more specific documentation of this point).

These examples refute Gilbert's association of broad definitions of rape with high prevalence rates. Ironically, Gilbert himself fails to define rape despite his emphasis on its vital importance in the incidence and prevalence rates that researchers obtain.

Gilbert (1994b) also takes issue with me for not having a subjective definition of rape, that is, for not allowing my respondents to decide whether or not they have been raped. More specifically, he objects that

a considerable proportion of the cases counted as rape and attempted rape in this [Russell's] study are based on the researchers' interpretation of experiences described by respondents. (p. 71)

Once again, this charge of Gilbert's is false. As described in Chapter 3, I and two staff members read all the qualitative information about rape that the interviewers had written down verbatim to make sure that respondents' descriptions of their rape experiences met the study's narrow definition of rape. Those cases that did not meet the definition were disqualified. Hence, the effect of this rigorous check subtracted a few cases from the number of rapes disclosed—thereby slightly reducing the prevalence of rape. For example, there were a few instances in which respondents had answered "yes" to the question on rape because they had consented to intercourse after being subjected to psychological pressure. These cases were disqualified because my definition of rape did not include psychological pressure.

My meticulous method of ensuring that rapes were correctly assessed probably has no equal in the field. Gilbert's way of describing my process (see the quotation above) makes it sound sloppy and subjective rather than exceptionally scrupulous and rigorous.

Feminists Formulate Overly Broad Definitions of Child Sexual Abuse

Although my primary definitions of child sexual abuse exclude non-contact experiences (see Chapter 11 for my definitions of incestuous and extrafamilial child sexual abuse), Gilbert also criticizes me for my allegedly overly broad definition of child sexual abuse (e.g., he refers sarcastically to my "supposedly more stringent definition of child sexual abuse" [1997, p. 109]). This reveals Gilbert's ignorance of the fact that most child sexual abuse prevalence research prior to mine included noncontact experiences in the definitions (e.g., Finkelhor, 1979; Gagnon, 1965; Kinsey et al., 1953; Landis, 1956). The same applies to many studies conducted *after* my survey (see Chapters 12 and 13 for several examples).

With regard to extrafamilial child sexual abuse between the ages of 14 and 17, I probably have the narrowest definition of all studies of child sexual abuse. Gilbert's charge that I "lump together" relatively harmless behavior with terribly damaging behavior in my definition of incestuous abuse overlooks the many experiences of sexual abuse that I excluded: for example, verbal propositions (e.g., requests by parents or other adult relatives to engage in sexual behavior or to pose for pornographic pictures); exhibitionism; voyeurism; being shown or forced to see pornography; and noncontact forms of sexual harassment (e.g., a father telling his daughter daily that women with large breasts like hers are sluts). Many researchers include some or all of these behaviors in their definitions.

I excluded being upset by witnessing male genital exposure from my definition of child sexual abuse even though I obtained data on this experience. Had I included this experience in my definition, my prevalence rate for child sexual abuse would have been much higher. For example, 27% of my 930 respondents answered "yes" to my question, "Before you turned 14, were you ever upset by anyone exposing their genitals?" The percentage of affirmative answers to this question would have been much higher than 27% had the question also been asked of respondents aged 14 to 17 years.[2]

Gilbert's complaint that advocacy researchers "give equal weight to experiences ranging from despicable violations . . . to mild acts" is also false. Including a broad range of sexually abusive experiences does not necessarily mean that these acts are given equal weight. I, for example, differentiated the victims of child sexual abuse in my survey into three groups: those who were very severely sexually abused in terms of the sex acts imposed on them, those who were severely sexually abused, and those who were least severely sexually abused (Russell, 1986).

When I examined the relationship between the degree of trauma that respondents reported and the severity of the sex acts that characterized the abuse, I found severity to be the most significant of all variables in predicting the degree of trauma reported by respondents. Analyses of the relationships between variables such as these could not be addressed if researchers limited their studies to the most serious forms of child sexual abuse. In short, studying a broad range of child sexual abuse experiences can provide invaluable information. Peters, Wyatt, and Finkelhor (1986) suggest that

> it makes sense, for research purposes at least, to gather data about a broader rather than [a] more restricted definition. Information once collected can always be ignored, but information not gathered is simply unavailable. With the broader definition, at least, samples can be trimmed for comparability to other samples using a somewhat different definition. (p. 46)

Gilbert consistently distorts my prevalence findings on child sexual abuse by reporting them as if my principal prevalence rate were the very high and broadly defined 54% rate that included noncontact experiences. I stressed that my motive to provide this broad definition of prevalence (which I described as "incomplete" and "inadvertently obtained" [Russell, 1984, p. 184]) was to illustrate that my primary 38% prevalence for child sexual abuse "would undoubtedly be even higher had I used definitions of both incestuous and extrafamilial child sexual abuse as broad as those used in some other studies" (p. 183). I also wanted to compare my prevalence rate to that of Wyatt, who included noncontact experiences in her high 62% prevalence rate (see Chapter 14 for this comparison).

Gilbert (1991b) also described my broad definition *before* my narrower definition, then claimed that: "children who merely receive 'unwanted kisses and hugs' are classed [by Russell] as victims" (p. 58). Gilbert omitted the word *sexual* preceding the phrase "kisses and hugs," without including ellipses. He repeats this same error in several later publications (e.g., Gilbert, 1994b, 1995). He uses the same strategy to distort my narrower definition of child sexual abuse. For example, he maintains that this definition "stretches from attempted petting to any exploitive contact such as touching on the leg or other body parts" (1994a, p. 21). This time the word *sexual* should have preceded the words *exploitive* as well as *touching*. Once again, no ellipses were included. Finally, Gilbert (1991c) also omitted the word *sexually* from the following question: "*Before you turned 14,* did anyone ever feel you, grab you, or kiss you in a way that you felt was [sexually] threatening" (p. 58).

Deliberate misquoting not only is unethical, but makes it appear that Gilbert *deliberately* misinterprets my study.

Feminists' Questions on Rape Exaggerate the Prevalence of Rape

Gilbert (1994b) is highly critical of feminist research for not using the terms *rape* and *attempted rape* in all of their screen questions. For example, he writes:

> Russell's estimates were derived from 38 questions, of which only one of these questions asked respondents whether they had been a victim of rape or attempted rape any time in their lives. And to this question, *only* [sic] *22% of the sample, or one-half of women defined as victims* by Russell, answered in the affirmative. (p. 71)

Gilbert appears to interpret the fact that "only" 22% of my sample answered *yes* to the question on rape to mean that the additional 22% prevalence of completed and attempted rape that I obtained from answers to several other questions—making a total prevalence of 44%—should not be counted as rape. He interprets my inclusion of the second 22% of victims in my prevalence rate as demonstrating his charge that feminists exaggerate their rape statistics.

Gilbert's comments reflect a lack of familiarity with the fact that many individuals in this society reserve the word *rape* for rape by strangers and that many women whose experiences fit the legal definition of rape do not use that word to describe their experiences.

It is also worth noting that Gilbert does not criticize the revised National Crime Victimization Studies for formulating only one question out of many that included the word *rape*. Nor does he criticize several researchers who did not use the term *rape* in their screening questions when they obtained low prevalence rates for rape and/or sexual assault (e.g., George et al., 1992; Sorenson et al., 1987). Gilbert's double standard exemplified here is repeatedly demonstrated in his criticisms of prevalence studies.

Advocacy Researchers' Failure to Take Account of Women's False Reports of Rape Exaggerates the Incidence Rates

Gilbert (1997) claims that "attempts to estimate the incidence of sexual assault are also contaminated by false reports of rape" (p. 131). He substantiates his statement by citing the police's judgment that approximately 8% of women's reports of rape to the police in 1992 were false. We noted in Chapter 4 the sexism that almost certainly accounts for this high rate of "unfounding." Furthermore, whatever motivation a few women may have for making false reports of rape to the police (e.g., to avoid being blamed for infidelity, to escape punishment by a parent or husband for staying out all night) are most unlikely to apply to women who participate in confidential interviews with researchers. As previously noted, there is general consensus among rape researchers that *under*disclosure, not *over*disclosure, is the problem prevalence researchers have to overcome. Finally, even if my prevalence rate for completed and attempted rape were reduced by 8%, it would still be extremely high.

Feminists' Use of Atrocity Stories to Exaggerate Prevalence Rates

According to Gilbert (1997), one of the ways in which so-called advocacy researchers/feminists exaggerate the prevalence of rape is

> by employing what Best (1990) describes as 'atrocity tales'—painful detailed anecdotes that typify the human suffering caused by the problem but fail to give the slightest hint of its incidence in the population. (p. 123)

In a footnote, Gilbert refers to my inclusion of "a series of case studies of sexual abuse" in my book *Sexual Exploitation* (1984) and "detailed descriptions" of case material in *Rape in Marriage* (1990) as examples of this phenomenon. However, he does not explain how quoting women's experiences of rape magnifies its incidence or prevalence. Furthermore, Gilbert's charge that these qualitative data are bereft of information on the incidence of rape is conspicuously incorrect as a description of my research. In addition, describing women's accounts of sexual assault as "atrocity tales" is very demeaning.

Advocacy Researchers Make Faulty Generalizations Based on Populations With High Prevalence Rates of Rape

Another method used by so-called advocacy researchers, according to Gilbert (1997), is to exaggerate their prevalence rates of rape "by measuring a group highly affected with the problem and then projecting the findings to society-at-large" (p. 123). Gilbert fails to provide references for this charge. Moreover, it does not apply to those who use representative samples of students or the general population. Indeed, the problem is quite the opposite; prevalence studies typically exclude the groups of women who are most prone to high rape rates, such as women in mental hospitals, prisons, brothels, and on the street, thereby underestimating the prevalence of rape.

METHODOLOGICAL ERRORS IN PREVALENCE RESEARCH

Clearly, Gilbert has invested a significant amount of time and energy in criticizing the methodology of prevalence researchers, particularly the research by Koss and myself. Yet ironically, Gilbert's critiques are fraught with methodological errors. For example, understanding the difference between the incidence of rape (typically based on the number of incidents of rape in the prior 12 months) and the lifetime prevalence of rape (the percentage of women who have been victimized by rape at some time in their lives) is an absolute necessity for individuals conducting or evaluating surveys that use one or both of these measures of the magnitude of rape. As previously noted, Gilbert contrasts BJS's National Crime Survey's 1987 *incidence* rate of 1 completed and/or attempted rape per 1,000 females with my study's lifetime *prevalence* rate of 44% for completed and/or attempted rape (Gilbert, 1991c). This is like comparing apples and oranges.

This same confusion is reflected in the following statement by Gilbert (1998) about the incidence rate reported by BJS's NCS in 1989:

> BJS findings reveal that 1.2 women in 1000 over twelve years of age were victims of rape or attempted rape. *This* [incidence rate] *amounted to approximately 135,000 female victims* in 1989. No trivial number, this annual figure translates into a lifetime *prevalence* rate of roughly 5 to 7 percent, which suggests that one woman out of fourteen is likely to experience rape or attempted rape sometime in her life. (p. 361; emphases added)

Gilbert (1998) here misinterprets BJS's finding of a 1.2 incidence of rape per 1,000 women (based on the number of rape *incidents* in the prior 12 months) as 1.2 *women* per 1,000 females. He also incorrectly translates this figure into "approximately 135,000 *female victims*" (p. 361). However, incidence rates are based on the number of *victimizations,* not the number of *victims.* This is further evidence of Gilbert's failure to understand the crucial difference between incident-based and victim-based statistics.

Gilbert goes on to maintain that 135,000 female victims in one year constitutes a lifetime prevalence rate for completed and attempted rape of approximately 5% to 7%. However, prevalence rates cannot be derived from incidence rates because women often experience more than one rape. Despite the fact that I pointed out this error in 1992 (Russell, 1992, p. 6), Gilbert has continued to make the identical error from 1991 until 1998.

CONCLUSION

After initially conveying that it was only feminist researchers who were reporting high prevalence rates for rape, Gilbert proceeded to attack the research of Dean Kilpatrick and his colleagues when they obtained a rape rate (13%) that he found disturbingly high. David Finkelhor and his colleagues also became a target. Gilbert (1995) was particularly critical of the screening questions used in a Gallup Poll survey that Finkelhor, Moore, Hamby, and Straus (1997) wrote up and criticized. Gilbert appears to have mistakenly assumed that this study was *conducted* by Finkelhor et al. (see Gilbert, 1995, p. 4). Gilbert seems not to notice that Finkelhor had already made the same criticism of the screen questions that Gilbert made. This is one example among many of what appears to be Gilbert's careless reading of the research he criticizes.

I wonder what Gilbert will say about the recent government-sponsored National Survey of Family Growth (Abma et al., 1997) that found a 20% prevalence for completed rape, and the even more recent government-funded study by Tjaden and Thoennes (1998a) that found an 18% prevalence for completed and attempted rape, and Lewis's Los Angeles Times poll (Finkelhor et al., 1990) that obtained a high 27% prevalence rate for child sexual abuse. It seems these high prevalence rates simply will not go away, despite Gilbert's and others' insistence that they are a "phantom" phenomenon created by feminists.

In general, it seems reasonable to conclude that the arguments made by the backlashers denigrating the research that substantiates the existence of an epidemic of rape and child sexual abuse in the United States have no merit. Furthermore, they are manifestations of a general backlash against feminism and other progressive movements. Despite the significant role in this backlash of some women who call themselves feminists, they are serving the interests of reactionary patriarchal forces invested in a return to a prefeminist era when male domination was more entrenched and accepted and freer from challenges. These female backlashers, as well as the male backlashers like Gilbert, have been able to leap out of obscurity into the limelight and to garner great attention and influence because they fit this reactionary agenda.

I have attempted in this chapter to demonstrate the lack of substance in the backlashers' attacks. In the next and final chapter, Bolen and I will stress the importance of urging the progressive forces in this country to devise strategies to address and combat the epidemic of sexual violence against females in this country.

NOTES

1. Gilbert's articles are typically without references, citations, or footnotes. Even in his one article that was published in a scholarly journal, he failed to cite page numbers when quoting others' material.

2. The 27% of respondents who expressed upset at seeing a man exposing his genitals cannot be added to the 38% who were sexually abused in childhood in some other way because these are overlapping categories.

17

◆

THE EPIDEMIC OF RAPE
AND CHILD SEXUAL ABUSE:
A NATIONAL EMERGENCY

DETERMINING THE SOUNDEST
PREVALENCE AND INCIDENCE RATES

Determining the soundest prevalence rates for rape and child sexual abuse was our major objective in writing this book. To this end, we evaluated the methodological soundness of seven representative studies that obtained prevalence rates on rape, nine representative studies that obtained prevalence rates on child sexual abuse, and six representative studies that obtained prevalence rates on child rape. Because the federal government sources obtain data only on incidence, not prevalence, we also evaluated their incidence rates for rape and child sexual abuse as well as incidence rates obtained by a few of the prevalence studies. The government studies are particularly important because they are often used to formulate social policies.

The Federal Government's
National Incidence Studies

We found that the methodology of the national incidence studies was so inferior for eliciting disclosures on rape and/or child sexual abuse that their estimates of the scope of these crimes are worse than useless. The Bureau of Justice Statistics' (BJS) revised National Crime Victimization Survey (NCVS) qualifies as by far the most significant of these methodologically inferior studies of rape rates. Their many methodological defects account for their gross underestimation of the incidence of rape. Their frequently stated conclusion that rape is a crime that occurs only infrequently is totally out of step with reality and with the findings of other surveys.

The NCVS's serious underestimate of the magnitude of the rape problem in the United States is extremely damaging. For many reasons—such as the prestige and authority with which these costly surveys are imbued, their national scope, their replication every year, and the fact that they represent the official government source on reported and unreported rape statistics—the annual incidence rates they obtain are widely used by politicians, journalists, and policymakers at all levels. Hence, the longer these surveys continue to "prove" that rape is an infrequent crime, the longer they will continue to be responsible for undercutting efforts to get the state and federal governments to recognize the epidemic dimensions of rape and to formulate appropriate policies to combat it.

The NCS/NCVS's low incidence rates of rape are also used by backlashers to undermine the credibility of methodologically sounder studies that have obtained much higher prevalence rates and/or incidence rates than the government surveys. For example, in an article in the *Wall Street Journal* in which Gilbert (1993) cited findings by the NCS, he denigrated the Violence Against Women Act of 1993 for giving "rape crisis centers $85 million to combat an epidemic that does not exist" (p. A18). He also charged that

> the act is designed to promote the cause of radical feminists, whose exaggerated claims of victimization deserve the critical scrutiny they are just beginning to receive from moderate feminists. (p. A18)

Even if unintentionally, the NCS/NCVS serve the interests of the backlashers, who use their statistics to foster denial about the epidemic of rape. Hence, as long as the Bureau of Justice Statistics continues to drastically underestimate the magnitude of rape in the United States, this federal government institution must be held responsible for serving as the "scientific" arm of the backlash dedicated to belittling the scope of the rape problem and efforts to ameliorate it.

Unlike the National Crime Victimization Surveys that endeavor to ascertain the incidence of unreported as well as reported rapes, the National Incidence Studies attempt only to collect information on child sexual abuse that comes to the attention of authorities. Limiting their efforts to compiling these cases ignores the majority of victims of child sexual abuse whose experiences are not disclosed to officials or anyone else. Because there is no obvious solution to this problem, the National Incidence Studies (NIS) must never be presumed to have estimated the true dimensions of child sexual abuse in the United States.

This problem aside, we pointed out in Chapter 10 that the National Incidence Studies suffer from numerous methodological problems that result in their estimates of the incidence of disclosed cases of child sexual abuse in the United States being inadequate, misleading, and sometimes sexist. For example, by limiting their definition of child sexual abuse to acts that are perpetrated or permitted by a parent or caretaker, most experiences of child sexual abuse are disqualified, especially cases of extrafamilial child sexual abuse. This form of sexual victimization constitutes a substantial majority of cases of child sexual abuse. In addition, only substantiated cases of sexual abuse are included in the NIS's incidence rates from child protective services sources. Furthermore, if NIS or child protective services or both are responsible for the failure to distinguish between fathers who sexually abuse their children and mothers who are judged to have failed to protect their children, we consider this to be exceedingly sexist.

Hence, the NIS's methodology contributes greatly to the vast underestimation and distortion of the problem of child sexual abuse in the United States. For example, it misrepresents the number of cases reported to child protective services by including only substantiated incidents of sexual abuse. This problem is further exacerbated because the child protective services system is now so overburdened (see Sedlak & Broadhurst, 1996b) that many cases of known or suspected sexual abuse are never reported, less than half of reported sexual abuse is investigated, and much investigated sexual abuse is not substantiated (see Chapter 10). In some of these cases, sexual abuse did not occur. In others, however, sexual abuse did occur. Thus, substantiated cases of child sexual abuse are simply the tip of the iceberg (see Sedlak & Broadhurst, 1996).

Prevalence Studies

We found that the methodology of some of the representative surveys we evaluated was so inferior for eliciting disclosures on rape and/or child sexual abuse that their estimates of the prevalence of these crimes have to be discounted. For example, Kilpatrick et al.'s (1985) first survey of child sexual abuse used only one screen question on child sexual abuse. Moreover, this question asked respondents if anyone had "tried to molest" them.[1] Most other studies that used only one screen question, whether for rape (e.g., Kessler et al., 1995) or child sexual abuse (e.g., Kercher & McShane, 1984; Kessler et al., 1995; Siegel et al., 1987) qualified as inferior, for this and usually other reasons.

Aside from the inferior studies, several other studies have moderately sound methodologies for assessing the prevalence of rape and child sexual abuse. However, studies in this category suffered from one or more methodological problems that presumably reduced women's disclosures of their experiences of rape and/or child sexual abuse (e.g., too few screen questions, use of inappropriate terminology in screen questions). A few of these studies also reported findings so contradictory to previous research (e.g., the Gallup Poll reported more cases of sexual abuse of boys than of girls) that our confidence in the validity of their findings was undermined. In some instances, the researchers inadvertently misreported their findings, on the basis of which they then drew faulty conclusions (e.g., data misinterpreted by Kilpatrick et al., 1992, and by Tjaden and Thoennes, 1998a, as showing that "rape is primarily a tragedy of youth").

In short, most of these studies suffered from problems with their design, execution, and/or interpretations. Most also appeared to make no effort to incorporate any special rape-appropriate and/or child sexual abuse-appropriate methodology designed to facilitate victims' abilities to remember or to recall such experiences (e.g., repeating the same question for different types of perpetrators to jog respondents' memories and/or to help them to recall forgotten experiences) as well as to encourage their willingness to disclose their usually well-concealed experiences of child sexual abuse (e.g., by eliminating victim-blaming interviewer applicants and questions).

In our evaluation of these studies, we commended numerous aspects of Wyatt's methodology, particularly in her study of child sexual abuse. The length of training that her interviewers received is unique, the ability of the interviewers to elicit disclosures was very impressive, and the interview schedule was presumably a crucial contributor to this achievement. We also noted that the major drawbacks of Wyatt's study included the small sample size, the fact that it was limited to one city, and the choice of an age range for her respondents that makes it difficult to compare her findings with those of other studies.

Despite the fact that Russell's survey was also limited to one city, we nevertheless concluded our evaluation of these studies by judging her survey to be the most methodologically sound and appropriate for assessing the prevalence rates for rape (24% for completed rape and 44% for completed and attempted rape), child sexual abuse (38%, excluding noncontact abuse), and child rape (7% for completed forcible rape, 18% for completed and attempted forcible rape, and 21% for completed and attempted nonforcible rape). Although we consider Russell's prevalence rates for these crimes to be the most valid of our sample of studies, there is an urgent need to conduct a methodologically superior study that is national in scope and draws on the best features of all the studies that have been conducted to date.

THE EPIDEMIC IS A REALITY

A second objective of our book was to determine if our evaluation of prevalence studies would reveal whether or not the rates of rape and/or child sexual abuse in the United States are occurring in epidemic proportions. Using the term *epidemic* simply to mean "widely prevalent" (*The American Heritage Dictionary,* 1992), we have no hesitation in concluding on the basis of Russell's and Wyatt's studies, as well as on the studies that we have described as moderately sound, that female sexual victimization is indeed occurring in epidemic proportions in the United States.

OTHER RESEARCH THAT VALIDATES HIGH PREVALENCE RATES

As feminist researchers (Herman, 1981; Russell, 1984) and backlashers (e.g., Gilbert, 1994b) have noted, the logical corollary of an epidemic of sexual victimization involving male perpetrators and female victims is that a substantial percentage of males have some propensity to rape and/or sexually abuse/assault girls and women. A few examples of the research that substantiates this inference are briefly described next.

Likelihood of Men Raping Women

According to Neil Malamuth (1986), research indicates that 25% to 30% of samples of male college students in the United States admit that there is some likelihood that they would rape a woman if they could get away with it.[2]

In another study, by John Briere and Malamuth (1983), 60% of 356 male students admitted that under the right circumstances there was some likelihood that they would rape a woman and/or force her to engage in a sex act against her will. Jacqueline Goodchilds and Gail Zellman (1984) found that 79% of their high school male and female subjects between 14 and 18 years of age thought it was acceptable to rape a girl in at least one of nine circumstances—for example, "if she gets him sexually excited" (p. 242). They concluded that both male and female adolescents see rape of females by males as an "ever-present and sometimes acceptable possibility" in women's lives (pp. 242-243).

Given these findings, it is hardly surprising that after reviewing a whole series of related experiments, Malamuth (1981) concluded that "the overall pattern of the data is . . . consistent with contentions that many men have a proclivity to rape" (p. 139). Clearly, the high prevalence of sexual victimization is neither a freak statistic nor a phantom epidemic. It is consistent with the high percentages of ordinary males who are willing to admit that they are motivated to rape women,[3] and moreover, that there is even some likelihood that they would do so if they could be assured of getting away with it.

Likelihood of Males Sexually Abusing Children

Malamuth found that 10% to 15% of male students reported some likelihood of sexually abusing a child if they could be sure of getting away with it (Malamuth, personal communication, July 1986). In a study of 193 male undergraduates, John Briere and Marsha Runtz (1989) found that (a) just over one fifth (21%) of the male undergraduates "admitted to at least some sexual attraction to some small children" (p. 71), and (b) 7% "indicated at least some likelihood of having sex with a child were it possible to do so without detection or punishment" (p. 71). However, Briere and Runtz hypothesized that "given the probable social undesirability of such admissions . . . the actual rates of pedophilic interest in this sample were even higher" (p. 71).

When Briere and Runtz applied a broad definition of pedophilia as having a sexual attraction to children, they estimated that 21% of their sample of male undergraduates would qualify as pedophiles.[4] These researchers concluded that

the current data offer strong support for the notion that male sexual response to children is relatively common in our society, even among normal (non-incarcerated and nonclinical) males. (p. 71)

Briere and Runtz's study question was about sexual attraction to "small children"—a phrase that suggests prepubescent rather than adolescent children. They concluded that their finding that 21% of their male subjects who admitted having some sexual attraction to small children is probably a gross underestimate of the percentage of males in the population who have some predisposition to abuse children sexually.

Had Briere and Runtz asked about their male subjects' sexual attraction to female adolescents at least five years younger than themselves, the percentage of those admitting an attraction would presumably have been substantially higher. Indeed, in a culture in which Brooke Shields was described at the age of 12 years as the most beautiful woman in the world, and in which female youthfulness has become eroticized for many males, a good case could be made for the notion that only a small percentage of men experience no sexual attraction toward postpubescent female children. While sexual attraction is not necessarily acted out, particularly if acting it out is illegal and/or stigmatized, it is an important factor in the occurrence of sexual abuse.

PREVALENCE RESEARCH MUST CONTINUE

Many researchers, clinicians, administrators, and activists in the field of sexual victimization of women and children might be tempted to believe that it is now time to leave the issue of prevalence and move on to other important issues, particularly those that will prove helpful to the victims of these crimes. While in no way wishing to argue that prevalence research is more important than many other issues, it is nevertheless vitally important for researchers to continue conducting studies on the prevalence and incidence of rape and child sexual abuse.

The prevalence of these and other forms of sexual victimization are not static variables. Because they have the potential to change over time (and according to Russell's research, rape increased dramatically over the years prior to 1978), research on the prevalence of rape and child sexual abuse must be ongoing. Furthermore, journalists, politicians, and other policymakers who require statistics on the scope of one or both of these forms of sexual victimization always want up-to-date figures.

If the inaccurate statistics of the National Crime Victimization Surveys provide the only up-to-date estimates on rape, it is virtually certain that these dangerous underestimates will continue to be used by individuals who need statistics on rape. This in turn would likely have a negative impact on the formulation and implementation of sound and much-needed ameliorative social policies on rape as well as on the allocation of appropriate amounts of funding to pay for these reforms.

Prevalence statistics are also a frequent by-product of rape or child sexual abuse research regardless of the specific focus. Although we have described the researchers whose studies we have reviewed as prevalence researchers, for several of them prevalence was incidental to their research on other topics. Kilpatrick, for example, has focused far more on the effects of rape on the victims than on prevalence. The National Survey of Family Growth had no intrinsic interest in rape and child sexual abuse other than as two examples among many of traumatic experiences. Its goal was to ascertain the association between all these traumas and mental disorders.

All studies that need a database of victims can (and often do) generate a prevalence rate. The more realistic their prevalence rates are, the more valid their databases will be. Hence, in order to evaluate their studies properly, they should be required by journals and other academic publications to report their prevalence rates.

THE POLITICS OF PREVALENCE

We would like to believe that this book will help to discredit once and for all the claims of the backlashers that the epidemics of adult rape, child rape, and child sexual abuse are but phantoms invented by feminists for ulterior motives. We earnestly wish that our thorough critique of the arguments of the backlashers will succeed in discrediting their persistent efforts over almost a decade to destroy the credibility of some of the best studies of sexual violence. But we know better than to believe our wishes will be realized because the reactionary, misogynist forces the backlashers represent are threatened by the revolution in awareness about sexual violence as well as by the reforms relating to sexual violence that feminists have accomplished in recent years. Hence, they have used the issue of prevalence methodology as a cover for their politically motivated attacks on high prevalence rates of female sexual victimization. We know this political motivation will not be moved by rational arguments or rigorous scientific data analysis.

And yes, there *is* a political aspect to high prevalence rates of female victimization. The fact that females predominate as sexual victims and males predominate as sexual perpetrators is profoundly political. And the higher the prevalence of sexual victimization is, the greater the indictment of male behavior and the patriarchal culture that has nurtured and condoned it. Some of the many individuals who would prefer not to face the crisis in gender relations that this reality connotes join the backlash and pillory the messengers.

However, the prevalence of female victimization is also a scientific methodology-related issue. The meticulous analyses of the methodologies of prevalence and incidence studies that we have undertaken in this book exemplify a scientific treatment of this issue. The analysis provides irrefutable evidence that female sexual victimization is a problem of mammoth proportions. By doing this rigorous analysis, we have debunked the backlashers' claim that the prevalence of female victimization is being overstated by so-called advocacy researchers with an ax to grind (see Chapter 5). Instead, we have shown that the studies upon which some backlashers rely for their figures are among the most methodologically inferior of all the studies we examined.

Having debunked the backlashers' arguments, and having resolved the centrality of methodology in the prevalence rates that researchers obtain, we will return to the political issue of what needs to be done about the unsafe lives that males' sexually predatory behavior imposes on American women and children.

MAJOR RECOMMENDATIONS

We strongly recommend that the methodology of the NCVS's section on rape either be radically overhauled as soon as possible or disbanded completely. If the methodology is to be revised, the NCVS researchers should be required to hire a staff of outside female and male experts free of gender biases who have demonstrated their abilities to conduct rigorous rape-appropriate prevalence research. These experts should have an equal or greater role than the NCVS researchers in formulating the revised methodology.

If the responsibility for obtaining rape statistics were removed from the NCVS, the financial savings that would result could be used to fund a team of qualified researchers to conduct an annual survey that does a first-rate job of measuring the incidence and prevalence of rape, as well as of obtaining information on numerous other important aspects of this crime. These studies should be particularly careful not to merge their data on the rape of males and females. Of these two options, we favor the second.

We strongly recommend that the NIS and other federally funded studies of the reported incidence of child sexual abuse be radically revised to include all cases of this crime that come to the attention of the authorities. In particular, these studies must include cases of extrafamilial child sexual abuse, for which there is currently no method of assessing the number of identifiable cases. This requires, however, that policies must be revised so that children who experience extrafamilial abuse—the most prevalent form of child sexual abuse—have the same right to protection as children who are abused intrafamilially.

We also strongly recommend that annual federally funded national representative studies of the prevalence of child sexual abuse be conducted so that statistics and additional information on numerous other important aspects of these crimes can be gathered on unreported as well as reported cases. If the annual survey of rape were to be conducted by a team of qualified researchers, as proposed above, this team could be expanded to include research experts who have demonstrated their abilities to conduct rigorous child sexual abuse-appropriate prevalence research. As we stated with regard to rape, these studies should also be particularly careful not to merge their data on the sexual abuse of male and female children.

We believe that the Internet is contributing to the epidemic dimensions of the victimization of women and girls by rape and child sexual abuse. For example, according to Kim McCarten, the editor of an on-line magazine called *Merge* (April, 2000), "*Wired* on-line magazine ran a story about a how-to site on raping women." After the Internet server hosting Daterape.org "pulled it down" in response to a feminist-led protest, "the date rape boys were briefly back in business—promising an upcoming live date rape on the Internet." Wire Company, their new server, got rid of these rapists' website once again. However, McCarten expressed certainly that "the sellers of date rape as sport are looking for another provider." Within a very short period, her conviction proved to be correct. McCarten also noted that "Daterape.org has recipes for date rape cocktails and gagging women" on its web site. Hence, we recommend that women demand that Congress investigate websites on the Internet that promote rape and child sexual abuse with a view to penalizing those responsible for contributing to sexual violence and violation of women and girls, as well as those web sites that show graphic examples of such crimes as they are perpetrated.

We also recommended in Chapter 4 that women organize to put strong pressure on their state legislatures throughout the country to implement the kind of radical reforms planned in Philadelphia where knowledgeable feminist women will be reviewing the police department's handling of sexual assaults "from start to finish" (quotation of Carol Tracy, the executive director of the Women's Law Project in Philadelphia, in Fazlollah, et al., 2000, p. A9). This will increase the numbers and rates of reported rapes instead of discounting them for sexist and political reasons.

CONCLUSION

The epidemic of rape and child sexual abuse in the United States must be treated as a national emergency as well as a national priority. These are gender crimes that have not been taken as seriously as they deserve. Continuing to treat these problems as the tragic but unavoidable fate of females is a form of gender discrimination, particularly in a country with the financial resources and know-how to mount a massive campaign to combat these crimes.

President Clinton's response to the crisis in Kosovo was to invest billions of dollars in an effort to end the horrendous abuses suffered by the ethnic Albanians living in that small territory. While we laud his concern, we wonder why the formulation of a national policy to ameliorate the problems of gender violence and sexual victimization of females in the United States is not also treated as a national emergency. Yes, women were raped and beaten and killed in Kosovo, and men were also tortured and killed. In the United States, children are being sexually abused and raped and sometimes killed, and women are being raped and beaten and sometimes killed, merely for being female. We applaud the fact that rape by enemy soldiers is now considered a war crime and treated as a heinous form of torture. But why are these crimes taken less seriously when they happen to American women and girls?[5]

We earnestly hope that this book will contribute to a widespread recognition that there is an epidemic of rape (including child rape) and child sexual abuse in the United States, and that this epidemic must be treated as a national emergency for as long as it takes to drastically reduce these crimes. We also earnestly hope that this book will help motivate many more individuals to demand that those with the power and resources to undertake a large-scale campaign to combat female sexual victimization recognize their responsibility to do so.

NOTES

1. However, the question did go on to define the meaning of sexual molestation. Nevertheless, stigmatizing words like *molest* and *rape* should not be used unless there are several questions on such acts that avoid such loaded terms.

2. In 1984, Neil Malamuth reported that in several studies an average of about 35% of male students indicated some likelihood of raping a woman (p. 22). This figure has decreased to between 25% and 30% since then, for reasons Malamuth does not know (personal communication, July 1986).

3. Motivation to rape is implicit in many subjects' admission that there is some likelihood that they would rape a woman if they would not be caught.

4. We personally disagree with using the term *pedophilia* as broadly as Briere and Runtz do in this research. Indeed, we think it is very important to differentiate between pedophiles and the larger number of mostly male individuals who have a sexual attraction to children and/or who act on it—but in a less compulsive and frequent manner.

5. Some rapes are taken seriously in the United States, but many rapes are not, for example, rapes that happen to poor women, women of color, prostitutes and drug addicts, wives, lovers, and dates. Furthermore, many of the penalties are very mild. Nor is rape in the United States prosecuted as a gender-based hate crime, although some rape is now considered torture in certain international contexts.

Appendixes

Appendix 1: Tables About Rape

Appendix 2: Tables About Child Sexual Abuse

Appendix 1:

Tables About Rape

TABLE A1.6.1 Comparison of Eight Representative Sample Surveys on Completed and/or Attempted Rape: Methodology and Findings

Researcher(s)/ Study Name	1 Russell	2 Wyatt[a, b]	3 Kilpatrick et al.[c, d]	4 Kilpatrick et al., National Women's Study[e, f]	5 Kessler et al., National Comorbidity Survey[g]	6 National Crime Victimization Survey (NCVS)[h, i]	7 National Survey of Family Growth (NSFG)[j]	8 Tjaden & Thoennes, National Violence Against Women Survey (NVAW)[k]
Date of fieldwork	1978	1981-1984	1983	1990-1991	1990-1992	1994	1995	1996
Publication date	1992, 1994	1992	1984, 1985	1992	1995	1997	1997	1998
Funder/sponsoring agency	NIMH grant	NIMH grant	NIMH grant	National Institute on Drug Abuse	Institute of Social Research, University of Michigan	Bureau of Justice Statistics (BJS)	Center for Disease Control and Prevention (CDC)	National Institute of Justice and Centers for Disease Control and Prevention
Location of study	San Francisco	Los Angeles County	Charleston County, South Carolina	National	National	National	National	National
Methodology								
Sample size (females only)	930	248	2,004	4,008	3,065	90,560 (male & female; about 45,280 females)	10,847	8,000

(continued)

269

TABLE A1.6.1 *(Continued)*

	1	2	3	4	5	6	7	8
Researcher(s)/ Study Name	*Russell*	*Wyatt[a,b]*	*Kilpatrick et al.[c,d]*	*Kilpatrick et al., National Women's Study[e,f]*	*Kessler et al., National Comorbidity Survey[g]*	*National Crime Victimization Survey (NCVS)[h,i]*	*National Survey of Family Growth (NSFG)[j]*	*Tjaden & Thoennes, National Violence Against Women Survey (NVAW)[k]*
Sampling method	Probability sample	Random-digit dialing & quota sample	Random-digit dialing sample	Random-digit dialing sample	Probability sample undermined by subsample methodology	Continuous representative sample	Probability subsample of 1993 survey	Random-digit dialing sample
Participation rate	(81%)[1] 64% (50%)	(73%)[2] 67% (55%)	84% 78%	80%	82% for sample 1 99%, 98%, 99% for 3 subsamples	95.1% household 92% individuals 87.5%[3] combined	79%	72% household 97% women 69.8% combined
Method of data collection	In-person interviews	In-person interviews	Telephone interviews	Computer-assisted telephone interviews (CATI)	In-person interviews	In-person and telephone interviews	Computer-assisted personal interviews (CAPI) & audio computer-assisted self-interviewing	Computer-assisted telephone interviews (CATI)
Definition of rape	Forced vaginal, threat of force, unable to consent	Forced vaginal, anal, foreign object	Forced vaginal, oral, anal	Forced vaginal, oral, anal, digital, foreign object	Intercourse by threat or force	Vaginal, oral, anal, foreign object, physical force, psychological coercion, threat of rape	Forced intercourse against will; first intercourse if involuntary	Vaginal, anal, oral, foreign object

270

	Russell	Wyatt[a,b]	Kilpatrick et al.[c,d]	Kilpatrick et al., National Women's Study[e,f]	Kessler et al., National Comorbidity Survey[g]	National Crime Victimization Survey (NCVS)[h,i]	National Survey of Family Growth (NSFG)[i]	Tjaden & Thoennes, National Violence Against Women Survey (NVAW)[k]
	1	2	3	4	5	6	7	8
Researcher(s)/Study Name								
Number of screening questions	18	2	2	4	1	6	2	5
Context of questions	Crimes against women	Sexuality	Crime	Crime	Morbidity	Crime	Fertility, family planning, and women's health	Violence against women
Interviewers trained by	Study personnel	Study personnel	Louis Harris	Survey research firm	Survey research center	Census Bureau	Study personnel	Survey research firm
Matched for gender?	Yes	Yes	—	—	—	90%	Yes	Yes
Matched for ethnicity?	Tried	Yes	—	—	—	—	—	Yes for Spanish speakers
Duration of interview	70 mins	5-8 hrs	—	35 mins	>1 hour	—	1 hr 40 mins	25 mins
Age range of respondents (in years)	18+	18-36	18+	18+	15-54	12+	15-44	18+
Mean age of respondents (in years)	42.7	—	42.0	44.9	—	—	—	—

(continued)

271

TABLE A1.6.1 *(Continued)*

	1	2	3	4	5	6	7	8
Researcher(s)/ Study Name	Russell	Wyatt[a,b]	Kilpatrick et al.[c,d]	Kilpatrick et al., National Women's Study[e,f]	Kessler et al., National Comorbidity Survey[g]	National Crime Victimization Survey (NCVS)[h,i]	National Survey of Family Growth (NSFG)[i,j]	Tjaden & Thoennes, National Violence Against Women Survey (NVAW)[k]
Age range of victims	0+	0+	0+	0+	0+	12+	0+	0+
Race/ethnicity of respondents	67% White[3]	49% White	66% White	85% White	76% White[4]	84.5% White	71% White[5]	82% White[6]
	10% African American	51% African American	34% minority	12% minority	11% African American	12% African American	14% African American	10% African American
	7% Latina	—	—	—	9% Hispanic	—	11% Hispanic	—
	13% Asian American	—	—	—	—	—	—	2% Asian Pacific Islander
	1% Native American	—	—	—	—	—	—	1% American Indian/ Alaska Native
	3% Other	—	—	—	3% Other	3.5% Other	5% Other	5% Other
	1	2	3	4	5	6	7	8

Researcher(s)/ Study Name	1 Russell	2 Wyatt [a,b]	3 Kilpatrick et al. [c,d]	4 Kilpatrick et al., National Women's Study [e,f]	5 Kessler et al., National Comorbidity Survey [g]	6 National Crime Victimization Survey (NCVS) [h,i]	7 National Survey of Family Growth (NSFG) [i]	8 Tjaden & Thoennes, National Violence Against Women Survey (NVAW) [k]
Findings								
Number of victims of rape/attempted rape	407	55	179	507	281	—	about 2,213[8]	1,408 (17.6 × 8,000/100)[10]
Number of incidents of rape/attempted rape	780	146	—	714	—	300,810 (estimated by NCVS) about 122 (actual number)[9]	—	876,064
Mean number of rapes per rape victim	1.9	2.7	—	1.4	—	—	—	2.9 (for incidence)
Incidence rates for rape/attempted rape per 1,000 females	36.7	—	—	—	—	Completed 1.5; attempted 1.3; combined 2.7	—	Completed and attempted combined (extrapolated) 8.8
Prevalence completed rape	24%	—	5%	13%	9.2%	—	20.4%	15%
Prevalence attempted rape	31%[6]	—	4%	—	—	—	—	3%
Prevalence rapes combined	44%	22%	9%	—	—	—	—	18%

(continued)

TABLE A1.6.1 *(Continued)*

	1	2	3	4	5	6	7	8
Researcher(s)/ Study Name	Russell	Wyatt [a,b]	Kilpatrick et al. [c,d]	Kilpatrick et al., National Women's Study [e,f]	Kessler et al., National Comorbidity Survey [g]	National Crime Victimization Survey (NCVS) [h,i]	National Survey of Family Growth (NSFG) [j]	Tjaden & Thoennes, National Violence Against Women Survey (NVAW) [k]
Percentage of rapes that were completed	37%	—	56%	—	—	54%	—	84%
Reported to police:								
Percentage completed rape	13%	—	—	16%	—	36.0%	—	—
Percentage attempted rape	8%	—	—	—	—	19.6%	—	—
Percentage completed and attempted rape	9.5%	13.7%	—	—	—	28.3%	—	—

SOURCES: a. Wyatt, 1985
         b. Wyatt, 1992
         c. Kilpatrick & Amick, 1984
         d. Kilpatrick, Best, Veronen, Amick, Villeponteaux, & Ruff, 1985
         e. Kilpatrick, Edmunds, & Seymour, 1992
         f. Resnick, Kilpatrick, Dansky, Saunders, & Best, 1993.
         g. Kessler, Sonnega, Bromet, & Hughes, 1995.
         h. Bureau of Justice Statistics, 1996.

i. Bureau of Justice Statistics, 1997.

j. Abma, Chandra, Mosher, Peterson, & Piccinino, NSFG, 1997.

k. Tjaden & Thoennes, 1998b.

NOTES:

1. Participation rates without parentheses indicate that this is the rate the researcher deems most appropriate.

2. For our evaluation of the validity of Wyatt's participation rates, see Chapter 6.

3. The overall participation rate was calculated by multiplying the household participation rate (95.1%) by the individual participation rate (92.0%).

4. These totals do not add to 100% due to rounding.

5. These percentages were calculated from the numbers in Abma et al. 1997, Table 21, p. 32.

6. These percentages were calculated from numbers provided in Tjaden & Thoennes, 1998b, Exhibit 4.

7. Twenty percent of Russell's sample were victims of one or more attempted rapes who had never been victimized by completed rape.

8. This figure was calculated by multiplying the prevalence rate (20.4%) by the number of respondents (10,847), yielding an estimate of 2,213 (Abma et al., 1997).

9. Based on only 122 incidents of completed rapes and attempted rapes in the prior 12 months; this 122 figure was calculated by multiplying the number of female respondents by the 1994 NCVS rape incidence rate of 2.7 per 1,000 females, that is, 45,280 × 2.7/1,000.

10. This figure was calculated as follows: (17.6× 8,000/100) = 1,408 (Tjaden & Thoennes, 1998b, p. 3).

— means no information

275

TABLE A1.8.1 FBI Statistics on Reported Crime: Murder, Aggravated Assault, Forcible Rape, and Unfounded Rates: 1932-1997

Year	Murder Rate Per 100,000 Inhabitants	Aggravated Assault Rate Per 100,000 Inhabitants	Forcible Rape Rate Per 100,000 Females[1]	Unfounded Rate for Forcible Rape (Percentage)	Unfounded Rate for Other Index Crimes (Percentage)
1997	6.8	382.0	70	8	2
1996	7.4	390.9[2]	71	8	2
1995	8.2	418.3	72	8	2
1994	9.0	430.2	77	8	2
1993	9.5	440.3	79	8	2
1992	9.3	441.8	84	8	2
1991	9.8	433.3	83	8	2
1990	9.4	424.1	80	9[3]	2[3]
1989	8.7	383.4	75	8[3]	2[3]
1988	8.4	370.2	73	9[3]	3[3]
1987	8.3	351.3	73	9[3]	3[3]
1986	8.6	346.1	73	9[3]	3[3]
1985	7.9	302.9	71	n/a[4]	n/a
1984	7.9	290.2	69	9[3]	3[3]
1983	8.3	273.3	66	10[3]	3[3]
1982	9.1	280.8	65	n/a	n/a
1981	9.8	280.9	69	n/a	n/a
1980	10.2	290.6	71	n/a	n/a
1979	9.7	279.1	67	n/a	n/a
1978	9.0	255.9	60	n/a	n/a
1977	8.8	241.5	57	n/a	n/a
1976	8.8	228.7	52	19	n/a
1975	9.6	227.4	51	15	4
1974	9.7	214.2	51	15	4
1973	9.3	198.4	47	15	4
1972	8.9	186.6	43	15	4
1971	8.5	176.8	40	18	4
1970	7.8	162.4	36	18	3
1969	7.2	151.8	35	18	n/a
1968	6.8	141.3	30	18	3
1967	6.1	128.0	27	18	3
1966	5.6	118.4	25	20	n/a
1965	5.1	106.6	23	n/a	n/a
1964	4.8	96.6	21	n/a	n/a
1963	4.5	78.4	17	n/a	n/a
1962	4.5	75.1	18	n/a	n/a
1961	4.7	72.7	18	n/a	n/a

(Continued)

TABLE A1.8.1 *(Continued)*

Year	Murder Rate Per 100,000 Inhabitants	Aggravated Assault Rate Per 100,000 Inhabitants	Forcible Rape Rate Per 100,000 Females[1]	Unfounded Rate for Forcible Rape (Percentage)	Unfounded Rate for Other Index Crimes (Percentage)
1960	5.1	72.6	17	n/a	n/a
1959	4.8	67.3	17	n/a	n/a
1958	4.7	65.5	17	n/a	n/a
1957	4.7	65.0	15	n/a	n/a
1956	5.0	87.4	29	n/a	n/a
1955	4.7	84.3	26	n/a	n/a
1954	4.8	85.0	24	n/a	n/a
1953	4.8	84.6	23	n/a	n/a
1952	5.0	81.5	23	n/a	n/a
1951	4.9	70.5	22	n/a	n/a
1950	5.1	73.4	22	n/a	n/a
1949	5.8	82.6	25	n/a	n/a
1948	6.0	75.8	25	n/a	n/a
1947	6.1	72.2	25	n/a	n/a
1946	6.5	67.5	24	n/a	n/a
1945	5.5	59.8	23	n/a	n/a
1944	4.9	54.8	22	n/a	n/a
1943	4.8	49.7	21	n/a	n/a
1942	5.5	52.1	20	n/a	n/a
1941	5.5	48.4	18	n/a	n/a
1940	5.4	45.8	18	n/a	n/a
1939	5.4	46.5	18	n/a	n/a
1938	5.3	44.5	17	n/a	n/a
1937	6.1	45.5	17	n/a	n/a
1936	6.2	46.2	16	n/a	n/a
1935	6.0	45.7	14	n/a	n/a
1934	6.7	49.4	13	n/a	n/a
1933	7.1	50.7	12	n/a	n/a
1932	7.0	45.9	12	n/a	n/a

SOURCE: FBI, *Uniform Crime Reports,* 1932-1997.

NOTES: 1. The forcible rape rates per 100,000 females were not reported from 1932 to 1963. For the years prior to 1964, the forcible rape rates per 100,000 females were calculated by multiplying by 2 the rates per 100,000 inhabitants, then rounding to the closest whole number.

2. This number was recorded as 388.2 in the UCR for 1996 and 390.9 in the UCR for 1987. Presumably, the more recent figure is more likely to be correct.

3. These unfounded rates were obtained from the FBI Uniform Crime Program database by the Information Specialist (names are not disclosed) at the Programs Support Section, Criminal Justice Information Service Division on 7/17/1997. For reasons unknown, they were not included in the annual reports for those years.

4. n/a = information not available

TABLE A1.8.2ª National Crime Surveys' Completed and/or Attempted Rape Victimization Rates for Females Aged 12 and Older: 1973-1995

Year	Number of Female Rape Victimizations (Estimated)	Rate of Female Rape Victimizations per 1,000 Females	Number of Females in U.S. Population	Adjusted Rate of Female Rape Victimizations per 1,000 Females[1]
1973	151,700	1.8	85,758,100	3.8
1974	159,400	1.8	87,094,200	4.0
1975	146,400	1.7	88,438,700	3.6
1976	129,300	1.4	89,572,400	3.3
1977	141,900	1.6	90,696,000	3.5
1978	153,000	1.7	91,837,900	4.0
1979	171,200	1.8	92,931,000	4.3
1980	151,400	1.6	96,135,600	3.8
1981	169,700	1.8	97,226,800	3.8
1982	140,500	1.4	98,284,800	3.2
1983	137,900	1.4	99,277,500	3.2
1984	164,480	1.6	100,031,350	3.8
1985	130,850	1.3	101,079,810	2.9
1986	122,200	1.2	102,054,010	2.6
1987	134,300	1.3	102,783,130	3.0
1988	119,780	1.2	103,606,290	2.6
1989	122,740	1.2	104,499,700	2.7
1990	106,660	1.0	105,437,010	2.6
1991	153,120	1.4	106,111,090	3.3
1992	83,080	0.8	107,150,610	2.7
1992/1993ᵇ		2.9		2.3
1994ᶜ		2.7		2.3
1995				1.7

SOURCES: a. Table 6 (modified from the original), BJS, 1994, p. 19.
b. Table 7, BJS, 1995.
c. Table 2, BJS, 1997, p. 7.

NOTE: 1. The NCVS adjusted these figures to make data comparable to data after the redesign. The NCS originally reported these figures as rates per 1,000 population, which included both males and females. In order to report the rates per 1,000 females, the NCS data were adjusted based on the estimate that 52% of the U.S. population in any given year were female.

TABLE A1.8.3 Raw Data for Figure 8.3: Cumulative Percentages of Five Cohorts of San Francisco Women Reporting Their First Experience of Completed and/or Attempted Rape in Russell's Survey in 1978

Years	Cohort 1 60+	Cohort 2 50 - 59	Cohort 3 40 - 49	Cohort 4 30 - 39	Cohort 5 18 - 29
Age Range at 1st Experience of Rape			*Percents*		
0 - 4	0.00	0.00	0.00	0.51	0.00
5 - 9	0.46	1.94	1.98	1.52	1.94
10 - 14	4.59	6.80	8.91	7.07	10.32
15 - 19	11.93	18.45	24.75	26.26	32.58
20 - 24	16.06	26.21	33.66	45.96	47.42
25 - 29	17.89	29.13	38.61	55.05	49.35
30 - 34	20.18	30.10	41.58	58.59	
35 - 39	21.56	32.04	43.56	58.59	
40 - 44	21.56	33.98	44.55		
45+	25.23	34.95	46.53		

Appendix 2:
Tables About Child Sexual Abuse

TABLE A2.12.1 Comparison of Nine Representative Sample Surveys of Child Sexual Abuse/Assault: Methodology and Findings

	1	2	3	4	5	6	7	8	9
Researcher/ Study Name	Russell	Kercher & McShane[a]	Wyatt[b,c]	Kilpatrick et al.[d,e]	Siegel et al.[f]	Lewis, L.A. Times Poll[g]	Murphy[h]	Kessler et al., National Comorbidity Survey[i]	Gallup Poll[j,k]
Date of fieldwork	1978	1980	1981-1984	1983	1983-1984	1985	ca. 1989-1990	1990-1992	1995
Publication date	1983, 1984	1984	1985	1985	1987	1990	1991	1995	1996
Funder/ sponsoring agency	NIMH grant	Criminal Justice Center, Sam Houston State University	NIMH grant	NIMH grant	Epidemiologic Catchment Area Program and NIMH	L.A. Times Poll	—	Institute of Social Research, University of Michigan	The Gallup Organization
Location of study	San Francisco	Texas	Los Angeles County	Charleston County, South Carolina	Los Angeles	National	Minnesota	National	National

(continued)

TABLE A2.12.1 *(Continued)*

	1	2	3	4	5	6	7	8	9
Researcher/ Study Name	Russell	Kercher & McShane[a]	Wyatt[b,c]	Kilpatrick et al.[d,e]	Siegel et al.[f]	Lewis, L.A. Times Poll[g]	Murphy[h]	Kessler et al., National Comorbidity Survey[i]	Gallup Poll[j,k]
Methodology									
Sample size (females only)	930	593	248	2,004	1,645	1,481	777 (males & females)	3,065	1,000 (men & women parents)
Sampling method	Probability sample	Random, from list of Texas drivers' licenses	Random-digit dialing sample	Random-digit dialing sample	Stratified probability household sample	Random telephone sample	Random-digit dialing sample	Probability sample undermined by subsample methodology	Random-digit dialing sample
Participation rate	(81%) 64%[1] (50%)	49% to 56%	(73%) 67%[2] (55%)	84% 78%	68% for household(s); no information for individuals	76%	65% (males & females)[3]	82% for sample 99%, 98%, 99% for 3 subsamples	57%
Method of data collection	In-person interviews	Self-administered questionnaires	In-person interviews	Telephone interviews	In-person interviews	Telephone interviews	Telephone interviews	In-person interviews	Telephone interviews

Researcher/ Study Name	Russell	Kercher & McShane[a]	Wyatt[b,c]	Kilpatrick et al.[d,e]	Siegel et al.[f]	Lewis, L.A. Times Poll[g]	Murphy[h]	Kessler et al., National Comorbidity Survey[i]	Gallup Poll[j,k]
	1	2	3	4	5	6	7	8	9
Definition: Sex acts	Range from attempted sexual contact to rape	Range from porn photographing to rape and prostitution	Range from non-body contact (e.g., solicitation) to intercourse	Range from serious sexual advances but no sex activity, to forced sex *excluding* all types of rape	Range from touching sexual parts to intercourse	Range from sex exploitation to sodomy	Range from exposure to intercourse	Touched genitals	Range from touching in sexual way to forced intercourse
Number of screening questions	14	1	8	1	1	4	6	1	4
Context of questions	Rape and child sexual abuse (csa)	Csa	Csa	Crime	Mental health	Csa	Csa and adult abuse experiences	Mental disorders	Disciplining children
Interviewer training	Yes	—	Yes	Probably not	Probably not	Probably not	Probably not	Probably not	Probably not
Matched for gender?	Yes	—	Yes	Yes	No	No	—	—	No
Matched for ethnicity?	Most times	—	Yes	—	Probably	—	—	—	—

(continued)

TABLE A2.12.1 *(Continued)*

Researcher/ Study Name	Russell	Kercher/ McShane[a]	Wyatt[b,c]	Kilpatrick et al.[d,e]	Siegel et al.[f]	Lewis, L.A. Times Poll[g]	Murphy[h]	Kessler et al., National Comorbidity Survey[i]	Gallup Poll[i]
	1	2	3	4	5	6	7	8	9
Duration of interview	1 hr 10 mins	—	3-8 hrs	—	—	30 mins	10-15 mins	> 1 hour	—
Age range of respondents	18+	Age can get driver's license	18-36	18+	18-40+	18+	18+	15-54	—
Mean age of respondents	36	—	—	42.0	41	—	—	—	—
Age range of victims	17 and under	17 and under	17 and under	—	15 and under	18 and under	17 and under	—	17 and under
Race/Ethnicity of respondents	67% White[4] 10% African American 7% Latina 13% Asian American 1% Native American 3% Other	85% White 5% African American 9% Latina	49% White 51% African American	66% White 34% African American	41% White — 47% Latina 12% Other	—	—	76% White[4] 11% African American 9% Hispanic	— — — 3% Other

284

Researcher/ Study Name	Russell	Kercher/ McShane[a]	Wyatt[b,c]	Kilpatrick et al.[d,e]	Siegel et al.[f]	Lewis, L.A. Times Poll[g]	Murphy[h]	Kessler et al., National Comorbidity Survey[i]	Gallup Poll[j]
Findings									
Number of csa victims	357	65	154	92	112	416	—	376	—
Prevalence of incestuous abuse	16%	—	21% contact, 23% non-contact	1%	—	8%	—	—	—
Prevalence of extrafamilial csa	31%	—	32%	5%	—	—	—	—	—
Prevalence of all csa experiences	38% (54% for broad definition)	11%	62% (contact & noncontact), 45% (contact)	6%	7%	27%	18%	12%	6% children, 30% mothers
Gender of perpetrator	96% male	—	98% male	—	—	98% male	—	—	—

(continued)

285

TABLE A2.12.1 *(Continued)*

SOURCES:
a. Kercher & McShane, 1984
b. Wyatt, 1985
c. Wyatt, Newcomb, & Notgrass, 1991
d. Kilpatrick, Best, Veronen, Amick, Villeponteaux, & Ruff, 1985
e. Kilpatrick, Edmunds, & Seymour, 1992
f. Siegel, Sorenson, Golding, Burnam, & Stein, 1987
g. Finkelhor, Hotaling, Lewis, & Smith, 1990
h. Murphy, 1991
i. Abma, Chandra, Mosher, Peterson, & Piccinino, NSFG, 1997
j. Finkelhor, Moore, Hamby, Straus, 197
k. Moore, Gallup, & Schussel, 1995

NOTES:
1. Participation rates without parentheses indicate that this is the rate the researcher deems most appropriate.
2. For our evaluation of the validity of Wyatt's participation rate, see Chapter 6.
3. Since 3% of the respondents failed to answer the questions on child sexual abuse, the participation rate for the relevant questions on child sexual abuse is 63%: $777 \times 97\% = 754$; $y\%$ of $1,195 = 754$; $y = 63\%$.
4. These totals do not add up to 100% due to rounding.

TABLE A2.15.1 Hazard Rate[1] for Ages of First and Last Completed and/or Attempted Rape for Respondents in Russell's Sample

	Hazard Rate	
	Age First Rape	*Age Last Rape*
0	0.0000	0.0000
1	0.0000	0.0000
2	0.0011	0.0000
3	0.0000	0.0000
4	0.0000	0.0000
5	0.0022	0.0000
6	0.0011	0.0011
7	0.0033	0.0011
8	0.0011	0.0000
9	0.0077	0.0032
10	0.0044	0.0022
11	0.0033	0.0000
12	0.0134	0.0054
13	0.0320	0.0077
14	0.0141	0.0099
15	0.0299	0.0145
16	0.0198	0.0251
17	0.0338	0.0245
18	0.0447	0.0277
19	0.0371	0.0339
20	0.0483	0.0395
21	0.0367	0.0318
22	0.0335	0.0422
23	0.0407	0.0368
24	0.0227	0.0278
25	0.0325	0.0457
26	0.0151	0.0437
27	0.0136	0.0141
28	0.0095	0.0233
29	0.0050	0.0179
30	0.0129	0.0258
31	0.0027	0.0172

(continued)

TABLE A2.15.1 (Continued)

	Hazard Rate	
	Age First Rape	*Age Last Rape*
32	0.0164	0.0204
33	0.0028	0.0079
34	0.0118	0.0221
35	0.0092	0.0087
36	0.0032	0.0060
37	0.0033	0.0093
38	0.0067	0.0063
39	0.0000	0.0032
40	0.0000	0.0099
41	0.0035	0.0000
42	0.0036	0.0068
43	0.0000	0.0000
44	0.0037	0.0107
45	0.0000	0.0148
46	0.0000	0.0000
47	0.0000	0.0078
48	0.0000	0.0000
49	0.0000	0.0041
50	0.0044	0.0043
51	0.0000	0.0000
52	0.0000	0.0000
53	0.0047	0.0046
54	0.0000	0.0000
55	0.0000	0.0049
56	0.0000	0.0000
57	0.0055	0.0053
58[2]	0.0000	0.0000

NOTES: 1. The hazard rate for first rape is computed by dividing the number of women who experienced their first rape at a given age by all women at risk to be raped. Women are only classified as being at risk to be raped for the first time if they have never been raped previously (and for the last time, if they have not yet experienced their last rape), and if they are old enough to be included in the calculations for that age. For example, 18-year-olds who have never been raped can be considered to be at risk for rape only up to the age of 18.

2. All hazard rates for first and last rapes beyond the age of 58 were 0.0000.

References

Abma, Joyce, Anjani Chandra, William Mosher, Linda Peterson, & Linda Piccinino. (1997). Fertility, family planning, and women's health: New data from the 1995 National Survey of Family Growth. National Center for Health Statistics. *Vital and Health Statistics, 23*(19).

Allen, Kathleen. (1997, April 17). Lower United States rape stats "misleading." *Tucson Citizen,* pp. C1, C9.

The American heritage dictionary of the English language. (1992). New York: Houghton Mifflin. Third edition.

Amir, Menachem. (1971). *Patterns in forcible rape.* Chicago: University of Chicago Press.

Armstrong, Louise. (1994). *Rocking the cradle of sexual politics.* New York: Addison-Wesley.

Bachman, Ronet, & Linda E. Saltzman. (1995). *Violence against women: Estimates from the redesigned survey* (NCJ 154348). Washington, DC: U.S. Department of Justice, Bureau of Justice Statistics.

Bachman, Ronet, & Bruce M. Taylor. (1994). Violence and rape by the redesigned National Crime Victimization Survey. *Justice Quarterly, 11*(3), 499-512.

Ballard, David T., Gary D. Blair, Sterling Devereaux, Logan K. Valentine, Anne L. Horton, & Barry L. Johnson. (1990). A comparative profile of the incest perpetrator: Background characteristics, abuse history and use of social skills. In Anne L. Horton, Barry L. Johnson, Lynn M. Roundy, & D. Williams (Eds.), *The incest perpetrator: A family member no one wants to treat* (pp. 43-64). Newbury Park, CA: Sage.

Bass, Ellen, & Laura Davis. (1988). *The courage to heal: A guide for women survivors of child sexual abuse.* New York: Harper & Row.

Besharov, Douglas J. (1994). Responding to child sexual abuse: The need for a balanced approach. *The Future of Children* (Center for the Future of Children), *4*(2), 135-155.

Bessera, Sarah, Nancy Jewel, & Melody Matthews. (1973). *Public Education and Research Committee of California. Sex code of California: A compendium.* Sausalito, CA: Graphic Arts of Marin.

Best, Joel. (1990). *Threatened children: Rhetoric and concern about child-victims.* Chicago: University of Chicago Press.

Biderman, Albert D., & James P. Lynch. (1991). *Understanding crime incidence statistics: Why the UCR diverges from the NCS.* New York: Springer.

Bolen, Rebecca M., & Maria Scannapieco. (1999, September). Prevalence of child sexual abuse: A corrective metanalysis. *Social Service Review, 73*(3), 281-313.

Bonilla, Margaret. (1993, Fall). Cultural assault: What feminists are doing to rape ought to be a crime. *Policy Review, 66,* 22-29.

Bovsun, Mara. (1997, June 5). One in five women forced to have sex. *United Press International,* p. 1.

Boyle, John. (1992, November). *National Women's Study: Final report on study methodology.* Unpublished report, not for citation without permission.

Bradshaw, Tausha L., & Alan E. Marks. (1990). Beyond a reasonable doubt: Factors that influence the legal disposition of child sexual abuse cases. *Crime and Delinquency, 36*(2), 276-285.

Breslau, Naomi, Glenn Davis, Patricia Andreski, Belle Federman, & James Anthony. (1991). Traumatic events and posttraumatic stress disorder in an urban population of young adults. *Archives of General Psychiatry, 48,* 216-222.

Briere, John, & Neil Malamuth. (1983). Self-reported likelihood of sexually aggressive behavior: Attitudinal versus sexual explanations. *Journal of Research in Personality, 17,* 315-323.

Briere, John, & Marsha Runtz. (1989). University males' sexual interest in children: Predicting potential indices of "pedophilia" in a nonforensic sample. *Child Abuse & Neglect, 13,* 65-75.

Bureau of Justice Statistics. (1994, July). *Criminal victimization in the United States: 1973-1992 trends: A National Crime Victimization Survey report* (NCJ-147006). Washington, DC: Government Printing Office.

Bureau of Justice Statistics. National Crime Victimization Survey crime trends, 1973-1997 and midyear 1998 [On-line]. [Retrieved March 2, 1999]. Available: http://www.ojp.usdoj.gov/bjs/glance/viotrd.tx

Bureau of Justice Statistics. (1995, August). *Special report: Violence against women: Estimates from the Redesigned Survey* (NCJ-154348). Washington, DC: Government Printing Office.

Bureau of Justice Statistics. (1996, May). *Criminal victimization in the United States, 1993: A National Crime Victimization Survey report* (NCJ-151657). Washington, DC: Government Printing Office.

Bureau of Justice Statistics. (1997, May). *Criminal victimization in the United States, 1994: A National Crime Victimization Survey report* (NCJ-162126). Washington, DC: Government Printing Office.

Bureau of Justice Statistics. (1998, April). National Incident-Based Reporting System (NIBRS) [On-line]. [Retrieved September 3, 1998]. Available: http://www.ojp.usdoj.gov/bjs/nibrs.htm

Burt, Martha R. (1980). Cultural myths and support for rape. *Journal of Personality and Social Psychology, 38,* 217-230.

Butterfield, Fox. (1997, February 3). '95 data show sharp drop in reported rapes. *New York Times,* Late Edition, pp. A1, A14.

Daro, Deborah. (1995). Current trends in child abuse reporting and fatalities: NCPCAs 1994 Annual Fifty State Survey. *The APSAC Advisor, 8,* 5-6.

De Jong, Allan R. (1988). Maternal responses to the sexual abuse of their children. *Pediatrics, 81,* 14-21.

Dietz, Christine A., & John L. Craft. (1980). Family dynamics of incest: A new perspective. *Social Casework, 61*(10), 602-609.

Draijer, Nel. (1990). *Seksuele traumatisering in de jeugd: Lange termijn gevolgen van seksueel misbruik van meisjes door verwanten.* Amsterdam: Uitgeverij Sua Amsterdam.

Eigenberg, Helen M. (1990). The National Crime Survey and rape: The case of the missing question. *Justice Quarterly, 7*(4), 655-671.

Ennis, Philip H. (1967). *Criminal victimization in the United States: A report of a national survey* (National Opinion Research Center, University of Chicago). Washington, DC: Government Printing Office.

Everson, Mark D., Wanda M. Hunter, Desmond K. Runyon, Gail A. Edelsohn, & Martha L. Coulter. (1990). Maternal support following disclosure of incest. *American Journal of Orthopsychiatry, 59,* 197-207.

Faller, Kathleen C. (1984). Is the child victim of sexual abuse telling the truth? *Child Abuse & Neglect, 8,* 474-481.

Faller, Kathleen C. (1990). Sexual abuse by paternal caretakers: A comparison of abusers who are biological fathers in intact families, stepfamilies and noncustodial families. In Anne L. Horton, Barry L. Johnson, Lynn M. Roundy, & Doran Williams (Eds.), *The incest perpetrator: A family member no one wants to treat* (pp. 65-73). Newbury Park, CA: Sage.

Farrell, Lynda T. (1988). Factors that affect a victim's self-disclosure in father-daughter incest. *Child Welfare, 67,* 462-468.

Fazlollah, Mark, Craig McCoy, & Robert Moran. (2000, March 21). Timoney to allow sex-case oversight. *The Philadelphia Inquirer,* p. A9.

Federal Bureau of Investigation. (1932-1998). *Uniform crime reports for the United States.* Washington, DC: Government Printing Office.

Federal Bureau of Investigation. (1984). *Uniform crime reporting handbook.* Washington, DC: U.S. Department of Justice, Federal Bureau of Investigation.

Federal Bureau of Investigation. (1998, April). *Implementing the National Incident-Based Reporting System* [On-line]. [Retrieved September 3, 1998]. Available: http://www.nibrs.search.org/frmain.htm

Finkelhor, David. (1979). *Sexually victimized children.* New York: Free Press.

Finkelhor, David. (1983). Removing the child—prosecuting the offender in cases of child sexual abuse: Evidence from the National Reporting System for Child Abuse and Neglect. *Child Abuse & Neglect, 7,* 195-205.

Finkelhor, David. (1984). Child sexual abuse in a sample of Boston families. In David Finkelhor, *Child sexual abuse: New theory and research* (pp. 69-86). New York: Free Press.

Finkelhor, David. (1994). Current information on the scope and nature of child sexual abuse. *The Future of Children* (Center for the Future of Children), *4*(2), 31-53.

Finkelhor, David, & Gerald T. Hotaling. (1984). Sexual abuse in the national incidence study of child abuse and neglect: An appraisal. *Child Abuse & Neglect, 8,* 22-33.

Finkelhor, David, Gerald T. Hotaling, I. A. Lewis, & Christine Smith. (1990). Sexual abuse in a national survey of adult men and women: Prevalence, characteristics, and risk factors. *Child Abuse & Neglect, 14,* 19-28.

Finkelhor, David, David Moore, Sherry L. Hamby, & Murray Straus. (1997). Sexually abused children in a national survey of parents: Methodological issues. *Child Abuse & Neglect, 21*(1), 1-9.

Fox, Richard. (1991, September 5). The truth about date rape: Radical feminist ideology encourages sexual assaults. *Daily Journal.*

Fuentes, Annette. (1997, November/December). Crime rates are down . . . but what about rape? *Ms., 8*(3), 19-22.

Gagnon, John. (1965). Female child victims of sex offenses. *Social Problems, 13,* 176-192.

George, Linda, & Idee Winfield-Laird. (1986). *Sexual assault: Prevalence and mental health consequences.* Unpublished final report submitted to the National Institute of Mental Health.

George, Linda K., Idee Winfield, & Dan G. Blazer. (1992). Sociocultural factors in sexual assault: Comparison of two representative samples of women. *Journal of Social Issues, 48*(1), 105-125.

Giarretto, Henry. (1982). A comprehensive child sexual abuse treatment program. *Child Abuse & Neglect, 5,* 263-278.

Giarretto, Henry. (1989). Community based treatment of the incest family. *Psychiatric Clinics of North America, 12,* 351-361.

Gilbert, Neil. (1991a, June 27). The campus rape scare. *Wall Street Journal,* p. A14.

Gilbert, Neil. (1991b, July 17). The phantom date rape epidemic: How radical feminists manipulated data to exaggerate the problem. *San Francisco Daily Journal.*

Gilbert, Neil. (1991c). The phantom epidemic of sexual assault. *Public Interest, 103,* 54-65.

Gilbert, Neil. (1993, June 29). The wrong response to rape. *Wall Street Journal,* p. A18.

Gilbert, Neil. (1994a, March/April). Miscounting social ills. *Society, 31*(3), 18-26.

Gilbert, Neil. (1994b, September/October). Was it rape? An examination of sexual abuse statistics. *The American Enterprise, 5*(5), 68-77.

Gilbert, Neil. (1995). *Was it rape? An examination of sexual assault statistics.* Menlo Park, CA: Henry J. Kaiser Family Foundation.

Gilbert, Neil. (1997). Advocacy research and social policy. In Michael Tonry (Ed.), *Crime and justice: A review of research* (pp. 101-148). Chicago: University of Chicago Press.

Gilbert, Neil. (1998, January/February). Realities and mythologies of rape. *Society, 35*(2), 356-362.

Gomes-Schwartz, Beverly, Jonathan M. Horowitz, & Albert P. Cardarelli. (1990). *Child sexual abuse: The initial effects.* Newbury Park, CA: Sage.

Goodchilds, Jacqueline, & Gail Zellman. (1984). Sexual signaling and sexual aggression in adolescent relationships. In Neil Malamuth & Edward Donnerstein (Eds.), *Pornography and sexual aggression* (pp. 233-243). New York: Academic Press.

Gordon, Margaret T., & Stephanie Riger. (1989). *The female fear: The social cost of rape.* Chicago: University of Illinois Press.

Gorey, Kevin M., & Donald R. Leslie. (1997). The prevalence of child sexual abuse: Integrative review adjustment for potential response and measurement biases. *Child Abuse & Neglect, 21*(4), 391-398.

Greenfeld, Lawrence A. (1997, February). *Sex offenses and offenders: An analysis of data on rape and sexual assault* (NCJ-163392). Washington, DC: Government Printing Office.

Haugaard, Jeffrey J., & N. Dickon Reppucci. (1988). *The sexual abuse of children: A comprehensive guide to current knowledge and intervention strategies.* San Francisco: Jossey-Bass.

Herman, Judith. (1981). *Father-daughter incest.* Cambridge, MA: Harvard University Press.

Hunter, Wanda A., Martha L. Coulter, Desmond K. Runyon, & Mark D. Everson. (1990). Determinants of placement for sexually abused children. *Child Abuse & Neglect, 14,* 407-417.

Jaudes, Paula K., & Martha Morris. (1990). Child sexual abuse: Who goes home. *Child Abuse & Neglect, 14,* 61-68.

Kamen, Paula. (1993, November/December). Erasing rape: Media hype an attack on sexual-assault research. *Extra!,* pp. 10-11.

Kangspunta, Kristina, Matti Joutsen, & Natalia Ollus. (Eds.), *Crime and criminal justice in Eruope and North America, 1990–1994.* Helsinki: European Institute for Crime Prevention and Control, affiliated with the United Nations (HEUNI).

Kanin, Eugene J. (1957). Male aggression in dating-courtship relations. *The American Journal of Sociology, 63*(2), 197-204.

Kanin, Eugene J. (1970). Sex aggression by college men. *Medical Aspects of Human Sexuality, 4*(9), 27-40.

Kanin, Eugene J. (1971). Sexually aggressive college males. *Journal of College Student Personnel, 12,* 107-110.

Kanin, Eugene J., & Stanley R. Parcell. (1977). Sexual aggression: A second look at the offended female. *Archives of Sexual Behavior, 6*(1), 67-76.

Kelley, Susan J. (1990). Responsibility and management strategies in child sexual abuse: A comparison of child protective workers, nurses, and police officers. *Child Welfare, 69,* 43-51.

Kelly, Liz. (1988). *Surviving sexual violence.* Cambridge, England: Polity Press.

Kercher, Glen A., & Marilyn McShane. (1984). The prevalence of child sexual abuse victimization in an adult sample of Texas residents. *Child Abuse & Neglect, 8,* 495-501.

Kessler, Ronald, Amanda Sonnega, Evelyn Bromet, & Michael Hughes. (1995). Posttraumatic stress disorder in the National Comorbidity Survey. *Archives of General Psychiatry, 52,* 1048-1060.

Kilpatrick, Dean G., & Angelynne E. Amick. (1984). *Intrafamilial and extrafamilial sexual assault: Results of a random survey.* Paper presented at the Second National Family Violence Research Conference.

Kilpatrick, Dean G., Connie L. Best, Lois J. Veronen, Angelynne E. Amick, Lorenz A. Villeponteaux, & Gary A. Ruff. (1985). Mental health correlates of criminal victimization: A random community survey. *Journal of Consulting and Clinical Psychology, 53*(6), 866-873.

Kilpatrick, Dean G., Christine N. Edmunds, & Anne Seymour. (1992). *Rape in America: A report to the nation.* National Victim Center, Arlington, VA, and Crime Victims Research and Treatment Center, Charleston, SC.

Kilpatrick, Dean G., Heidi S. Resnick, Benjamin E. Saunders, & Connie Best. (1998). Rape, other violence against women, and post-traumatic stress disorder. In Bruce Dohrenwend (Ed.), *Adversity, stress, and psychopathology* (pp. 161-176). New York: Oxford University Press.

Kilpatrick, Dean G., Benjamin E. Saunders, Lois J. Veronen, Connie L. Best, & Judith M. Von. (1987). Criminal victimization: Lifetime prevalence, reporting to police, and psychological impact. *Crime and Delinquency, 33*(4), 479-489.

Kinsey, Alfred C., Wardell B. Pomeroy, Clyde E. Martin, & Paul H. Hebhard. (1953). *Sexual behavior in the human female.* Philadelphia: W. B. Saunders.

Kirkpatrick, Clifford, & Eugene J. Kanin. (1957). Male sex aggression on a university campus. *American Sociological Review, 22,* 52-58.

Kocen, Lynne, & Josephine Bulkley. (1985). Analysis of criminal child sex abuse statutes. In Josephine Bulkley (Ed.), *Child sexual abuse and the law: A report of the American Bar Association* (5th ed., pp. 1-20). Washington, DC: American Bar Association.

Koss, Mary P. (1992). The underdetection of rape: Methodological choices that influence the magnitude of incidence estimates. *Journal of Social Issues, 48*(1), 61-75.

Koss, Mary P. (1996). The measurement of rape victimization in crime surveys. *Criminal Justice and Behavior, 23*(1), 55-69.

Koss, Mary P., Christine A. Gidycz, & Nadine Wisniewski. (1987). The scope of rape: Incidence and prevalence of sexual aggression and victimization in a national sample of higher education students. *Journal of Consulting and Clinical Psychology,* *55*(2), 162-170.

Koss, Mary P., & Mary R. Harvey. (1991). *The rape victim: Clinical and community interventions* (2nd ed.). Newbury Park, CA: Sage.

Koss, Mary P., Lori Heise, & Nancy Russo. (1994). The global health burden of rape. *Psychology of Women Quarterly, 18,* 509-537.

Landis, Judson T. (1956). Experiences of 500 children with adult sexual deviance. *Psychiatric Quarterly Supplement, 30,* 91-109.

Largo, Tom, et al. (1999). *1996 survey of violence against women in Michigan.* Unpublished manuscript.

Law Enforcement Assistance Administration. (1975, June). *Criminal victimization surveys in 13 American cities.* Washington, DC: Government Printing Office, LEAA.

Leventhal, John M. (1990). Epidemiology of child sexual abuse. In R. Kim Oates (Ed.), *Understanding and managing child sexual abuse* (pp. 18-41). London: W. B. Saunders.

Lyon, Elanor, & Katherine Kouloumpos-Lenares. (1987). Clinician and state children's services worker collaboration in treating sexual abuse. *Child Welfare, 66,* 517-527.

MacDonald, John M. (1971). *Rape: Offenders and their victims.* Springfield, IL: Charles C Thomas.

Malamuth, Neil M. (1981). Rape proclivity among males. *Journal of Social Issues, 37,* 138-157.

Malamuth, Neil M. (1984). Aggression against women: Cultural and individual causes. In Neil M. Malamuth & Edward Donnerstein (Eds.), *Pornography and sexual aggression* (pp. 19-52). New York: Academic Press.

Malamuth, Neil M. (1986). Predictors of naturalistic sexual aggression. *Journal of Personality and Social Psychology, 48,* 953-962.

Margolin, Leslie. (1992). Sexual abuse by grandparents. *Child Abuse & Neglect, 16,* 735-741.

McCarten, Kim. (Ed.). (2000, April 17). *Merge* [On-line feminist magazine]. Personal communication. Available E-mail: Mergemag@scn.org.

Michael, Robert, John Gagnon, Edward Lauman, & Gina Kolata. (1994). *Sex in America: A definitive survey.* New York: Warner Books.

Monto, Martin, & Norma Hotaling. (1998). *Predictors of rape myth acceptance among the male clients of female street prostitutes.* Unpublished manuscript.

Moore, David W., George H. Gallup, & Robert Schussel. (1995, December). *Disciplining children in America: A Gallup Poll report.* Unpublished report. Princeton, NJ: Gallup Organization.

Muehlenhard, Charlene L., Barrie J. Highby, Joi L. Phelps, & Susie C. Sympson. (1997). No, rape statistics are not exaggerated. In Mary Roth Walsh (Ed.), *Women, men, and gender: Ongoing debates* (pp. 243-252). New Haven, CT: Yale University Press.

Murphy, John E. (1991). An investigation of child sexual abuse and consequent victimization: Some implications of telephone surveys. In Dean D. Knudsen & Joann L. Miller (Eds.), *Abused and battered: Social and legal responses to family violence* (pp. 79-87). New York: Aldine De Gruyter.

Myer, Margaret H. (1985). A new look at mothers of incest victims. *Journal of Social Work and Human Sexuality, 3,* 47-58.

National Incident-Based Reporting System. (1998, April). BJS/Search NIBRS Project National Incident-Based Reporting System [On-line]. [Retrieved September 3, 1998]. Available: http://www.nibrs.search.org

National Victim Center. (1995). Extensions of the criminal and civil statutes of limitation in child sexual abuse cases. *INFOLINK, No. 54.*

Newman, Graeme (Ed.). (1999). *Global report on crime and justice.* Published for the United Nations Office for Drug Control and Crime Prevention. Centre for International Crime Prevention. New York: Oxford University Press.

Oates, R. Kim, & Anne C. Donnelly. (1997). Influential papers in child abuse. *Child Abuse & Neglect, 21*(3), 319-326.

Paglia, Camille. (1992). *Sex, art, and American culture.* New York: Vintage Books.

Pellegrin, Alicia, & William G. Wagner. (1990). Child sexual abuse: Factors affecting victims' removal from home. *Child Abuse & Neglect, 14,* 53-60.

Pence, Donna M., & Charles A. Wilson. (1994). Reporting and investigating child sexual abuse. *The Future of Children* (Center for the Future of Children), *4*(2), 70-82.

Peters, Stefanie D., Gail E. Wyatt, & David Finkelhor. (1986). Prevalence. In David Finkelhor (Ed.), *A sourcebook on child sexual abuse* (pp. 15-59). Newbury Park, CA: Sage.

Pollitt, Katha. (1993, October 4). Not just bad sex. *New Yorker, 64*(4), 220-224.

Population projections. (1978, July). *San Francisco almanac.* Sacramento, CA: California State Department of Finance.

Radford, Jill, & Diana E. H. Russell. (Eds.). (1992). *Femicide: The politics of woman killing.* New York: Twayne/Macmillan.

Resnick, Heidi S., Dean G. Kilpatrick, Bonnie S. Dansky, Benjamin E. Saunders, & Connie L. Best. (1993). Prevalence of civilian trauma and posttraumatic stress disorder in a representative national sample of women. *Journal of Consulting and Clinical Psychology, 61*(6), 984-991.

Riede, Gregory A., Timothy Capron, Patrick M. Ivey, Richard Lawrence, & Carol E. Somolo. (1979). *A Texas study of child sexual abuse and child pornography.* Huntsville, TX: Sam Houston State University.

Riger, Stephanie, & Margaret T. Gordon. (1981). The fear of rape: A study in social control. *Journal of Social Issues, 37*(4), 71-92.

Rogers, Carl M. (1982). Child sexual abuse and the courts: Preliminary findings. *Journal of Social Work and Human Sexuality, 1,* 145-153.

Roiphe, Katie. (1993). *The morning after: Sex, fear, and feminism on campus.* Boston: Little, Brown.

Roiphe, Katie. (1993, June 13). Rape hype betrays feminism: Date rape's other victim. *The New York Times Magazine,* pp. 26-30, 40, 68.

Russell, Diana E. H. (1975). *The politics of rape: The victim's perspective.* New York: Stein & Day.

Russell, Diana E. H. (1982). *Rape in marriage.* Bloomington: Indiana University Press.

Russell, Diana E. H. (1983a). The incidence and prevalence of intrafamilial and extrafamilial sexual abuse. *Child Abuse & Neglect, 7*(2), 133-146.

Russell, Diana E. H. (1983b). The prevalence and incidence of forcible rape and attempted rape of females. *Victimology: An International Journal, 7,* 1-4.

Russell, Diana E. H. (1984). *Sexual exploitation: Rape, child sexual abuse, and workplace harassment.* Beverly Hills, CA: Sage.

Russell, Diana E. H. (1986). *The secret trauma: Incest in the lives of girls and women.* New York: Basic Books.

Russell, Diana E. H. (1990). *Rape in marriage.* Bloomington: Indiana University Press.

Russell, Diana E. H. (1992). My turn. *Violence Update, 2*(7), 6, 11.

Russell, Diana E. H. (1999). The great incest war: Moving beyond polarization [new introduction]. *The secret trauma: Incest in the lives of girls and women* (2nd ed., pp. xix-xliv). New York: Basic Books/Perseus.

Russell, Diana E. H., & David Finkelhor. (1984). The gender gap among perpetrators of child sexual abuse. In Diana E. H. Russell, *Sexual exploitation: Rape, child sexual abuse, and workplace harassment* (pp. 215-231). Beverly Hills, CA: Sage.

Salter, A. C. (1992). Epidemiology of child sexual abuse. In W. O'Donohue & J. H. Geer (Eds.), *The sexual abuse of children: Theory and research* (pp. 108-138). Hillsdale, NJ: Lawrence Erlbaum.

Sapp, Allen D., & David L. Carter. (1978). *Child abuse in Texas.* Huntsville, TX: Sam Houston State University.

Saunders, Benjamin E., Dean G. Kilpatrick, Rochelle F. Hanson, Heidi S. Resnick, & Michael E. Walker. (1999). Prevalence, case characteristics, and long-term psychological correlates of child rape among women: A national survey. *Child Maltreatment, 4*(3), 187-200.

Saunders, Benjamin E., Lorenz A. Villeponteaux, Julie A. Lipovsky, Dean G. Kilpatrick, & Lois J. Veronen. (1992). Child sexual assault as a risk factor for mental disorders among women. *Journal of Interpersonal Violence, 7,* 189-204.

Sauzier, Martha. (1989). Disclosure of child sexual abuse: For better or for worse. *Psychiatric Clinics of North America, 12,* 455-469.

Schoenberg, Nara, & Sam Roe. (1993, October 10). Rape: The making of an epidemic. *The Blade, 1,* pp. 8-9.

Schwartz, Martin. (Ed.). (1997). *Researching sexual violence against women.* Thousand Oaks, CA: Sage.

Schwartz, Martin, & Walter DeKeseredy. (1994, December). People without data attacking rape: The Gilbertization of Mary Koss. *Violence Update, 5*(4), 5, 8, 11.

Schwartz, Martin, & Mary Koss. (1998, November). *The backlash against feminist rape research.* Paper presented at the annual meeting of the American Society of Criminology, Washington, DC.

Searles, Patricia, & Ronald J. Berger. (1987). The current status of rape reform legislation: An examination of state statutes. *Women's Rights Law Reporter, 10*(1), 25-43.

Sedlak, Andrea J., & Diane D. Broadhurst. (1996a). *Executive summary of the Third National Incidence Study of Child Abuse and Neglect: Final report.* Washington, DC: U.S. Department of Health and Human Services.

Sedlak, Andrea J., & Diane D. Broadhurst. (1996b). *Third National Incidence Study of Child Abuse and Neglect: Final report.* Washington, DC: U.S. Department of Health and Human Services.

Siegel, Judith M., Susan B. Sorenson, Jacqueline M. Golding, M. Audrey Burnam, & Judith A. Stein. (1987). The prevalence of childhood sexual assault: The Los Angeles Epidemiologic Catchment Area Project. *American Journal of Epidemiology, 126,* 1141-1153.

Sirles, Elizabeth A., & Pamela J. Franke. (1989). Factors influencing mothers' reactions to intrafamilial sexual abuse. *Child Abuse & Neglect, 13*(1), 131-139.

Sirles, Elizabeth A., & C. E. Lofberg. (1990). Factors associated with divorce in intrafamily child sexual abuse cases. *Child Abuse & Neglect, 14*(2), 165-170.

Skogan, Wesley G. (Ed). (1976). *Sample surveys of the victims of crime.* Cambridge, MA: Ballinger.

Sommers, Christina Hoff. (1994). *Who stole feminism? How women have betrayed women.* New York: Simon & Schuster.

Sorenson, Susan, Judith Stein, Judith Siegel, Jacqueline Golding, & Audrey Burnam. (1987). The prevalence of adult sexual assault: The Los Angeles Epidemiological Catchment Area Project. *American Journal of Epidemiology, 126,* 1154-1164.

Sparks, Richard F., Hazel G. Genn, & David Dodd. (1977). *Surveying victims: A study of the measurement of criminal victimization.* New York: John Wiley.

Tjaden, Patricia, & John M. Boyle. (1998, July). *National violence against women survey methodology report*—Draft. [Unpublished manuscript].

Tjaden, Patricia, & Nancy Thoennes. (1998a, November). *Prevalence, incidence, and consequences of violence against women: Findings from the National Violence Against Women Survey.* National Institute of Justice. Centers for Disease Control and Prevention: Research in Brief. U.S. Department of Justice.

Tjaden, Patricia, & Nancy Thoennes. (1998b, April). *Stalking in America: Findings from the National Violence Against Women Survey.* National Institute of Justice. Centers for Disease Control and Prevention: Research in Brief. U.S. Department of Justice.

U.S. Department of Health and Human Services, National Center on Child Abuse and Neglect. (1995). *Child maltreatment 1993: Reports from the states to the National Center on Child Abuse and Neglect.* Washington, DC: Government Printing Office.

U.S. Department of Health and Human Services, National Center on Child Abuse and Neglect. (1996). *Child maltreatment 1994: Reports from the states to the National Center on Child Abuse and Neglect.* Washington, DC: Government Printing Office.

U.S. Department of Health and Human Services, National Center on Child Abuse and Neglect. (1998). *Child maltreatment 1996: Reports from the states to the National Center on Child Abuse and Neglect.* Washington, DC: Government Printing Office.

U.S. Department of Justice, Federal Bureau of Investigation. (1996). *Uniform Crime Reports for the United States—1995.* Washington, DC: Government Printing Office.

van Dijk, Jan, & Patricia Mayhew. (1993). Criminal victimization in the industrialized world: Key findings of the 1989 and 1992 International Crime Surveys. In Anna Alvazzi del Frate, Ugljesa Zvekic, & Jan van Dijk (Eds.), *Understanding crime: Experiences of crime and crime control* (pp. 1-50). Rome: United Nations Interregional Crime and Justice Research Institute.

Williams, Linda M. (1994). Recall of childhood trauma: A prospective study of women's memories of child sexual abuse. *Journal of Consulting and Clinical Psychology, 62,* 1167-1176.

Winfield, Idee, Linda K. George, Marvin Swartz, & Dan G. Blazer. (1990). Sexual assault and psychiatric disorders among a community sample of women. *American Journal of Psychiatry, 147,* 335-341.

Wulkan, Donna, & Josephine Bulkley. (1985). Analysis of incest statutes. In Josephine Bulkley (Ed.), *Child sexual abuse and the law: A report of the American Bar Association* (pp. 52-80). Washington, DC: American Bar Association.

Wyatt, Gail E. (1985). The sexual abuse of Afro-American and White-American women in childhood. *Child Abuse & Neglect, 9,* 507-519.

Wyatt, Gail E. (1987). *Factors affecting the sexual experiences of Afro-American women* (Final Report to NIMH Center for the Prevention and Control of Rape, NIMH Grant RO1MH33603). Washington, DC.

Wyatt, Gail E. (1992). The sociocultural context of African American and White American women's rape. *Journal of Social Issues, 48*(1), 77-91.

Wyatt, Gail E., Michael Newcomb, & Cindy M. Notgrass. (1991). Internal and external mediators of women's rape experiences. In Ann W. Burgess (Ed.), *Rape and sexual assault: III. A research handbook* (pp. 29-55). New York: Garland.

Wyatt, Gail E., & Stefanie D. Peters. (1986a). Issues in the definition of child sexual abuse in prevalence research. *Child Abuse & Neglect, 10,* 231-240.

Wyatt, Gail E., & Stefanie D. Peters. (1986b). Methodological considerations in research on the prevalence of child sexual abuse. *Child Abuse & Neglect, 10,* 241-251.

Wynkoop, Timothy F., Steven C. Capps, & Bobby J. Priest. (1995). Incidence and prevalence of child sexual abuse: A critical review of data collection procedures. *Journal of Child Sexual Abuse, 4*(2), 49-66.

Index

legal, 4, 8, 21-24
National Comorbidity Survey, 105
National Crime Surveys, 64
National Crime Victimization Surveys,
    67-69, 127, 128, 247
National Incident-Based Reporting
    System, 60
National Survey of Family Growth,
    107, 109-110, 111
National Violence Against Women
    Survey, 112-113
National Women's Study, 97-98, 101,
    102 (n6)
Russell's San Francisco survey, 34,
    246, 247-248
sexual assault and, 8, 22-23, 24-26
Uniform Crime Reports, 22, 34, 52, 64
Wyatt's Los Angeles County survey,
    89, 91-92
DeKeseredy, Walter, 242
Denial, 13, 173. *See also* Disclosure
reluctance; Recall problems
Dietz, Christine, 143
Disclosure reluctance, 26-28, 40
child sexual abuse, 154-156, 165, 169,
    212
interview duration and, 100
interviewer-respondent matching and,
    42
Los Angeles Epidemiologic Catchment
    Area Project, 186, 187
National Crime Victimization Surveys,
    75
recall problems and, 13
respondent age and, 131
DiTullio, Barbara, 62
Dodd, David, 28
Donnelly, Anne C., 239
Double standard, 86 (n2), 266 (n5)
Draijer, Nel, 46-47, 48 (n8)
Driver's license sampling method, 170, 171-
    172
Drugged victims. *See* Victim incapacitation

Edelsohn, Gail A., 143
Edmunds, Christine N., 188. *See also*
    National Women's Study
Eigenberg, Helen M., 66, 75, 79, 81, 83-84,
    85, 246

Ennis, Philip H., 40
Epidemiologic Catchment Area Program.
    See Los Angeles Epidemiologic
    Catchment Area Project
Ethical issues, 156
Evaluation methodology:
    fieldwork dates, 101-102 (n1)
    inclusion criteria, 7-8, 17 (n1), 26, 147,
        157 (n1)
Everson, Mark D., 143
Exhibitionism, 164, 248, 254 (n2)
Extrafamilial child sexual abuse, 146
    Murphy's Minnesota survey, 197
    National Incidence Studies, 150-151,
        257
    research recommendations, 264
    Russell's San Francisco survey, 150,
        151, 160, 163, 177, 208
    survey comparisons, 207-208, 208
        (table)

Fabrication, 28, 40, 51, 222, 251
Face-to-face interviews (FFI), 41, 76, 77,
    89, 107
Faller, Kathleen C., 143, 151, 155
False memory syndrome theory, 15, 141
Farrell, Lynda T., 155
Fazlollah, Mark, 61-62, 265
Federal Bureau of Investigation (FBI), 21,
    22, 64, 67. *See also Uniform Crime
    Reports*
Federman, Belle, 2, 95
Female-on-female rape, 21, 52, 60, 67
Female-on-male rape, 21, 23, 52, 60, 67
Femicide, 23, 29 (n1), 86 (n7)
Feminist activism, 1-2, 6-7, 239
    backlash agenda and, 6, 243-245, 254
    law reform and, 22, 23, 26
    See also Backlash
FFI. *See* Face-to-face interviews
Finkelhor, David, 2, 12, 14, 37, 44, 76, 143,
    145, 148, 151, 152, 153, 154, 155, 156,
    157 (n3), 165, 166, 169, 189 (n9), 200,
    201, 203 (nn3,5), 209, 210, 212 (n1),
    228, 242, 244, 249. *See also* Los
    Angeles Times Poll
Flunitrazepam ("Roofies"; Rohypnol), 101,
    125
Forcible rape, definitions, 21, 22, 60

About the Authors

Diana E. H. Russell is Professor Emerita of Sociology at Mills College, Oakland, California, where she taught sociology and women's studies for 22 years. She is author, coauthor, editor, or coeditor of 15 books (see the list at the beginning of this volume). Her book *The Secret Trauma: Incest in the Lives of Girls and Women* was the corecipient of the 1986 C. Wright Mills Award for outstanding social science research that addresses an important social issue.

She obtained a Postgraduate Diploma from the London School of Economics and Political Science (with Distinction) in 1961. She was the recipient of LSE's Mostyn Lloyd Memorial Prize, awarded to the best student studying for the Postgraduate Diploma in 1961. She subsequently received a Ph.D. from Harvard University in 1970.

Dr. Russell, who lives in Berkeley, California, has lectured widely in the United States and abroad about the political situation in South Africa, rape, incest, child sexual abuse, pornography, femicide, and all forms of violence against women.

Rebecca M. Bolen is Assistant Professor at the Boston University School of Social Work where she teaches courses in human behavior and child sexual abuse. She was awarded an M.A. in Social Work from the University of Tennessee (Nashville Branch) and her Ph.D. from The University of Texas at Arlington (School of Social Work). Dr. Bolen was a doctoral research fellow for the National Center on Child Abuse and Neglect in 1994-1995 and was a 1998 corecipient of the outstanding dissertation award presented by the American Professional Society for Abused Children.

Dr. Bolen's research focus is in the areas of child sexual abuse and female victimization, with a more specific emphasis on factors that place females and children at such great risk for sexual violence as well as those factors that then predict outcome in victims. She has made numerous presentations and has several papers in professional journals.